# DISTANCE EDUCATION THROUGH TELEVISION

ENCYCLOPAEDIA OF DISTANCE EDUCATION SERIES

# DISTANCE EDUCATION THROUGH TELEVISION

*Edited by*

**M. Husain**

**ANMOL PUBLICATIONS PVT. LTD.**

**NEW DELHI - 110 002 (INDIA)**

**ANMOL PUBLICATIONS PVT. LTD.**
4374/4B, Ansari Road, Daryaganj
New Delhi - 110 002
Ph.: 23261597, 23278000
Visit us at: www.anmolpublications.com

*Distance Education Through Television*

First Edition, 2004

ISBN 81-261-1534-3



PRINTED IN INDIA

---

Published by J.L. Kumar for Anmol Publications Pvt. Ltd., New Delhi - 110 002 and Printed at Mehra Offset Press, Delhi.

# Contents

# Preface

Distance education, a mode of upgrading educational qualification as pastime in yore days has presently become a popular mode of education. Paucity of time and adverse circumstances in life may hamper the formal classroom education of someone.

Distance education as an educational endeavour is developing a momentum of unprecedented dimensions—covering most of the university and lower level disciplines with a large number of enrolment. More and more open universities are being established all over the world and more and more non-educational agencies, governmental and non-governmental, engaged in in-service training/instruction are now turning to DE to meet the overwhelming pressure of numbers, diversity of needs and growing awareness about the importance of professionalism. The overall scene points to what may be called a 'utilisation explosion' of DE courses and DE methodology all over the world.

The institution of education has entered a phase of 'change' manifest in the progressive expansion and application of Distance Education methodology. This change is a social imperative and yet we in the developing countries display an inexplicable unpreparedness for meeting the demands being made by this 'change'—we must comprehend it, plan for it, effect it, sustain it and thus build for the future.

The present work, in four volumes, is an endeavour to focus on vital issues pertaining to Distance Education. Attempts are made to gather the well researched material, based on the empirical findings of different scholars of repute from various settings.

The information contained herein is drawn from various authoritative sources. Hence no claim of originality. We are deeply beholden to all those whose works and views are cited or substantially borrowed herein for making the work comprehensive and more useful. Besides those, we are grateful to one and all who have rendered the assistance while executing the plan of the work. Finally, Mr. J.L. Kumar, Managing Director, Anmol Publications Pvt. Ltd. deserve all appreciation for undertaking the publication of the present venture.

—MH

# 1

# Methodological Introduction

## The Need for a Scientific Assessment of the Results Achieved in Adult Education

The past 50 years have seen a radical change of direction in child education, and have revealed the problem of assessing results in a new light. With the traditional type of education, the effect of lessons was judged merely from examinations and competitions. But other criteria were needed for the new type of education, whose aim is not so much the increase of knowledge as the development of character. Often enough it has relied solely on a vague intuitive judgment as regards the pupils' evolution. At its best, however, it has had recourse to scientific psychology, measuring levels, comparing processes of evolution and experimenting in methods of techniques. The science of teaching, in short, has become an "experimental" one.

Adult education long remained unaffected by these changes. Its teaching processes were undefined, its aims and methods uncertain. But it was to develop along new lines under the impetus of technological progress and labour reforms, which made recreation an increasingly important factor in the worker's lives. New problems arose from the need to provide recreation and entertainment, and to develop the personality through the acquisition of new knowledge or skills. The growing mechanization of leisure through the use of radio, films and television brought tremendous cultural possibilities within the reach of wider circles of the population, while at the same time exposing them to serious dangers. It could offer a new challenge to mind and body or, alternatively, induce an attitude of interia. This latter danger was further aggravated by the fact that exactly the same news and ideas were offered simultaneously to millions of people.

The major objectives of adult education in our technological society were thus crytalized, whilst its responsibilities were increased. Instead of ignoring or scoring these powerful instruments—the chief source of entertainment for the mass of population—it was essential to try to combat their evil effects and promote their use in such a way that they could exert a constructive influence. It was the duty of educators to endeavour to awaken an active response in the general public by a discriminate use of the great communication media, and by suitable treatment and commentary of the subjects.

By "active response" we mean a reaction that brings the critical faculties into play; the audience not to be content with mere passive enjoyment of a play or film but being led on to a discussion of its value. Instead of remaining mere lookers-on at sporting events, spectators should wish to engage in games and physical exercises themselves. Instead of lending only half an ear to broadcasts, listeners should take them seriously and follow them up by study of their everyday environment, by joining a study circle or through independent reading; they should draw upon the best broadcasts for instructions as to how to improve their daily lives, instead of merely escaping into an imaginary or ideal world; that they should use their sparetime occupations for developing their instinct for action, taste for invention and pleasure in creation. In short, as Georges Friedmann put it, adult education had to help develop all man's faculties by extending the practice of "active" recreation.[1]

In order to carry out so complex a task, educators had to consider ways and means, and the actual chances of success. Many of their traditional methods and techniques seemed likely to fall short of such novel and ambitious aims. Yet superficial or half-way solutions might lead to a worse state of things than that which they were intended to remedy. Adult education accordingly felt the need for a more careful assessment of its results. The rules of qualitative and quantitative observation, and if possible of experimentation, had to be applied to all its aspects, in the light of its own particular aims. Recourse had to be had to the social sciences. The psycho-sociology of "active response" had to be developed, in close relationship with experimental educational policy and methods for the organization of recreation.

## A Plea for a Psycho-Sociology of "Active Response", Applied to the Study of the Cultural Impact of Television

### *Two Experiment's Scattle and Iowa State Colleges*

Several attempts have already been made to study the results of child education through television. Although it bears on children, this research is of interest to us; for it concerns the use of leisure for cultural purposes and employs a method that is a "cross" between pedagogy and sociology, which is the right approach to the psycho-sociology of "active response". We shall give only one example, illustrating the development of the reading habit among children under the impact of television.

In Seattle a 13-week experimental series of telecasts, each, half an hour long, was initiated over station KING-TV in December 1951. The purpose of this programme was to stimulate children to read books. Its formal was designed by Gloria Chandler, long experienced in the making of recordings and transcriptions for children.

"Shown on the television screen is a group of children, their backs to the viewer, seated at the feet of a young storyteller. In her hands is a book from which she is telling the story. The backdrop is a huge open book with the inscription *Telaventure Tales . . . Once Upon a Time.* Across its pages moves Benjamin Scribble, a "non-realistic" character who serves instead of a live announce. He is the storyletter's helper knows all the authors and all the books.

"In the first half of the programme an episode from some recent book is related by the storyletter. A few live scenes are enacted to vary the story technique. The second half of the programme involves a game in which the television audience participates. Scenes from a number of books are presented, and the viewers are invited to write in the name of the character portrayed, the book, its author and "why I like this book".

"The immediate results were remarkable. By the second programme the Seattle Public Library and all its branches had reported that every book by the author featured on the first programme had been borrowed. The programme's influence extended into rural areas. The King Country Public Library's report indicated that all the books by all the authors mentioned on this programme disappeared from the shelves of its 38 branches and two bookmobiles."[2]

This is a type of experimental research whose spirit, assumptions, methods and techniques should be applied not only to the study of children's recreation but also for that of adults.

Another experiment, which was concerned with the constructive development of the leisure time activities of rural populations was conducted by Iowa State College in the United State of America. This university has a television station which for eleven hours a day broadcasts programmes with a constant emphasis on cultural and educational issues for a population of roughly 600,000 persons, most of them living on the land. It also operates a centre for research on "television discussion" techniques. The most interesting experiment conducted by Iowa State College is the programme entitled "The Whole Town's Talking", intended to encourage discussion of problems which are of general interest to all communities. The participants are the people themselves. The programmes are "live" telecasts focused on problems of direct concern to a particular community; they are discussed by the townsfolk in front of the camera and the participants are encouraged to take a vote on the issues raised in all the discussion, so as to show that talking is not enough but that some definite stand must be taken that will lead to action.

"When we entered Cambridge (a village of 600 inhabitants, which had a school problem), we found an apathetic, dispirited community, afraid to discuss its problems. In the past few weeks we have watched a ferment growing in this town. We have watched people as they began to talk about their problems in the open—for the first time. This talk need not, must not, end with the television programme. At this moment we do not know what direction this process of involvement will take. But this much we do know. By using glamour and excitement of present-day television, we can literally start a whole town *talking*."[3]

### Assessment of the Results of Tele-clubs' work

It was along the lines of these all too rare experiments that we tried to solve our own methodological problem. Our first concern was to find out the main preoccupations of tele-club leaders. When these leaders try to develop the effectiveness of their work, they seek to select from among all that "interests the public", which is most "worth while", what "enriching"—what leads to "self-improvement", etc. But what exactly do we mean by these expressions? Is there a clearer criterion for the assessment of results? And how exactly can the results be measured?

One obvious way to judge the interest aroused by telecasts is from what people think of them, the degree of approval or disapproval, the number of people who, among the different categories of viewers, show approval of disapproval, etc. We can also ascertain the effects and cultural possibilities of telecasts from the impression they leave, their impact on tastes, knowledge and opinions, the desires and activities to which they have given rise, and so forth. For an objective assessment of the impact of a telecast on the life of viewers, we can check up on attendance and participation in discussions, or on changes in attitude and behaviour in professional, domestic or social life after a series of telecasts, etc.

For each particular problem we had to choose the most appropriate angle of approach, and put our questions in such a way as to obtain the clearest and most reliable answers possible. The questions were worked out during preliminary field enquiries by a team including the various research-workers—ethnographers, sociologists and psychologists, the producers of the broadcasts, the teachers entrusted with the commentaries and the agricultural engineer responsible for land re-allocation in the Department of the Aisne. For five days, most members of the team met for a preparatory course at the Institut National d'Education Populaire at Marly-le-Roi.[4]

## Field Observation and Experiment

Our study of the interest aroused by the telecasts, and of their possible cultural influence, was not easy, as we could question only a small number of people. We therefore had to use several dovetailing methods and techniques so as to have as many cross-checks as possible—direct and indirect questions; questions to which only one or questions to which any reply could be given; subjective interrogation and objective observation; description, analysis and statistics.

Whenever possible we tried to give our observations a statistical framework. Figures cannot, of course, take the place of analysis. But they establish the dimensions and the relative importance of a social phenomenon, give some idea of differences and variations, and provide a standard for comparison. To avoid giving the impression of pedantic reliance on statistics, we had no hesitation in rounding off our figures to the next number or the nearest ten.

Last but not least, we made the fullest possible use of field experiments for the study of our subject. The experimental method is, after all, no more than a systematic, rational testing of our hypotheses. A tele-club is not of course a laboratory, and we deliberately refrained from resorting to the artificial devices often used for the study of group dynamics on the pretext that they afford better means of isolating and assessing the effect of any given factor. Indeed we scrupulously avoided any methods that would not elicit genuine reactions on the part of countryfolk, who are specially hostile to surveys. Our experimental study had to be made part of the every-day life of the group. The reliability of our results thus offset any possible incompleteness.[5]

**The Questionnaires**

Accordingly, we had to devise questionnaires for observing and interpreting the results of the work of tele-clubs, television programmes and the "Etat d'urgence" series. If these questionnaires were to yield sufficiently reliable results, they had to be understood and accepted by the rural television, public whom it was necessary to make active partners in this enquiry. Our methods had to be supple if they were to reveal any changes in attitude over the short period of five months. Conventional "tests" had to be ruled out as they were not suited to these particular aims and working conditions. Nor was uniformity a desirable quality, for our methods had to register results with many facets and facilitate the maximum amount of cross-checking.[6]

To begin with, each tele-club had to be fully seen against its local background as a whole—with general facts about the environment in order to interpret certain reactions of the clubs. Hence the need for a descriptive *survey of each individual locality* (Method No. 1). Then, as the main purpose of the 13 telecasts in the series "Etat d'urgence" was to encourage modernization, we wished to register the reaction of tele-club members to this problem before they viewed the telecasts, so as to compare it with their attitude to the same problems after the series had been completed and find out whether there had been any change of attitude. Hence the *two references (initial and final) on reactions to the modernization of public, collective and domestic equipment* (Method No. 2).

But such a methods of assessment was apt to be rather superficial. We felt it essential to jot down the reactions of spectators during and after each telecast, during the ensuing discussion and even in the course of their everyday remarks and behaviour. We therefore developed a *Log-book* to be kept for each of the 13 telecasts of "Etat d'urgence" (Method No. 3).

Lastly, it was helpful to compare the reactions elicited by our experimental telecasts with reactions to other programmes. This would also give an idea of the possible cultural contributions of the various types of telecasts and the main activities of the tele-clubs. Hence the *general survey of the Television Francaise programmes* (Method No. 4).

All four methods of assessing results were applied for a period of six months by the teacher-observer, guided or assisted by the team of research-workers. Except for the surveys of each individual locality, the enquiries were all conducted by direct interviews. The answers were written down, either by the teacher and his assistants, or (after a long interview) by the person questioned. An important safeguard was that in all cases the interviewer had a personal acquaintance, often of long standing, with the persons to whom he addressed his questions.

**Experimental Tele-clubs**

Such observations could not be carried out in all tele-clubs. A few had to be selected, to serve as samples.[7] There could be no question of "drawing lots" for them. We knew that first-rate teacher-observers were needed to lead the discussions and shoulder the heavy burden of the enquiry. Accordingly we first selected some 50 tele-clubs out of 180. Then the number was reduced to 15—in 10 localities for experiment and 5 auxiliary localities—upon which we drew as required. The number of persons questioned ranged between 225 and 231, depending on the subject of enquiry.

I. Everyone knows that the basic principle of experimentation is the isolation of a given factor so as to enable its action to be studied in detail. We neither wished nor were able to isolate, in turn, all the factors exerting an influence on the reactions of our televiewers. Furthermore, as we were unable to eliminate factors of less interest to us, we neutralized them by the way in which we selected our samples. This was the procedure adopted in regard to regional differences and variations in the make-up of the villages. Tele-clubs in France first developed in the area covered by the Paris transmitter and have become most popular in the Department of the Aisne. Yet the way of life varies even from one part of this Department to another; and very wide differences are found in neighbouring Tardenois, Brie and Champagne areas.

The various villages may also differ considerably in their economic and social make-up. The French countryside is a complex subject for study. In the so-called rural districts in which our tele-clubs operate, every degree of urbanization is to be found, from the compact, well-equipped village near a town, with agricultural occupations in the minority, such as

Etampes (Aisne) to the village distant from any town and consisting of scattered, comfortless hamlets—such as Montfaucon (Aisne). Similar differences are found as regards land tenure in our various localities. On the outskirts of the Brie district, around Chateau-Thierry, we encounter mainly small farms of less than 20 hectares, cultivating several types of crop (e.g. Viffort and Fossoy). Near Epernay, in Champagne, holdings are even smaller; but they are wealthier, this being a wine-growing district (e.g. Venteuil and Chatillon in the Marne). North of Chateau-Thierry, or in the Aube Department, we find large estates with "big" landowners and their farm labourers (e.g. Dammard in the Aisne and St. Aubin in the Aube).

The tele-clubs surveyed were therefore so selected as to provide a fair cross-section of these various regional, economic and social types. For an understanding of reactions to telecasts on modernization special account had to be taken of economic and social factors. Our samples will therefore be described on this basis.

The localities selected belong to the following regions: nine communes from the Department of the Aisne (Montfaucon, Viffort, Fossoy, Gramaille, Montreuil-aux-Lions, Nesle-la-Montagne, Nogentel, Etampes); six communes from other Departments: Marne (Chatillon, Venteuil), Oise (Coudray-St. Germer, Les Marais), Eure-et-Loir (Boullay-Mivoie), Aube (St. Aubin).

Our 15 experimental tele-clubs reflect the following differences in economic and social conditions:

### A. Ten main localities

Communities where agricultural occupations predominate:

1. A fairly isolated village with an agricultural population working on small or medium-sized farms (several

crops). The tele-club is the only cultural activity: Montfaucon.

2. Another isolated village of the same type: Viffort.
3. Similar, but closer to the town : Fossoy.
4. An isolated village with small and medium-sized vine-yards, the tele-club being attached to a very active school co-operative (cine-club) : Venteuil.
5. An isolated village with a mixed population (one-third of the inhabitants employed in industry and other non-agricultural occupations), but where wine-growers (small and medium-sized holdings) are in the majority. The tele-club is the only organized cultural activity: Chatillonsur-Marne.
6. An isolated village with a predominantly agricultural population working for two big landowners. A high proportion of the inhabitants are of foreign origin. The tele-club operates as part of a very energetic rural centre engaging in many activities: Dammard.
7. An isolated village of much the same type (a small number of very large estaes, and a steady tendency towards concentration), but with almost as many industrial workers as farm labourers. The tele-club is practically the only organized cultural activity: St. Aubin.

Communes where non-agricultural occupations predominate:

8. A village, near the chief town of a district, where most of the inhabitants are employed in industry, but with a large minority of agricultural workers mostly employed on small and medium-sized farms (though some of the estates are fairly large). The tele-club was founded recently and is the only local cultural activity: Nesle-la-Montagne.

9. A village also very close to the chief town of the district, with a population consisting mainly of industrial workers (roughly 50 per cent), but still engaging in a certain amount of rural activity (about 30 per cent). The School Friendly Society conducts various cultural activities. The tele-club is the oldest in the region: Nogentel.

10. A village which in fact is a suburb of the chief town of the district. Agricultural work occupies less than 3 per cent of the total population. High proportion of retired persons and people with private means. The tele-club has been operating for three years along with a cine-club, even though the town is so near: Etampes.

### B. Five auxilliary localities

The ten localities just described were the main operational base for the enquiry. The following five communes were unable to supply all the information requested of them, or to fill in all the questionnaires. However, they constituted most useful auxiliary localities for the purpose of our enquiry:

1. An isolated village with an agricultural population consisting mostly of labourers employed on a few large farms. The tele-club is the only cultural activity: Cramaille (comparable to Dammard).

2. A village of 253 inhabitants, the majority of whom work on mixed farms: one-third of the population farm labourers: Boulaye-Mivoie (comparable to Montfauco).

3. A village of 646 inhabitants 10.5 miles from the chief town of the district. The majority of the population in non-agricultural occupations, but a strong agricultural minority. A high proportion of workers, both industrial and agricultural. Of the latter, the great bulk work on small and medium-sized farms: Montreuil-aux-Lions.

4. A village of 315 inhabitants with an agricultural majority, working, for the most part, small and medium-sized farms. Barely 10 per cent are farm labourers. A number of foreigners: Coudray-St. Germer.

5. A village of 376 inhabitants, the majority in non-industrial occupations. Office and factory workers, who work in Beauvais. Those living on the land work small and medium sized farms for the most part: Aux Marais.[8]

II. Our aim was to neutralize regional differences and variations in economic and social conditions but, on the other hand, to isolate as far as possible the reactions of certain categories of viewers, whom it is specially important to understand if adult rural education is to be developed through television.

1. In the first place, reactions differ according to occupation. In fact, they are affected not only by the nature of the work, but also by the corresponding economic status, social relations and cultural level. We mean, more accurately, socio-occupational categories.

   Fifteen such categories were selected for our enquiry, but statistical requirements obliged us to regroup these in various ways, according to the working method used (Methods Nos. 2, 3 and 4).

   (a) To begin with we picked out the small farmers,[9] for whom the "Etat d'urgence" series was mainly designed. One of the most urgent problems in rural education in connexion with the equipment of town and countryside is how to familiarize over 300,000 small farmers with the benefits of progress.[10] The reactions of this category of televiewer was therefore of prime importance to us. We included in it the few rural craftsmen (6 per cent of our sample)—farriers, saddlers, etc. Their outlook is very similar to that of the small farmers who are their clients. Like the small farmers, they feel they are being left "high and dry" in their village.

(b) Our next category consists of farm labourers and the big farmers. France has almost as many farm labourers as small farmers. When studying reactions during programmes, special attention was given to these farm labourers, as also to the big farmers; but we were unable to treat the latater separately in the statistical study of the initial and final referenda on modernization, or in the general survey on programmes, since the number of individuals concerned was so small. We had to group together all workers—agricultural and non-agricultural—and all non-manual professions, including managers or owners of large farms.

(c) The regrouping of agricultural and non-agricultural workers does not mean that we were unmindful of the difference between these two categories. But, all in all, these differences seemed less material than the similiarity in attitudes towards the television programme and the particular problem of modernization. This remark is borne out by a comparison of the attitude of this united category with that of the small farmers and the non-manual professors.

(d) Non-manual workers, for their part, are less numerous in the localities with predominantly agricultural occupations, but are naturally far better represented in localities where the majority of occupations are non-agricultural. Despite the very real differences in social status as between office workers, teachers and managers of large farms, they have all gone beyond the *certificat d'eludes* (primary school leaving certificate) in their studies. They are not manual workers; they have more extensive general knowledge, a greater gift for self-expression, practice in writing etc. We are quite aware that this new category, evolved to meet statistical requirements, does not reflect any real economic and social unit; but in the tele-club discussions, its members did in fact stand out from the manual workers who had not carried their studies beyond the primnary school, and especially from the small farmers. This difference was of particular interest to us in our study of rural tele-clubs.

2. As to the other categories, we studied reactions according to sex. In country and town alike, adult education in France is all too often planned by men for men. This bias is particularly unfortunate in the villages, where the womenfolk have an even heavier burden of work than their town sisters. They have little spare time and often lose all desire for self-instruction, satisfied to remain a mere timid echo of their husbands. We were specially interested in their reactions, with a view to a more balanced development of adult education through television.

   Lastly, we studied reactions on an age basis. The main reason for this decision was, of course, the general drift towards the towns—mainly on the part of young people. We wanted to know what age groups were most resistant or most favourable to modernization, and how these different age groups were going to react to the "Etat d'urgence" series. At the outset we identified five age categories, regrouped for reasons of statistical convenience into three larger categories:

> young people under 25 years of age, mostly unmarried; men from 26 to 39 years of age; and men over 40 years of age. We were unable to sub-divide these groups further.[11]

Finally, this study of differences led on to an investigation of the extent to which the variations observed between a few samples of each category could serve as a basis for valid general conclusions. By applying the laws of probability to small samples[12] we were able to establish, for the observation of different attitudes, the probable percentage of error in any general conclusion. If the percentage of error was between 10 per cent and 5 per cent, we took it that the difference was *significant* (S.D.); if the percentage was 5 per cent or less, we assumed that the difference was *highly significant* (H.S.D.).

Whenever it was impossible to apply the law of probabilities, we cross-checked quantitative and qualitative observations and testimony so as to make our generalized findings as reliable as possible. When the scientific checks were inadequate—either because we had too small a sample to carry out a statistical test, or because the necessary cross-checks could not be made with our particular experiment or method of assessment—we did not use the replies, interesting as they might have been to confirm or disprove our hypotheses.

The psycho-sociology of leisure does not merely seek to record opinions or behaviour. It aims to furnish its own particular replies to the complex problems of adult education policy and methods, and to supply more effective aid to those who are endeavouring to create or transform recreation centres with a view to arousing a more active response on the part of the public.

But such considerations do not lead the scientific spirit to abate its insistence on independence and precision. Its function, then, is to : devise methods and techniques suited to each problem; assess as accurately as possible the degree of probability of the results obtained by the different methods; to distinguish as clearly as possible in the analysis of the replies between observation on the one hand and explanation or forecast on the other.

We endeavoured to adhere to these principles.

## References

1. Georges Friedmaun, Ou va le travail humain ? Paris, NRF, p. 257.
2. The account of this experiment is taken from Charles A. Siepmann, Television and Education in the United States, Paris, Unesco, 1952, pp. 103-4.
3. Siepmann, op. cit.
4. Cf. Notes on Methods. The organization of team work for the survey, p. 225.
5. Notes on Methods, General remarks on the use of observation and experimentation in the psycho-sociology of the active employment of leisure, p. 229.
6. The four questionnaires and the instructions for their use can be supplied by Unesco's Department of Mass Communication to those who wish to consult them.
7. Cf. Notes on Methods, The problem of sampling, p. 230.
8. See Appendix I, Description of communes in which the experimental tele-clubs are situated, p. 235.
9. These include both tenant farmers and farmers who work their own land.
10. The working population of France amounts to roughly 20 million persons.
11. Appendix III, The population under survey after statistical regrouping, p. 250.
12. Cf. Notes on Methods, The theory of small samples and the application of Pearson's criterion to the investigation, p. 232.

# 2

# Television and Video

## The Variety of Educational TV Delivery Systems

In the 1950s, as soon as television became a practical reality, it was seen to have great educational potential and many attempts were made to set up television-based mass-education systems. In the USA, a notable effort was made to introduce educational television into the public schools, with the aid of some $ 25 million, supplied by the Ford Foundation. Due to the decentralized nature of North American education, a large number of local 'instructional television broadcast stations' were set up. In the UK, the BBC was not far behind in setting up a regular programme of television for schools. These early broadcasts were 'live' transmission of classroom lectures, using a certain amount of close-up shots and special camera angles to break up the monotony of the 'talking head' format, so prevalent in the early days.

## Live Broadcasting

This approach to instruction by television was more or less dictated by the technology available at the time. Video recording was not yet invented, so all programmes had to go out live. Any errors committed during shooting would also be broadcast, so the tendency towards conservative, well tried progrmme formats and unadventurous camera work reinforced. An alternative use of the medium at this time followed the entertainment trends. The techniques already developed for the shooting of film were modified to the 'instantaneous' medium of television. Instead of cutting and assembling a final version of the film from a series of separate takes of a number of scenes, the television director was forced to use a number of cameras set up at different vantage points and cut between them on the basis of split-second decisions taken as the programme was acted out and transmitted. This required enormous effort in the prior rehearsal of a programme, as well as great skill on the part of the production team. As the resources, in terms of both time and human skills, available for the early educational programmes were much more limited than was the case for entertainment programming, a very noticeable difference in quality between educational and general television programmes was apparent.

However, even these early programmes showed how the television medium could enhance the power of education. Two special benefits were noticeable.

- Control over size and viewpoint, achieved by the camera position and lens characteristics, could present a much clearer and more precise visual image than could normally be achieved by a teacher with a large class of students. All could get the view that only one or two privileged students in the front row would get in conventional classroom situations. Of course, film and even slides or photos (even drawings) may also be used to focus the student's viewpoint, but the television camera did this instantly with little need for preparatory work on the part of the instructional designer, laboratory crew or artist;
- Immediate distribution of the programme to a theoretically unlimited audience. One first-class teacher, using one set of exceptionally well produced demonstration materials, could be multiplied. More

students could be reached with smaller educational resources, provided, of course, that the necessary technological resources were installed, in working order and switched on.

There were, of course, serious limitations as well. One was the lock-step nature of the 'instant' transmission, which forced all students wishing to study a given topic to study it at one and the same time. School timetablign systems generally had difficulty in synchronizing class sessions with broadcast times. The inability, on the part of the teacher, to preview a live broadcast, made it difficult to build an appropriate overall lesson plan that would take the utmost advantage of the TV programme. One way to overcome this latter weakness was to prepare very detailed lesson outlines and supply printed support materials that the teacher could use with the broadcast. But then the danger was that the teacher would feel that all the teaching tasks had been pre-planned by the TV producers. This often led to the total rejection of the medium by some teachers, and to the delegation of all responsibility for instructional success of the lesson to the programme, by others. In both cases, the long-term result was not very good for the acceptance of televised instruction.

Live, open broadcast television continues to be used in education, but not very extensively. We see its use most frequently in what we may term *educational* television (as opposed to *instructional* television) - in programmes that do not have specific pre-determined instructional objectives, but have educational value either as a source of information on current events (newsreels), opposing points of view (debates), interesting or famous persons (interviews), and so on. It is of course possible to build such programmes into an instructional system, as one form of stimulus component, but the teacher must devise appropriate practice tasks, in which the learners apply what they saw on TV to tasks that lead to the achievement of specific worthwhile instructional objectives.

From the user's view point, the technical aspects of open-broadcast transmission systems, whether of live or recorded programmes, are minimal. It is sufficient to have a TV receiver in working order and an appropriate antenna, in order to receive a clear signal from the transmitting station. Typical link-ups are illustrated in Figure 2.1.

**Recorded Broadcasts**

There are yet other reasons why the early promise of the television medium was not realized. One of these was the natural distrust of the teaching profession of a medium that appeared poised to take over their jobs. Another reason was that television systems and their owners, realizing the extent of resistance on the part of teachers, decided to promote the role of television in teaching, as an 'enrichment' medium that would not be seen as a threat by teachers. In so doing, they avoided intensive and adventurous instructional designs, settling for itsy-bitsy pieces of one-way broadcasting that the teacher had to build into his/her own instructional plan. But teachers were not skilled at doing this, nor were they equipped in terms of basic information about the structure of each programme well in advance of its transmission.

The situation improved markedly in the 1970s, with the increasing use of video recording. First, the TV stations were able to pre-record their programmes. This offered several advantages and new capabilities:

- Transmission time was no longer the problem it had been as the stations could record programmes at times that were convenient for them, and then broadcast at times that were convenient to the schools.
- Programmes could be assembled in a similar manner to films, scenes being edited with precision, errors being re-shot, effects such as flash-backs and scene repetitions being used to good instructional effect.

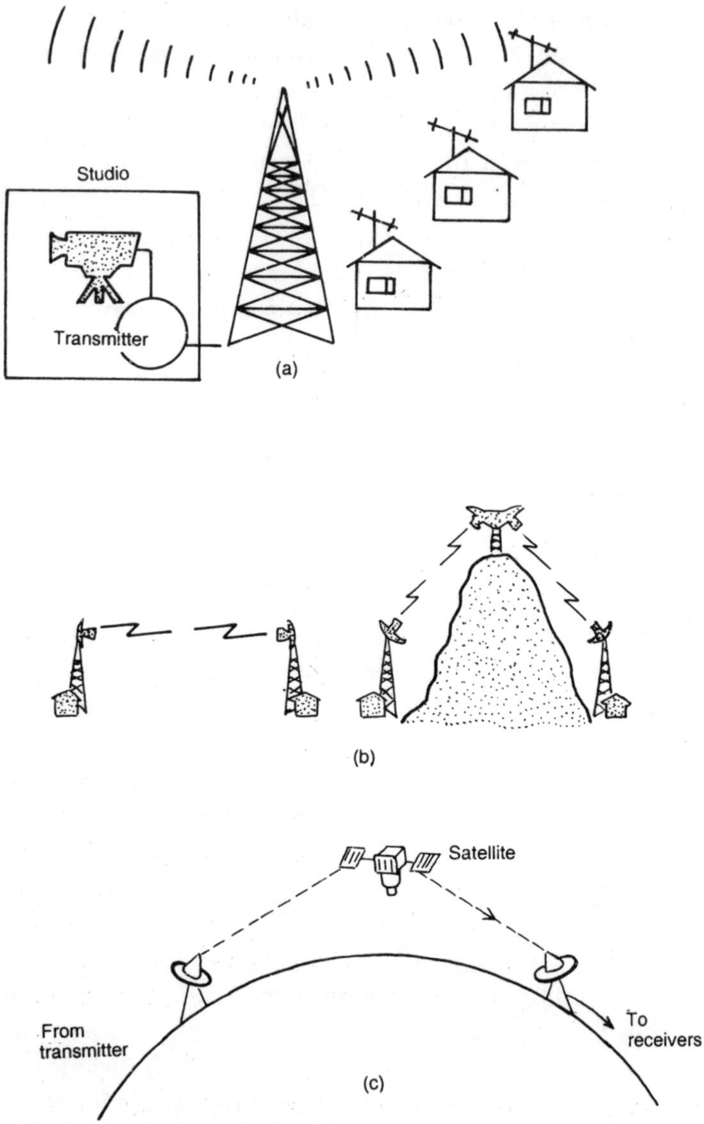


**Fig. 2.1:** Types of broadcast television systems. (a) In an open-broadcast system, signals are transmitted over air-waves to receivinng antennae. (b) Microwave television involves sending signals point to point. Retransmission is necessary to circumvent barriers. (c) Satellite transmission over long distances

- Programmes could now, in theory, be field-tested on samples of the student population and the results used as indicators of necessary revisions (in reality this was seldom done due to financial and scheduling restrictions).

- Programmes, once recorded, could be stored for repetition to future groups on other occasions - this brought the cost of instructional television programming down considerably, as the initial development and production costs could be recovered over a number of years use.

- Programme quality improved, as the relative facility with which programming or shooting errors could be corrected, coupled to the lower cost per showing of recorded programmes, led producers to experiment with more adventurous programme designs and more elaborate and well prepared studio props - specially built demonstration and laboratory equipment, colour, animated sequences etc. In general, the quality of educational and instructional television programmes approached the production quality standards (termed 'production values' in the profession) of general broadcast television.

Figure 2.2 illustrates the set-up of a studio that should be able to produce near-broadcast quality educational/ instructional television programmes. This basic set-up may be enhanced by the addition of more cameras (especially one for transmitting pictures, graphics or captions from printed artwork) a telecine chain (for the incorporation of existing clips of film, slides, etc. into the programme), and a special effects generator which, in this microchip age, can bring the skills of clever fading, split screen, blow-ups, inversions or you-name-it, to the fingertips of any video editor.

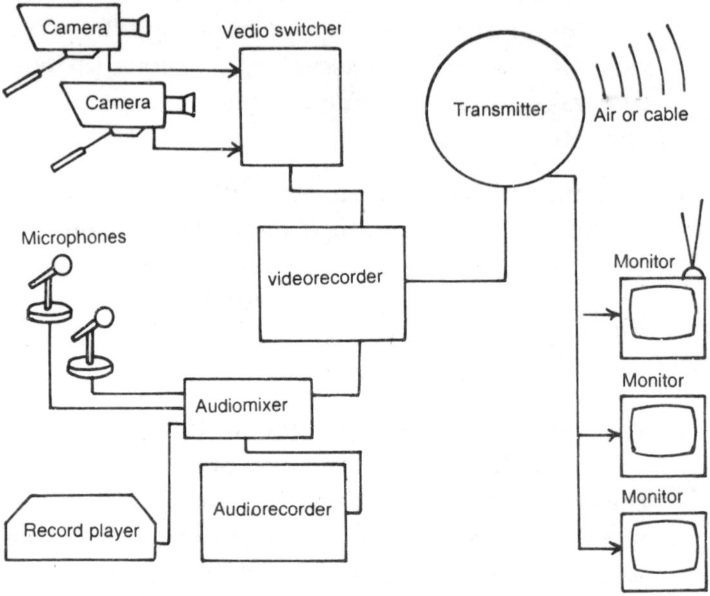


**Fig. 2.2:** A basic television system, with recording capabilities and mixing of several sources.

## Successes and Failures of Broadcast TV

As video recording equipment became increasingly available in the schools, a number of further advantages were gained:

1. Time scheduling limitations were further eliminated, as schools could now record broadcast programmes and then replay them to student groups at any locally convenient time, or even several times to different groups at different times (this advantage was also not fully exploited in some cases, due to copyright restrictions which have only recently been releaxed);
2. By recording the programme in advance, the teacher could preview it and thus build other instructional

activities around it in a much more systematic manner;

3. The teacher may also select only parts of the programme for a given lesson, may decide to show all or part of it more than once to the same group and, in general, may adapt the progrmme to the specific course objectives that are to be achieved.

Nowadays, most instructional television is pre-recorded and many systems allow a limited amount of local recording and replaying in order to gain the advantages outlined above. However, the impact of broadcast instructional television in schools and other institution is still quite small. It is notable that the majority of recognized 'success stories' lie outside the formal educational establishment. A USA success story is 'Sesame Street', which is possibly so successful exactly because it is aimed at a pre-school audience, watching at home. A success story from the UK, at quite a different level of education, is the Open University, also outside the main stream of established institutions. As an alternative university, designed from the start to rely entirely on mediated instruction and to fill a 'vacuum' - hidden demand for home-study university-level education - the OU did not encounter the resistance of an established organization of teachers as would be the case if large-scale TV based instruction were to be proposed for all universities.

It is interesting to note, in this context, that most of the successful large-scale projects involving mass media (especially television) as major components of formal educational systems have been in the developing countries, where, once more, the TV-based systems have filled some form of vacuum created by inadequate conventional resources, absence of an established body of teachers, special geographical or demographical problems that render conventional methods inefficient, and so on. Once more, we are led to believe that what has kept television down in education have been the teachers, rather than any limitations of the medium itself.

However, developing nations have not had a clear run of successes either. Over the years, there have been more failures than successes. Often this has been due to inappropriate or unskilful use of the medium by the programme producers or their sponsors. Topics which should not be taught through television (such as colour or pattern recognition, which called for a level of picture quality well beyond what was possible with the TV technology of the time, or topics which require group interactions between course members) led to poor programmes which only served to get the medium a bad name. Administrative or technical inadequacies often led to irregular broadcasts, poor picture quality, or total system breakdown (as in the classic Mexican case study which showed that over 70% of TV classroom hours planned were not being received by the student groups due to signal or receiver breakdowns). This has led to a decline in the number of instructional TV systems 'in business', which is well illustrated by the data presented for Latin America in Fig. 2.3 (Tiffin, 1980).

Let we think, however, that such trends are limited to developing nations, let us remember the $ 25 million invested by the Ford Foundation into the development of ITV in the USA. Berkman (1976), when commenting this investment, states:

> '... scant more than a decade later, I defy anybody to show me where this multi-megabuck-backed experiment - by far, still, the largest ever in American education - rates even a footnote in the education texts ...'

Since Berkman's writing there are signs, however, that in the USA, Instructional TV has started a slow and painful upward trend. It seems that the systems have slowly learnt from their early mistakes and have begun to gain a stronger position in education. This revival has been likened to the 'Phoenix' - it was necessary to burn oneself up in order to be reborn from one's own ashes. Some of the reasons for this slow and painful rebirth will become clear in this and later chapters. But we must not expect such a revival to occur automatically. In Latin America there is as yet no sign of one—and with the current economic crises in the continent ...?

**Closed Circuit Television (CCTV)**

Perhaps, all in all, more success has been experienced through the use of the many thousands of Closed Circuit Television (CCTV) systems installed in many modern schools and just about all universities in the developed world (not to mention the many industrial and commercial training centres which are wired up for CCTV). Basically, a CCTV system is a local installation, linking one or more studios to a series of classrooms, usually by means of permanent cables installed in the building. More ambitious systems may link several associated institutions and may allow transmission from any of the classrooms to any or all of the other classrooms or sites 'wired in' to the system. Such systems may transmit 'live' lectures to several rooms, or may be used for the selective distribution of pre-recorded programmes on topics of interest to the system or certain groups of students. In many cases, the programmes are locally produced, by or with the cooperation of the teachers, so that a strong sense of ownership of the system and its programming can be fostered. Also, the owners of the system, who have invested a considerable sum setting it up, are close enough to the users to be able to monitor and evaluate the use made and the benefits gained by the organization. There is less likelihood of total rejection of the medium by the system, although we do sometimes hear horror stories of expensive CCTV systems that were installed and then hardly used at all.

The overall success of this method of employing TV in education and training may be judged by the quantity of locally produced programmes and the growing availability of commercially produced videotapes that find a ready market. In the UK, for example, there has, since the early 1970s, existed an interchange system of videotapes between universities. This was instigated by the then National Council for Educational Technology (NCET, later just CET), through the regular collection of information and publication of a catalogue *HELPIS,* or Higher Education Learning Programmes—Information Service. In its first early 1970s' version, this catalogue contained barely 100 titles of university-produced videotapes. The number slowly increased during the 1970s, reaching somewhat over 300 titles by 1978/9. By 1982, however, the number had shot up to over 3000 titles and has contained to rise so much that the service was taken over by the British Universities Film and Video Council, a body devoted exclusively to the dissemination of information about audiovisual materialsthat are available for use at university level.

In the USA, the production and commercialization of videotapes for educational and training use had also mushroomed, the amount of material on the market being so large that no single cataloguing organization is handling all the materials, potential users and media librarians being therefore forced to use several catalogues in order to obtain full coverage of what is available. And these numbers do not, of course, include the vast amount of video that is annually produced by business for its own internal training purposes. For the time being, there does not seem to be any slowing down in the production and use of special-purpose instructional videotapes.

Closed-circuit television involves basically, camera equipment and viewing or monitor equipment, linked by a cadle, to give a 'closed circuit'. In practice nowadays, the term

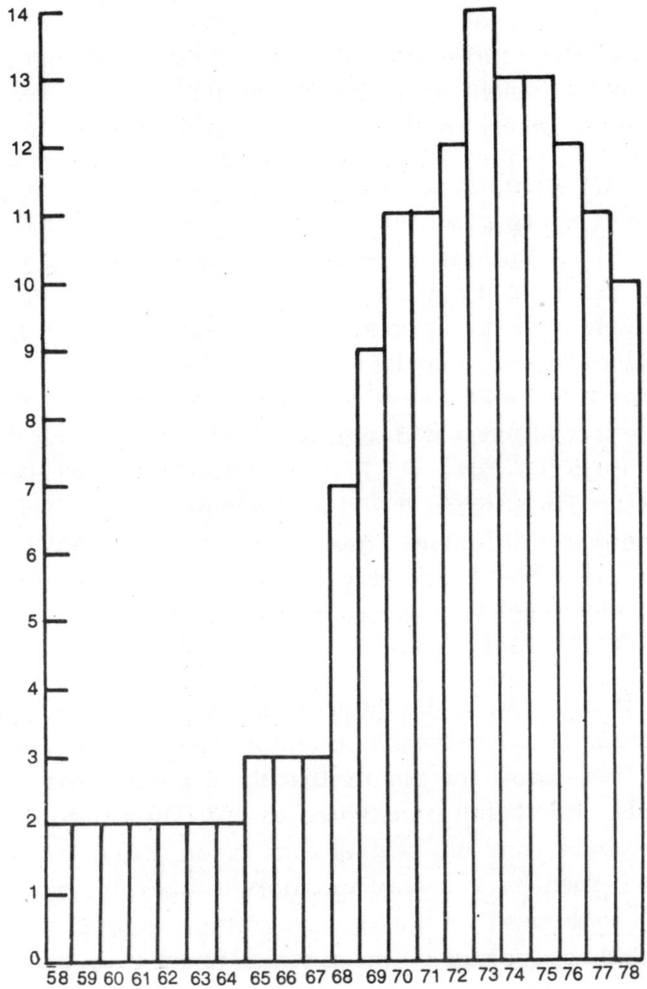


**Fig. 2.3:** The number of fully operational ETV systgems in Latin America (from Tiffin, 1980).

is sometimes used to describe systems which are not linked by cable, but by wireless waves over a limited area. The method is employed by a number of American school boards, often using an intermediate transmission station or even satellite to give wider coverage. Technically, such systems are really local broadcast or open-circuit systems and we will not discuss them further, particularly as the problems at both ends of the system - camera and monitor - are in any case very similar whatever transmission method is used.

The monitor, or viewer, is essentially a television receiver which picks up its signal from a cable or land-line rather than through an aerial. The signal may be at video frequencies, or at normal VHF frequencies. In the latter case, the monitor is no different from a normal TV, and in fact a standard receiver may be used by simply plugging the land-line into the aerial socket. In practice however, it is better to use a special receiver designed for the job. For one thing, it will probably have a 27 inch screen size for classroom viewing. For another, it will give a better picture. Schools or training establishments already equipped with TV receivers for outside broadcasts may, however, find it economically attractive to utilize these as at least an extra or spare viewer in a CCTV system.

In addition to the large receivers, one for each remote classroom, one needs small monitors, one for each camera in use. These show the picture that the camera is focussed on, whether it is being transmitted or not. The producer of the programme may use several cameras in different locations. He wll then have several monitors to keep his eye on. He refers to these to see how the programme is progressing and to select appropriate points at which to cut from one camera to another. Hence the name monitor. Further monitors may be used to show the producer the final products as transmitted and to keep other personnel 'in the picture'.

Obviously, the more complex the CCTV system envisaged, the more receivers and monitors are required and the pennies have to be watched.

Simple TV cameraswhich give adequate results when used as a visual aid (e.g. to blow up detail) are not very expensive. For more ambitious work a more versatile camera is required and the cost mounts. Also you do not get far without extra lighting, a selection of lenses (or a zoom lens), and at least one monitor. For one thing, the monitor acts as a view finder and check on adjustment combined. If the picture at the monitor is OK, it will be OK at the receiver - that is as long as no faults develop in the receiver or the connecting cables. Many modern cameras have built in monitors.

As soon as more ambitious projects are attempted, you not only need monitors to keep tabs on what is happening, you also need more than one camera. If you wish to change your viewpoint, this can sometimes be accomplished by 'panning' or by coming in closer or by usinga zoom lens. Skill is required to perform these actions. A safer way, and sometimes the only way, is to move and adjust one camera while the other is transmitting. When everything is under control, then you can cut to the new camera position. Few training presentations would need more than two cameras, but few would not benefit from the use of more than one.

By the time you have invested in a battery of cameras and monitors, you will need a camera crew, or alternatively, remote control. There is nothing about the system which cannot be adjusted by remote control. The only barrier is cost.

Many small CCTV systems do not really warrant the title of an installation. One or two cameras, three or four receivers, and drums of cable are stored in a locked room and are pulled out when required - probably once a year about Easter time, and again on Open Day.

A successful CCTV installation however, requires permanent land-lines, particularly if the several receivers are very remote from the camera. It also requires careful planning from where are we likely to transmit, and to where?

Such an installation must be built up around a central studio. Most standard transmission would be screened from the studio, where facilities and equipment are available. Monitoring of programmes is also performed at the studio, preferably from a soundproof booth. Finally the studio acts as a switchboard. Cable from the studio to remote classrooms or workshops may be used as required for the transmission of programmes or for the receiving of signals from cameras 'on location'.

Finally, of course, any modern CCTV system will be equipped with video recording and replay facilities. In practice, much greater use will normally be made of pre-recorded tapes than of live broadcasting. If live broadcasts are to be made they will generally first be tape recorded, edited and improved as necessary before transmission. In that case, tape reproduction and editing equipment will be necessary. Occasional programme production would not however warrant the outright purchase of this extra equipment, as it may be hired by the hour at many professional studios.

**Individual Study of Pre-recorded Video**

Of course, not all these tapes get used by means of group instruction, through closed circuit TV systems. Many are used on an individual basis, by students in resource centres, non-print media libraries, or in some form of self-directed open learning system. This is a third important way of using television/video in education and training. Whereas the other two forms - open broadcast TV and CCTV - may be used for the transmission of either live or recorded programmes, this third 'resource centre' form may of course only be used with a supply of pre-recorded programmes. Furthermore, these

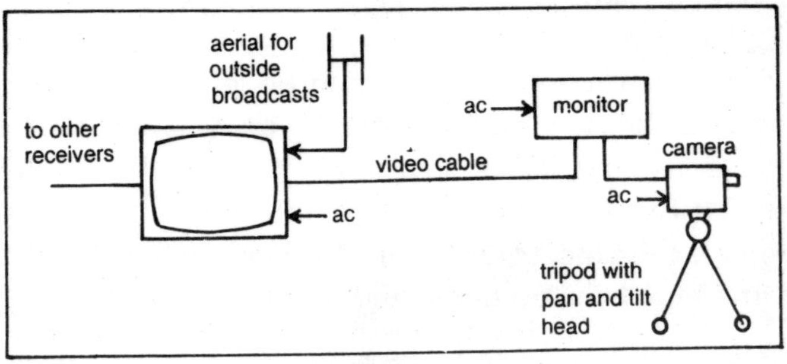


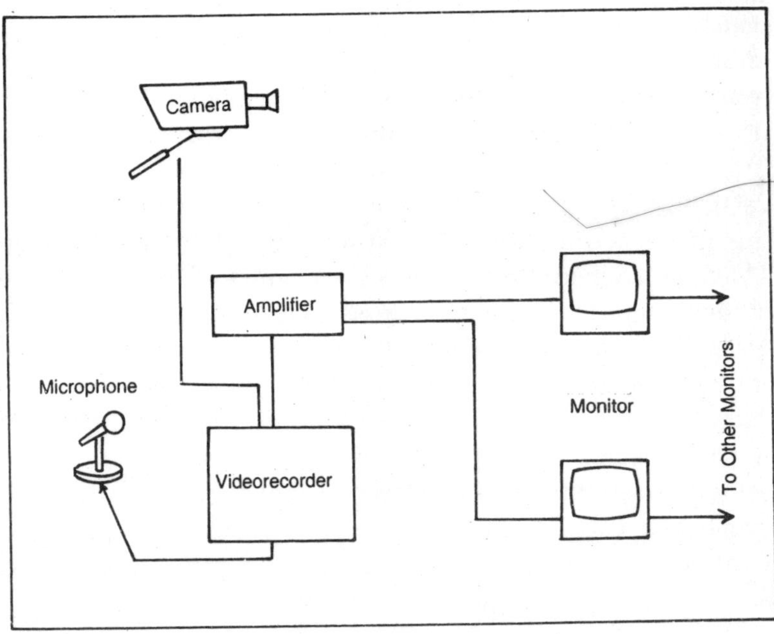


**Fig. 2.4:** Two basic forms of CCTV system. (a) Basis of a very simple I-camera CCTV system for live-broadcast only. This system also doubles as an open-broadcast reception system as it employs receiver/monitors in all classrooms. (b) A simple CCTV system capable of both live and recorded broadcasting. Note that the use of video monitors precludes its use for open-broadcast reception (though it could of course be modified by having a central RF tunner feeding a video signal to the amplifier).

programmes should be designed with individual study in mind. They should contain explanatory information that, in the group instruction made, would be left for the instructor or course leader to supply. They may be designed with built-in questions and tasks that may require the student to momentarily stop the tape, rewind and review certain sections of the tape, complete a workbook in synchronization with the taped instructions, and so on.

If a student may independently study a videotape, can be or she also independently study open broadcast TV? Of course, there is nothing to stop an individual student from watching, say, an Open University broadcast, at home, entirely alone - indeed most Open University students do exactly this. However, in terms of the programme's structure, no adaptation is possible to the needs or difficulties of the individual student. The programme must be designed to cater, as best it can, to all the students that are likely to take the given course, and in a system like the British Open University, where there are few if any entry prerequisites, the student population in one course may vary a great deal in terms of all manner of individual characteristics that may influence learning. The programme is a 'one-to-many' form of communication in its conception. It matters not at all whether it is watched by a group gathered together in front of one TV set in a classroom, or by one lone student at home. During the broadcast, each student receives the same message and treatment in both cases (although what happens before and after the broadcast may be quite different).

When, however, an individual student (or perhaps a pair) watches a pre-recorded videotape, then some form of adaptation to individual learning needs *may* take place. Even when the programme was designed as a lock-step 'one-to-many' communication, the student may stop, take notes, rewind and review, or otherwise adapt the presentation to his/her needs. It is better still when the programme is so structured as to help this adaptation to occur - a 'one-to-one' structure.

It is important to note the meaning I give here to 'one-to-one' programme structure. The essential aspect is that the programme as it were speaks directly to the student and the student may in some way influence the programme. As an analogy, reading a book - any book - is a one-to-one learning situation, in that the reader may stop and start at will, re-read a page, copy a paragraph or workout a problem using the content being read (even if he has to invent the problem for himself). Of course, a well-structured textbook, with clear paragraph headings, a good indexing system, well chosen and explained examples, and suggested practice problems, will be much more of a one-to-one learning experience. However, neither of these books, read out aloud at a fixed pace, without the opportunity for individual pace, route and style of reading, would qualify as one-to-one. Please note that neither of the books is a rigidly programmed text, nor are unique pre-specified instructional objectives implied. It is merely that in the one-to-one situation, each learner can exert a modicum of control over what to learn, when to learn and how to learn.

**Teletext as a Medium of Instruction**

The inclusion of Teletext at this point surprise some readers, but I do this for a very good reason, in that Teletext, although not as yet much used in education, is a practical example of a 'one-to-one' learning situation, using *open-broadcast* television. But Telext is not really television, you say. It uses the hardware of television, but presents only text messages and the simplest of graphics. Very true, but there are other, more sophisticated systems just around the corner of technological progress and there are already some promising experiments in the use of today's admittedly crude Teletext systems.

Teletext is one of the family of new telecommunication media which Tyler (1979) defines as:

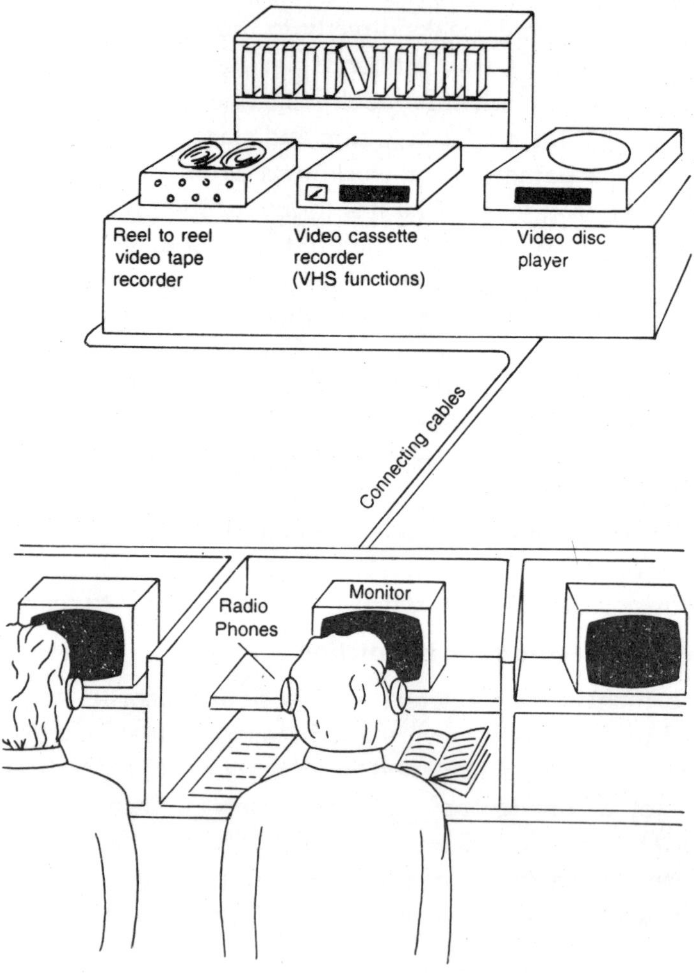


**Fig. 2.5:** A typical self-study resource centre. Carrells can receive any one of several formats of video recordings, from a central battery of players.

'... systems for the widespread dissemination of textual and graphic information by wholly electronic means, for display on low cost terminals (often suitably equipped television receivers) under the selective control of the recipient, and using control procedures easily understood by untrained users...'

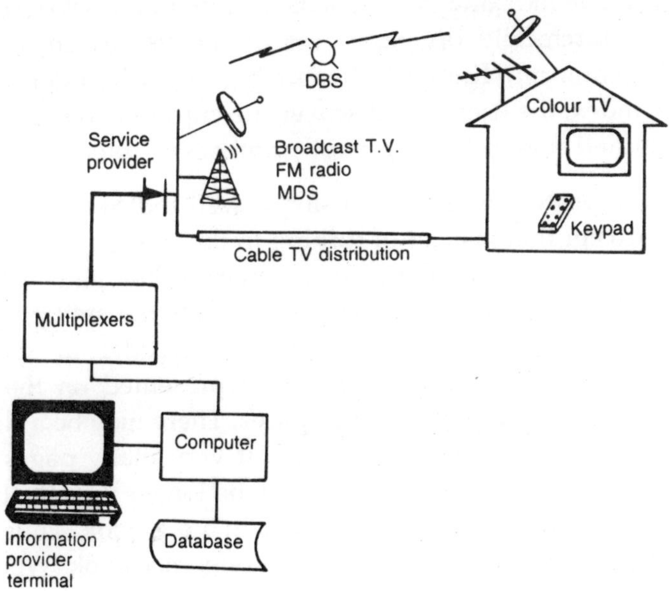


**Fig. 2.6:** A typical components of a Teletext system. The information provider composes the 'pages' of information. The service provider broadcasts these pages in intervals between video broadcast pictures. This may occur by FM broadcast, satellite, cable, etc. The user (our student) selects the desired pages with the keypad and studies them on the screen of his home TV set. (Adapted from Tydeman *et al.*, 1982.)

The 'family' includes such proprietary systems as Prestel and Telidon, which are somewhat more complex, allowing for two-way communication between the user and a distant database. Teletext, on the other hand, is simpler, in that it is a one-way communication medium, but which is, nevertheless under the control of the user. Examples of other proprietary systems include Ceefax and Oracle.

The principle of Teletext is quite simple. A number of screens, or 'pages' of text or graphics are stored in a distant database, just like the pages of a book. They are numbered and indexed, just like a book, to indicate the information that they contain. The indexing system is itself stored on a set of pages as a hierarchically organized set of menus (or any other convenient form). Knowing the number to key in order to get at the index, the user may discover the current content of the system and may select the page numbers of interest.

The process is just like using a well indexed reference book, except that instead of turning to the desired pages, the user keys in their numbers on a numerical key pad. All the pages stored in the database are periodically transmitted, and the desired page is captured by the decoder (a special attachment to the television set) and presented on the TV screens for as long as the user requires. There may be a slight delay in accessing the desired page if very many pages are stored, but the waiting time is usually no longer than the time it takes to find a given page number in a big book. Thus the use of Teletext is just like the use of a reference book (Woolfe, 1987).

There are some important differences between Teletext and a printed book, however. The information in Teletext is updatable at any moment. Current events may be used as real-life case studies in a social science programme, for example. The pages stored in the system may be changed daily or weekly, in step with a series of broadcast ITV programmes - thus the student may watch a half-hour instructional programme and then may access a series of summary pages or practice problem sheets, in order to reinforce and evaluate his understanding of the topic.

The potential applications are many, though not at all sophisticated. The one-way communication capability does not allow full-blown CAL routines, for example, although simple programmed instructions routines of the 'branching text' variety could be implemented. The medium will do nothing that may not be done by means of other, simpler, media, but, in certain applications, it may be more effective, more efficient or more economical. It is presented here to extend somewhat beyond the commonplace the concept of educational television and, principally, to illustrate a possible one-to-one use of open broadcast television. Further educational applications are discussed in Tydeman *et al.* (1982) and Anderson (1987).

### A Schema of Educational TV Systems

In the preceding sections, we have examined a number of common (and some not so common) ways of using television in education and training. We have used several terms to distinguish between and classify them:

- Open broadcast/local system or network;
- One-way/two-way transmission of information;
- Live/recorded programmes;
- One-to-many/one-to-one programme structures.

We can bring together all the examples that we have discussed so far into a table or matrix which will better illustrate their similarities and differences (Figure 2.7).

Note that we have only examined one half of this schema so far - the upper half, dealing with one-way transmission systems. We shall leave the other half—two-way transmission systems — to later chapters. These are important new developments in the use of the television medium that put the emphasis on interactivity. I present the whole schema here,

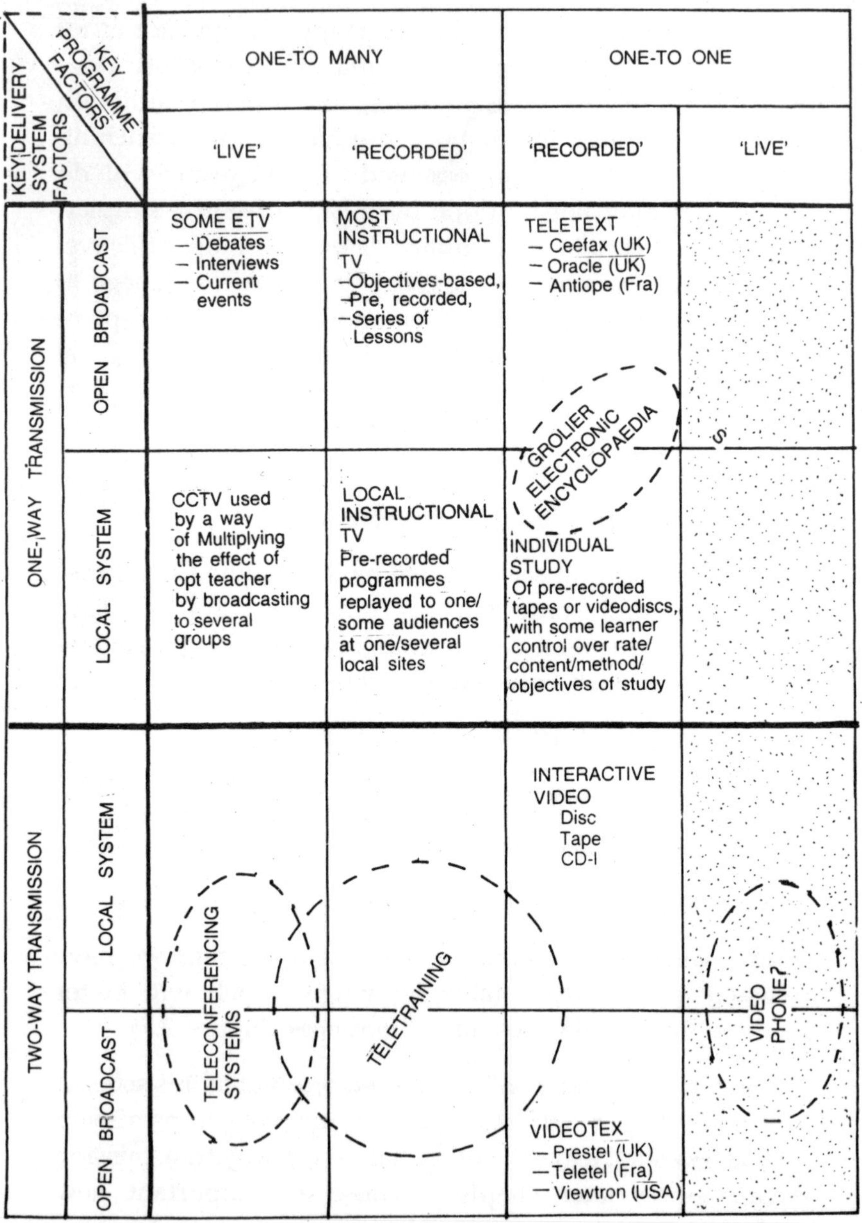


**Fig. 2.7** A schema of educational and training application of TV systems

however, to establish a context and advantage of this form is the case of updating information - during the 1986.

There is one entry in the top half of our schema which was not discussed earlier. It has been left till now as an 'afterthought', as it were, which illustrates the usefulness and the limitations of the schema we have constructed. The 'Grolier Electronic Encyclopaedia' is a specific case that illustrates the merging of technologies that is currently occurring. A few years back, the Grolier Encyclopaedia (a set of some 20 or more volumes in its text form) was transformed into electronic form and offered as a database to be accessed from a distance. One advantage of this form is the ease of updataing of information - during the 1986 World Cup year, for example, a greater amount of detailed information on soccer was included to meet the seasonal demand and was later withdrawn again as demand subsided. Moreover recently, the same encyclopaedia has been made available on a CD-ROM disc. This has of course lost the rapid updating facility, but has gained a sophisticated key-word indexing system that allows rapid searches of the 'small print', right through the complete work, on a personal microcomputer, at zero search fee. The first version is an 'open broadcast, one-to-one' system that is used very much like Telextext (although the technical details are quite different).The second is a local, stand-alone one-to-one system, which has little to do with television as we understand it, except that the information output is presented on a cathode ray tube.

We have also not classified all common uses of video on our schema. For example, the use of video recording of class activities for later evaluation and feedback (as in microteaching systems, interviewing or sales training, etc.) has not been mentioned. Here, the video feedback is one component in a more complex, multi-media instructional system. We have restricted ourselves to the analysis of systems in which TV or video are the principal delivery systems. The limitations of our schema are obvious. However, it is a useful way to view the whole field of television and video in education - provided you do not try to interpret the classifications too rigidly.

## Current and Future Growth in Video Usage

Lest some of the comments made earlier have led you to think that I believe television and video to be underused in education and training, I present here some recent statistics, taken from the 1985 Higher Education Utilization Study (HEUS-85) sponsored in the USA by the Chronicle of Higher Education. According to this report, nearly all US universities (92%) have video distribution facilities and equipment, and seven out of ten have central reception facilities for picking up special education video broadcasts. The two tables presented in Figure 2.8 illustrate the variety and modern sophistication of the delivery systems in use. We might add that some school systems are also big users of the newer distribution technologies - at the time of writing, the State of New York school system has over 100 operating or projected local instructional TV networks using microwave or cable linkups between remote sites. Whereas the early dreams of mass TV-based education did not materialize, today we see a trend toward TV-based variety, individualization and catering for minority interests.

The situation in the UK and Europe is similar, as shown by the variety of video applications in Higher Education which are described in the book edited by Zuber-Skerritt (1984).

## The Benefits of TV and Video

### *Research: TV versus Film*

On the face of it there is little difference, from the audience's point of view, between a television or a cine film presentation. McLuhan (1964) argued that the 'here and now'

| Video Facilities Available in US Colleges and Universities | All Institutions |
|---|---|
| Any central reception facilities | 69% |
| Community cable system drop(s) | 47 |
| Master TV antenna | 33 |
| Rotatable satellite receive-only dish | 12 |
| Fixed satellite receive-only dish | 11 |
| Other microwave reception equipments | 7 |
| ITFS reception equipment | 6 |
| Satellite transmission antenna (uplink) | 2 |
| Any distribution/exhibition facilities | 92 |
| Special video or film screening/projection room | 63 |
| Campus close-circuit TV (on campus origination) | 34 |
| Campus building wired by community cable TV system | 34 |
| Community cable TV system educational/access channels | 31 |
| Non-commercial television broadcasting station | 11 |
| ITSF transmission equipment | 5 |

(a)

| Uses of Video Technologies in US Colleges and Universities | All Institutions |
|---|---|
| One-way presentation of instruction to students on campus | 84% |
| Promotion/recruitment | 64 |
| Counselling | 60 |
| Outreach | 54 |
| Staff development | 49 |
| One way presentation of instruction to students off-campus | 35 |
| Pictorial enhancement of programmed instruction using computers | 26 |
| Conferencing or two-way communications between faculty members and off campus students | 8 |
| Conferencing or two-way communications between faculty members and students in multiple locations on campus | 6 |
| Other | 5 |

(b)

Fig.: 2.8 (a) Video facilities available in US colleges and universities. (b) Use of video technologies in US colleges and universities (HEUS-85).

aspects of a TV image, coupled with qualities such as less precise definition and presence in your own home, make the TV image a much more acceptable, and hence a much more powerful, medium of communication than the cine film. There is evidence to support this view, particularly from measures of the relative success of advertising on the two media.

However, when both media are removedto the relatively artificial setting of the classroom or workshop, there seems to be very little difference. Munday (1962) compared the effect of television and film presentation of lessons in social studies and geography. He found no difference in the amounts learned through the two media. A similar French study (Bertran, 1962) again found no significant differences in the respective effectiveness of TV and film in general, although those students who knew that the TV presentation was live did respond much more favourably to the presentation. They remembered slightly more and were influenced in their attitudes very much more than students who thought they were watching a filmed recording. This finding tends to suggest that TV is a more powerful medium than the cinema ever was - not because more people watch television, but because people accept its message more readily, get more involved emotionally and are participants rather than observers.

One major use of instructional television automatically utilizes this 'here and now' quality: the use of a CCTV system to increase the size of the audience, by allowing one teacher to address several classrooms or schools at once. We would normally arrange for someone technically competent and gifted as a communicator to deliver a carefully planned and prepared presentation. In addition however, if the speaker is known to the audience either personally or by repute, their level of involvement will be greater.

This use of CCTV is valuable for economic reasons. It

enables one to make the best use of highly skilled or qualified personnel, cuts down the need for duplication of expensive demonstration apparatus and allows a careful presentation to be viewed by many. The imaginative use of the TV camera can also produce a better presentation. For example, the use of close-ups can focus the audience's attention on particular points, or can blow-up the details of a demonstration so that all can see clearly. One can show an operation from the operator's point of view, or cut-in a pre-recorded sequence from a workshop to illustrate the relevance or importance of the task to be learnt. In short, the principles of design of instructional films, outlined earlier, can be applied to produce an altogether better presentation than would be possible in the 'live' teaching situation.

**Research: The Instructional Effects of TV**

There has probably been more recently reported research on the use of television in education than on cine films. However, as Peggie Campeau (1972) points out, most of it is subjective and poorly designed. Those studies which are properly controlled geneally repeat the pattern of 'no significant difference' found earlier in the bulk of research into film. There are hundreds of reported studies comparing TV with traditional methods, but no conclusive results.

For example, Chu and Schramm (1967) carried out a review of 207 studies involving 421 separate comparisons. At the college and adult level, results of 235 comparisons indicated that 176 found no significant differences between televised and conventional instruction, 29 favoured television over conventional instruction and 30 favoured conventional methods.

Dubin and others (1969) conducted a more rigorous review of studies in which experimental classes taught by television were compared with control classes receiving no televised instruction. They identified 42 studies that could be considered to be comparable on the basis of several criteria, namely, instruction lasted at least one term; identical, written course-content examinations were used for groups being compared; similar methods of instruction were experienced by both groups, etc. First, when teaching methods were matched, face-to-face instruction was superior to two-way instructional television, and then only when the lecture method was used by each medium. ('Two-way' television provided students and lecturer with audio facilities for exchanging questions and initiating discussions, thereby approximating to a 'live' instructional situation). Second, *one*-way instructional television produced the same amount of learning as face-to-face teaching by lecture, by a combination of lecture-discussion-demonstration, or by discussion alone. Third, instruction by either method yielded no significant differences when the studies were grouped by the broad subject-area headings of humanities, social sciences and science/mathematics. In attempting to explain the odd finding that two-way television was definitely inferior to face-to-face teaching, the authors suggested that the need for students and lecturer to use the fairly complicated technical apparatus necessary for two-way communication may have been the cause.

In more recent and more rigorous 'meta-analyses' of a group of 74 video-based studies, Cohen, Ebling and Kulik (1981) found very slight benefits for the video mediated instruction as opposed to conventional instruction, but the benefit was of the order of 1 or 2 percentage points only.

The trouble with surveys of this nature, and with comparative studies generally, is that in looking at a mass of evidence concerning the 'total course' we may be masking real differences which exist between media for certain aspects of the learning which is taking place. By lumping together the results of a number of studies, we are aggravating this situation. The greater the sample of studies we take, and the more all-inclusive they are, the more likely we are to cancel out any differences which exist and to end up with 'no significant difference'. As Briggs and others (1966) point out, we should be classifying studies according to the categories of learning taking place. But the 'traditional' categories as used by Dubin - humanities, etc - are not precise enough. We ought to be using such categories as procedures, discriminations, or concepts, as outlined in the opening chapters of this book. We ought also to be investigating learning differences between individuals.

Smith (1968) conducted a series of experiments on the effect of television broadcasts on the attainment and attitudes of students taking City & Guilds 'G' courses at technical colleges in England. The largest experiment involved students in 27 technical colleges watching a BBC television series on emgineering science. Some students watched the broadcasts. The control group did not. In all, over 800 students were involved in the study, and were carefully matched for ability. There were no significant differences between groups on the attainment test used to assess the instructional effects of the two treatments. On the other hand, large and significant differences both in ability and attainment were found when the scores for individual colleges were analysed separately. The television broadcasts appeared to have a greater impact on students who were above average ability, and to have more effect on performance in mechanics.

Research of this nature suggests that there may indeed the difference between media which have been obscured in earlier studies. However, more research at this 'micro' level is still needed before a comprehensive picture emerges.

Another 'micro' approach has been suggested by Salomon (1976, 1979). He suggests that three groups of factors may make a difference in learning from mediated instruction - technology of transmission; content; and symbolic code of the message. The first is the one most often studied in comparative research and generally has not rsulted in very significant differences. The second is not really a media factor except in as much as certain media can transmit the given content and others cannot. The third group - symbolic codes - is the one that Salomon considers worthy of further research. He also singles out certain characteristics of TV (e.g. the ability to show a process in action) as potentially significant in the promotion of appropriate learning through TV. He quotes research (Salomon and Cohen, 1976) which supports his views. However, not all researachers (e.g. Clark, 1983) agree that this line of research is worth pursuing. Clark believes the only benefits of media are related to costs and efficiency, and practical constraints that may be overcome, not any psychological differences.

### Some Practical Benefits of Video

Whether Clark is correct or not on the psychological effects of video instruction being negligible, practical experience, especially in training applications, has often shown enormous benefits of video-based systems. Some examples follow.

Video is an unusually successful training medium. It saves time, money and resources. It adapts to a wide variety of situations and requirements, and at the same time, it guarantees consistency in repeated viewing.

Even though it usually takes about ten times as long to create a video training programme as it does to prepare and present traditional classroom training, video ultimately saves far more time at the point of delivery and when the material must be repeated. With a well-designed video programme, you save up to 75% of the time it would take to deliver the same message in traditional lecture style. If training time can be reduced by as much as 75%, money and other resources can certainly be saved as well (Marlow, 1981).

In designing traditional media materials like slides and transparencies, you have the advantage of compression. You can cut out unnecessary information and deliver only as much information as is directly related to the objective. This also holds true in video programme design. When you compares information, the student can learn in less time that it would usually take in a classroom setting. The objectives of the training can be attained in much less teaching and learning time (Robson, 1978).

By reducing the time spent by staff, management and instructors, video can reduce the cost of training and communications. If it takes less time to communicate corporate messages through the use of video, staff and management time is saved. If it takes less time for train new workers, they become productive that much sooner. If the training process itself takes less time, instructional staffs may be reduced, on their time may be employed more economically. Thus, video effectively creates cost savings throughout the corporation (Dranov *et al.,* 1980).

Time and money are saved when video replaces the travelling instructor. Using a video network (video players placed in field offices), learners in regional or international offices can benefit from on-site training without the instructors having to travel to each location.

Seldom is the viewer ready to receive information at the same time as the trainer is ready to deliver it. Video enables you to bring these two times together and allows the learner to adjust information reception to his or her own schedule. No longer are you locked into prescheduled information delivery. The learner now controls the schedule of viewing.

This is particularly useful for organizations like hospitals, law enforcement agencies, transportation and high technology manufacturing that require workers to be scheduled round the clock.

With well-designed video training, insntructors do not have to be present to deliver information. Thus, video can assume the responsibility of training 24 hours a day.

Another significant advantage of using video in training is its ability to deliver information consistently. All viewers receive the same information in the same style of delivery. The videotape records the lecture or programme and preserves its style and meaning exactly as the presenter originally intended them. Individual differences of a number of instructors in the interpretation, style or philosophy is never a problem. All viewers receive the same message every time they view the tape (Dranov *et al.*, 1980; Anderson, 1976).

This is extremely important when it comes to teaching attitudes and philosophy, as in supervisory or management training. The presentation of the organization's policy and philosophy is not left to individual interpretation. Instructors need not feel the pressure of presenting the material over and over again in a consistent, organized manner. All viewers, whether they are impressionable new employees receiving their first exposure to the company or seasoned sales personnel in offices around the country, receive consistent information - information that has been designed, written and controlled by the organization. Video creates a reliable, constant delivery system, readily available, delivering the same corporoate message each time.

Video, like film, has another advantage that contributes to training, and this is motion. Through motion you can provide performance feedback, role modelling, product and safety demonstrations, process examples and motor skill development. Motion helps to deliver the message. If used effectively, it increases the training reception. In some situations, such as skill development, motion is essential for effective learning (Anderson, 1976; Heinich, Molenda and Russell, 1985).

Video is a visual medium, and it has the ability to hold interest through colour, motion and sound. If used properly, video can create interest through visual stimuli. According to some experts, visual images hold interest, and add to retention and recall of information (Kearsley, 1984, Kemp, 1980).

One case study that I have come across was a project carried out for the Ford Motor Company in South Africa by a small video-training consultancy group. A small team, working with portable video equipment from a van equipped with editing facilities, developed all the operator training required as on-the-job short videoclips to *demonstrate* each step, using previously trained operators as evaluators and guides in a 'TWI' type of overall training system. The in-service, video-based training was so effective that the company closed down two operator training centres that it had previously been supporting.

## Selecting and Using TV/Video for Instruction

### *Adopt, Adapt, Repurpose or Produce?*

Let us suppose that your local educational or instructional television system is currently planning to broadcast a programme, or a series which seems to match the overall objectives of part of a course that you will be teaching. You will be faced with the decision of whether to include the programme or series in your teaching. Assuming that this is the first time this particular offering will be broadcast, you have no past experience on which to base your decision. Also, as this will be a broadcast that is synchronized with the local teaching schedule and (possibly) is protected by copyright so that you cannot, legally, make a preview copy, your decision is limited to whether or not you will *adopt* the programme/ series as developed and produced by the network.

On the other hand, if you can obtain a preview copy of

the tapes or, better still, tape the broadcast and use the tapes with your group, then your decision is less restricted. You may decide to adopt the programme 'as is', but you may also decide to use only some parts, or to modify the sequence of presentation of certain scenes, or to stop at key points for group discussion. In other words, you may be free to *adapt* the original programmes to better suit the objectives that you wish to pursue, or the learning habits of your particular group of students. In this case you will be acting in much the same way as when you preview and analyse a film before using it in your teaching.

In both the above cases, you have come across, or been offered, a video production that was designed for instructional purposes that are similar to yours but was in fact designed and developed by someone else. The situation is somewhat different when you set about designing and developing a course or a lesson, decide that some objectives require, or would benefit from, the video medium, and then set about obtaining the necessary video sequences.

You may, for example, wish to show some examples of heated discussions and arguments as material for analysis by a human relations class. If you have access to a video/film library, you may be lucky and find just what you need in some old films that perhaps were never intended for instruction. Having identified the scenes, you mark them in some way for later identification, or get them transferred to a fresh videotape, so that you can conveniently present them at the appropriate moment in the lesson. You are, in effect, inventing new uses for old video - the term which is now often used for this is *repurposing.*

But suppose that you do not find what you need to complete your lesson design. Either you change your design, abandoning your plans to use video, or you decide to *produce* the sequences that you require.

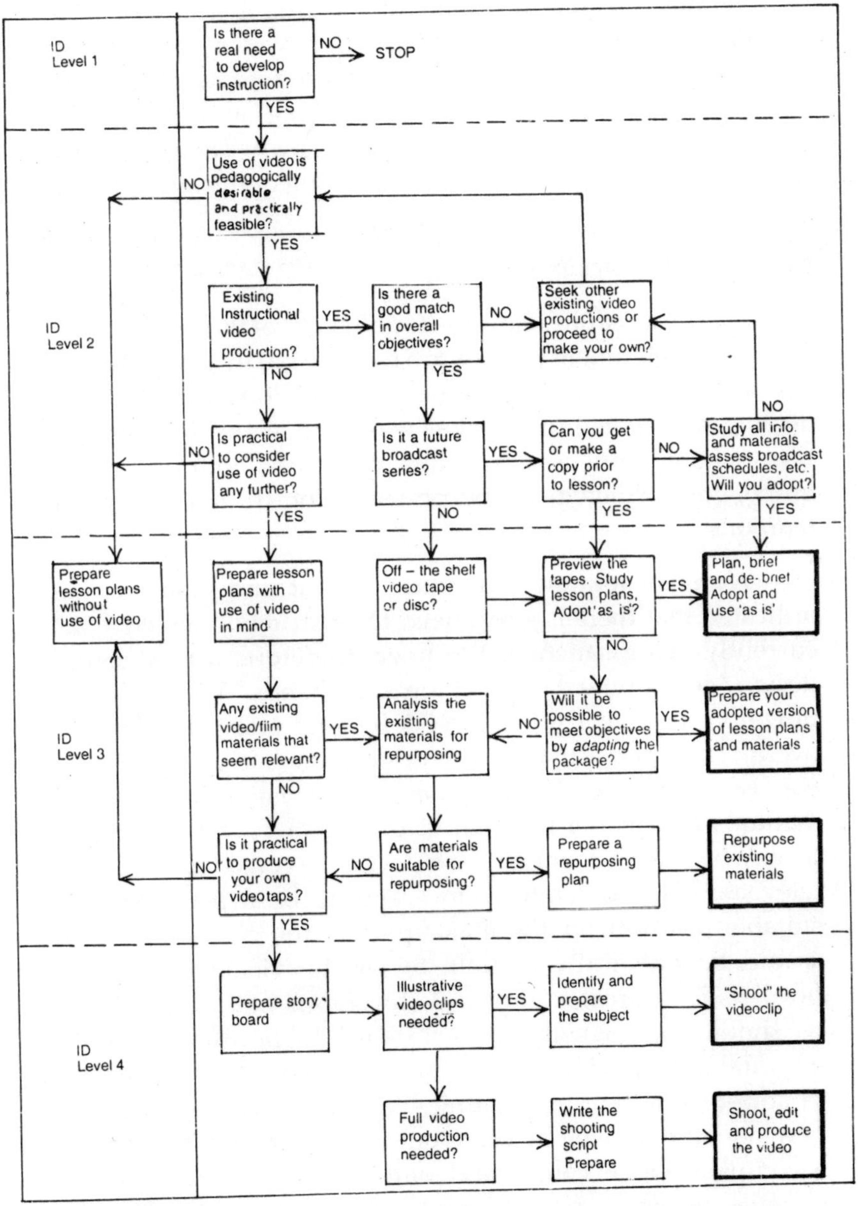


**Fig. 2.9:** Summary of the procedures for selecting or developing video for instruction. (Note how the procedure flows through the four ID levels.)

In this section, we shall be dealing with these four alternative courses of action. We shall, however, only discuss the general principles involved, as space does not permit the inclusion of a whole video repurposing and production course - this would require a book of its own. The flow charts in Fig. 2.9 illustrate in summary the scope of our work in this book.

## Initial Media Decisions

Fig. 2.9 illustrates how the four 'levels' of the instructional design/development process are (or may be) involved in your decision-making. This is particularly obvious when we are dealing with a medium such as television as the decisions we take may be influenced by a host of factors, both macro and micro, both pedagogical and practical (logistical, economical, temporal, etc).

We shall assume that initial, 'front end' analysis has indicated that there is a real need for instruction which is not currently being satisfied. We have, therefore, a new course design/development project on our hands. We therefore, move on to what I term 'level 2 ID' and start planning the overall course objectives, content, structure, etc. As we do this, we also get involved in considering alternative instructional methods and media for each of the major course objectives. It may be that at this point we decide to consider the use of television/video. If television seems to be a pedagogically suitable medium for the major part of the course, and if it would be practically feasible to use television extensively (available resources, equipment, development time, etc.), then we should check whether some existing TV production would be suitable as, obviously, it will be much cheaper and quicker to adopt (or adapt) an existing TV course than to develop a new one. It may well be quite out of the question to develop a complete video course and only if we find a reasonably suitable existing series of programmes can we consider the intensive use of video in our project.

The procedures for such overall level 2 media selection are outlined in the third section. Figures 2.10 presents a more detailed, TV-oriented, set of questions which may further assist you to make the overall decision on whether the use of TV is both desirable and feasible.

Of course, in reality, the sequence may be a little different. You may already know of a TV series that you would like to use, or that your local educational authorities are recommending. It may be that the course objectives are not 'crying out' for the use of video. It may be that you could teach the whole course without any television, but here is this interesting series of programmes offered to you 'on a plate'. Too good to resist! But beware! It is still just as important to check that the TV course objectives match those of the course that you propose to give. It is still important to check as closely as possible that the teaching methods, the content and the examples and problems presented are appropriate for your students. So the sequence of the flow chart may, in reality, vary, but its content and spirit remain valid.

If the objectives of the existing TV series are reasonably close to your own, then you should investigate the material further. If at all possible, get copies of all the materials, the printed supporting study material, teachers' notes, and broadcasting schedules as well as tapes of the programmes themselves. In the case of current TV offerings, this may be difficult and you will be forced to make a decision on the incomplete information that you *can* get hold of. You will decide whether to adopt the series or not.

## Adopting and Adapting Existing Instructional TV

If you *do* decide to adopt the series, you will possibly receive some outline lesson suggestions in the teachers' notes supplied by the programme producers. But whether you do or not, you should still plan the lesson, paying particular attention to the *briefing* and *de-briefing* of the students. If you

| | | Yes | No |
|---|---|---|---|
| 1. | PEDAGOGICAL DESIRABILITY | | |
| A. | Must both audio and visual information be presented? | ______ | ______ |
| B. | Must presentations of audio and visual information be synchronized? | ______ | ______ |
| C. | Must motion be shown? | ______ | ______ |
| D. | Must information on other media (such as slides, graphics) be shown? | ______ | ______ |
| E. | Is extremely fine picture quality and detail unimportant? | ______ | ______ |
| F. | Are there ways to get active student response to programme content, either during the programme itself or after the programme is used? | ______ | ______ |
| G. | Is it desirable to present information in a fixed sequence? (not applicable to videodisc) | ______ | ______ |
| H. | Is it desirable to present information at a fixed space? | ______ | ______ |
| II. | PRACTICAL FEASIBILITY | | |
| A. | Is there space available to accommodate television? | ______ | ______ |
| B. | Is appropriate (size, format) equipment available for either producing or presenting programmes? | ______ | ______ |
| C. | Is television tc be used in a way that does not impose undue constraints on teaching time? | ______ | ______ |
| D. | Do students and staff have skills to use equipment or are they willing to acquire these skills? | ______ | ______ |
| E. | Can the skill levels required for using television be acquired easily? | ______ | ______ |
| F. | Is television affordable? Is its cost reasonable in light of its potential benefit? | ______ | ______ |

**Fig.: 2.10:** A check-list to assist in the assessment of the desirability and feasibility of using television as a principal medium of instruction. (Adapted from Locatis and Atkinson, 1984).

have had the opportunity to preview the programme, then you will be able to alert students for specific events or situations that they will witness, and prepare their 'mind set' so that they attend to what is important. You will also be able to develop some follow-up exercises or discussion topics which relate directly to the programme's content. If you were not able to preview, then it is even more important that you plan an introduction and follow-up that address the objectives you wish to achieve. You would do well, also, to prepare some 'contingency plans' in case the programme misfires completely and you have to implement some alternative instructional activities. The final report of the School TV Utilization Study (Dirr *et al.*, 1979) reported that, although most teachers (in the USA) who used instructional TV broadcasts in their classroom teaching did spend some time preparing their students and then follow up the programmes, the time so spent was very short - less than five minutes on preparation and ten minutes on follow-up. This may, in part, be forced on the teachers by the relation of TV programme duration to overall class duration. However, to get the most out of a TV-based lesson, the briefing and de-briefing times should be much longer - often longer than the programme itself. This should be taken into account when scheduling class times for TV lessons.

If you do get to preview the programme, it may well happen that certain aspects of it will immediately seem ill adapted to the needs or the capabilities of your particular student group. You may have the chance to plan some adaptations to the original. The most common and simple (and often most essential) adaptation to a 20- or more minute programme is to build in some pauses at key points, allowing discussion or reinforcement of important concepts midway through the presentation. Unless the programme is a dramatization or case study, or is basically descriptive, then it will introduce a new key concept or principle every few minutes and it may be desirable to make several stops in a half-hour video. Procedural 'how to do it' presentations often benefit from progressive application practice step-by-step. There may be a stop every minute or two, each stop lasting longer than the previous video segment. This was the format actually built into the very successful South African operator training programmes, mentioned earlier in this chapter.

**Opening Activities (The Briefing)**

- What introductory material has been supplied with the programme? Is it adequate? Must I supplement it?
- Does the programme attract student attention/interest inthe topic? How can I enhance this before the broadcast?
- Does the programme explain its objectives? How should I explain our objectives in using the programme?
- What prior learning is assumed? What must I do to get students to recall/refresh this before the broadcast?
- What key points or events should students be looking for? How can I get them in the correct 'mind set'?

**Adaptations to the Programme (Only if Showing a Video)**

- Are anys tops desirable? Where? Why? What activities should be planned for each stop?
- Are any sections worth repeating? Which? Why? At what point in the lesson? How can this be done in practice?
- Are any sections irrelevant? Which? How can I skip them? What about continuity? Will I need to say/do something?
- Would any changes in sequence be beneficial? What are they? How can this be arranged in practice?
- Are any sections weak/unclear/inadequate/incomplete? How can they be improved? Do I have any suitable materials? How can I integrate these with the programme?

**Closing Activities (The De-briefing)**

- What supplementary materials were supplied with the programme? Are they adequate? How can they be improved?
- How can I encourage transfer of learning? What transfer activities can I include in the de-briefing session?
- How can I evaluate the learning? Are any tests supplied? What other instruments or activities may I use as tests?
- How can I evaluate students' reactions to the programme? Do I have an appropriate instrument? Should I do it 'live'?
- What further remedial/enrichment activities should I have 'up my sleeve' in case the programme 'misfires'?
- What summary should students prepare/receive for later review/study? What further references/homework/projects should I give them to take away?

**Fig: 2.11:** A check-list to assist in the planning of a lesson around an existing instructional television programme.

Other adaptations that may be made include the repetition of a particularly important or difficult segment, the elimination of any irrelevant segments, presenting the final summary segment first, as an advance organizer, etc. You may also interface or add on any other existing materials which you think will enrich or clarify the original programme. These will not, of course, be edited into the programme tape, but will be shown during an interval or as part of the briefing or de-briefing process. All of this is, of course, dependent on whether you will be showing a videotaped version of the programme. If you are forced to use the direct broadcast, then you are limited to the design of the 'before' and 'after' activities.

**Repurposing Existing Material**

So far we have been assuming that a reasonably well designed instructional video production has been selected as the backbone of our lesson and all we have to do is to build other essential lesson components around it and, possibly, just fine-tune some of the programme's sections for the special needs of our specific student group.

If no suitable programme is located, it is necessary to reassess the feasibility of using video, as the time and cost involved in producing your own programmes may be prohibitive. There is the intermediate possibility of repurposing some existing video or film segments. This is still quite time-consuming, though faster and cheaper than starting from scratch.

Depending on this reassessment of the feasibility of using video, you will now proceed to the lesson planning stage (level 3 ID) with one of two possible mind-sets:

- to plan your lessons on the basis of other media, avoding the use of video if at all possible, or
- to plan your lessons with the use of video in mind, looking for opportunities to use this medium creatively and to good instructional effect.

In the latter case, you should once more explore the existence of suitable material. This time, however, you are looking for specific scenes or segments - videoclips - that are required by your own instructional design. You need not limit yourself to video that was originally produced for education, nor even to video - any old film sequences that illustrate what you want to show may also be repurposed. One project for a psychology course required a large number of examples of different styles of behaviour, to illustrate such concepts as introversion, extroversion, and schizophrenia. These were located by searching through several films in a local film library - mostly well known Hollywood movies. The selected scenes - very short segments - were then transferred to one videotape for convenience of presentation. The example set was so designed as to include several illustrations of each behaviour type, obvious and less obvious in ascending order of difficulty. They could be used for initial demonstration, for practice in recognition and as a final test.

This was a commercial project, so copyright permission was sought to reproduce the scenes selected, some interlinking 'talking head' sequences were actually produced to explain the examples, and the segments were edited and assembled professionally. However, it is often possible to produce very effective instruction by simply marking the segments of existing tapes, setting them to the starting points, stacking the cassettes in the order in which the lesson plan calls for them and just loading them into the cassette player as required during the lesson. This avoids all the copyright and editing problems, at the cost of some inconvenience in use. It all depends on how often the particular lesson will be taught, how many different source tapes are involved, whether the tapes are of the same video standards (VHS, BETA, etc), whether any cine film sources are involved, and so on.

The key difference between adapting an existing programme and repurposing is that in the latter case, the

**Detailed Lesson Plan**

Follow the general lesson planning procedure outlined. Plan in great detail, so as to specify *when* a video segment is necessary, *why* it is necessary - how it will be used, *what* is the required content, scene, examples, etc.

Consider the value of video for:

*Opening the lesson -*
Gaining attention/stimulating interest.
Presenting an introduction/overview of the topic.
Reviewing the prerequisites.

*Implementing the instruction -*
Explaining/defining/demonstrating.
Providing examples/practice exercises.
Providing evaluation exercises/feedback.

*Closing the lesson -*
Illustrating generality/promoting transfer.
Providing enrichment beyond the objectives.
Providing a summary/wider context.

**Analysis of Candidate Audiovisual Segments**

- Does the segment fulfil the purpose for which it is being considered (see the list above)?
- Is the content appropriate to the purpose, audience? Will they relate to the examples, language, characters?
- Is the visual imagery and style appropriate, not outmoded, understandable by the target audience?
- Is the segment clear, free of 'distractors', well filmed, supported by useful and well spoken commentary, etc.?
- Is the length of the segment appropriate?

**Analysis of Practical/Logistical Constraints**

- Will copyright clearance have to be obtained?
- Are all video segments produced in the same standard tape width/ line and field-rate standard/colour system/etc?
- Are there facilities for transfer to one common standard, telecine, editing, assembly, captions, voice-over, etc.?

**Fig. 2.12:** A check-list to assist the process of repurposing of existing video or film material for new objectives.

source material was not developed initially to reach the objectives that you have in mind, indeed it may not have been intended for educational use at all. You design the lesson plan and then seek out the video material that meets your specification. This is often easier said than done. Although you avoid the hassles of video productiion, you may spend a lot of time in the viewing theatre. Sometimes in turns out to be easier and faster to make your own videoclips.

**Producing Your Own Material**

When adaptation or repurposing of existing materials is impractical or impossible, you may consider producing your own material. This may be quite easy and cheap, or difficult, time consuming and expensive, depending on the type of video content specified in your lesson plans.

If you require a series of examples of naturally occurring objects, phenomena or situations, to be used as 'vignettes', or 'videoclips' (moving snapshots) in an otherwise teacher-delivered lesson, then production of the necessary video material depends primariuly on locating the examples. As they occur naturally, just as you want to show them, the preparation and planning is minimal - selection of viewpoint and camera angle, type of shot (general wide angle, close-up, etc) and possibly some special lighting. The procedure is not that different from still photography, except that you are trying to capture the important aspects of motion as well as the essential visual content of your 'snapshot'. Provided that your programme does not require shots of the mating habits of rare spiders found only in the depths of the Amazon jungle, your production expenses are likely to be modest. Of course, some camera and lighting skills are required, but these are easily mastered. We shall not discuss them here as many excellent specialist books exist and in fact the best way to learn is to do it.

If, on the other hand, your lesson plan calls for dramatized case studies, composed of a number of scenes and involving several characters, then we are talking of a full-scale production. You will either require a studio set up with several cameras and a control room, competent and well rehearsed actors (not to mention the detailed scripting), a camera crew and bags of time, or you may follow the cinema

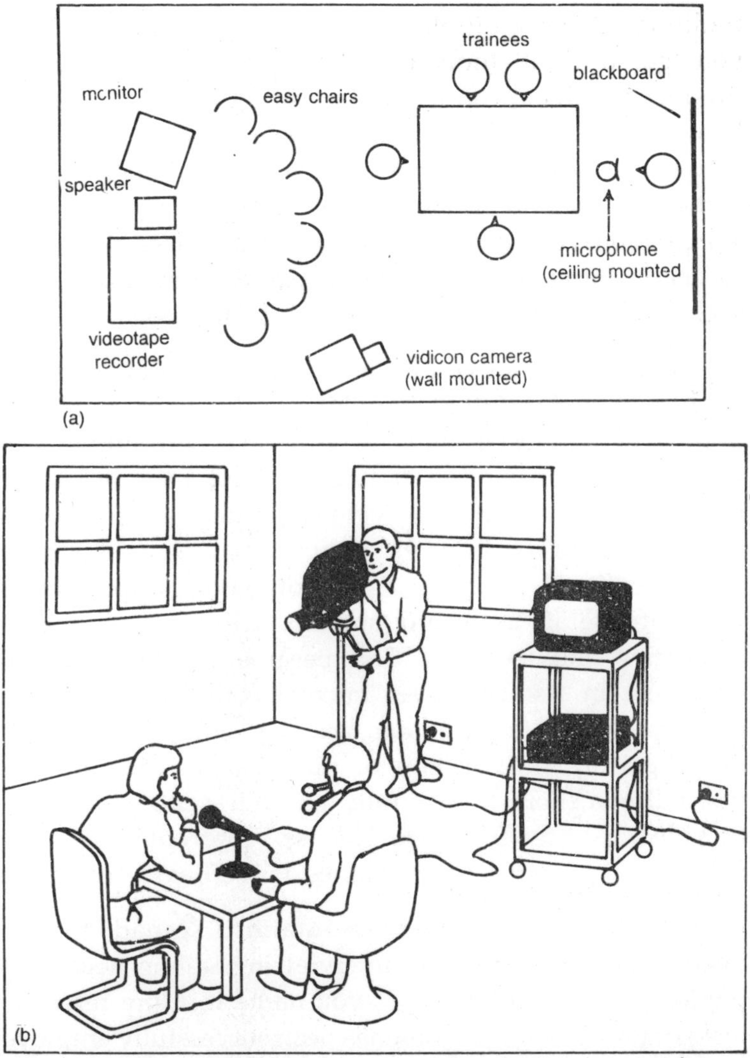


**Fig. 2.13:** Two room layouts prepared for single-camera video recording. (a) The layout used for teacher training at the University of Aberdeen, Scotland. This is set up for self-confrontation in the context of microteaching (McAleese, 1985) (b) A set-up suggested for interpersonal skills training. Note the portability of the equipment. This set up may be used for the taping of model examples for later demonstration, or for student practice and self-confrontation (Heinich, Molenda and Russell, 1982).

tradition, taking multiple shots of each separate scene until you 'get it right' (only one camera is needed) and then produce the final product on the editing console (many long hours will be consumed here). Either way, the time, cost, variety of resources and people involved is much higher, as is the level of skill and experience, if anything approaching a professional production is required. Once more, we shall not go deeply into this area. Interested readers may refer to books such as Kirk (1973) or Combes and Tiffin (1978).

Whether or not you have the resources, time or interest to get involved in full-blown video productions, it is, in this day and age, almost essential to be familiar with simple, single camera, video recording techniques, and have access to a portable single-camera-plus video cassettee system. Not only is this useful for schooting videoclips to be used as illustrations in conventional teaching; a possibly more important and frequent use is to record student activity as a form of evaluation and feedback. This became popular in teacher education in the 1960s, as 'microteaching' - a method of developing specific classroom teaching skills, by watching a model performance (usually on film or tape), then practising the skill in a short, five-minute, 'micro lesson', which would be videotaped for feedback. This 'self-confrontation' proved to be a very powerful (if sometimes dangerous) feedback tool.

In the 1970s, self-confrontation spread to most interpersonal skills training - interviewing, selling, negotiating, public speaking, supervision, you name it. More recently, a form of group-confrontation has been successfully employed, in which the class activities of a whole group are recorded during, say, a simultation-game, and the tape is replayed during de-briefing to evaluate more precisely the group dynamics that developed, the climate of the group, etc.

### Delivering and Evaluating Instructional TV Lessons

If you have gone through the paces of detailed lesson

planning, as described earlier, then you are well prepared to deliver your lesson. Of course, a large part of the lesson delivery will be taken care of by the video programme, but you will still be responsible for the opening and closing activities, for discussion or exercise activities during any planned stops in the programme, for overall timekeeping and direction, and for final evaluation. When you are using repurposed material as video snapshots in your presentation, then your role is even closer to that of the conventional instructor. But however much your role is reduced during an instructional TV lesson, it is still very important and, indeed, has some unique characteristics that may require some special skills on your part.

One very obvious set of special skills is concerned with the operation of the TV or video equipment that will be used. You should make sure that you are fully conversant with all operational aspects of your system, including basic troubleshooting and correction. Nothing disrupts a TV lesson more than a scrolling picture or distorted sound that the teacher tries, but fails, to correct.

Another, less obvious, but even more important set of skills is concerned with being able to view and listen to the transmission from the students and teacher's viewpoints at one and the same time. Particularly when you have not had the opportunity to preview the programme, your success in the de-briefing session will depend on how well you identify points that will be obscure or difficult for your students, examples that will require reinforcing or supplementing with other, more meaningful ones, key facts that students should remember and therefore be questioned on at the end of the lesson, etc. To some extent, this is a function of your knowledge of the topic and experience of teaching it to the specific type of students you now have. However, it is very easy to get lulled by the broadcast into only half paying attention (because you know the content already) or paying the wrong sort of attention - for example, attending to the programme as *you,* from the vantage point of your interest, experience and knowledge of the topic, rather than from the vantage point of the students, their knowledge and their learning skills and difficulties.

Yet another set of skills is involved in executing the de-briefing or closing activities. In this stage, it should be the students who do most of the talking, they who suggest new applications for the knowledge presented. The instructor acts more as a facilitator of the group's activities, yet must be ready to take on the role of tutor when required. The skills of the lecturer are, however, largely redundant.

Part of the instructor's role to evaluate the lesson. In terms of learning, you should have developed, and will now apply, valid evaluation instruments, be they tests, observation checklists, or whatever. You should also evaluate the process adopted in the TV programme, in order to improve it if possible for the future. And don't forget to evaluate your own performance. In all these process aspects, it is a good idea to enlist the help of the students. One way to do this is by means of a student's evaluation questionnaire. An example of a possible questionnaire is shown in Fig. 2.14.

## Television and Video Equipment

### *Operating Standards*

An image (such as that formed on the tube of a TV camera by its lens) has to be split up into a very large number of discrete points and the information about those points (ie, brightness and colour) must be transmitted one point at a time. In current TV system this is done by 'scanning' the image - looking at each point in a line, from left to right, and then line by line down the image, from top to bottom. The scanning process may vary in two ways: the number of lines into which the picture is divided, and the rate at which the

**Part I: Instructors**

A. *Instructor in The Classroom*

1. Were the classroom instructor's objectives for the course made clear?
   1. Never stated — 1 2 3 4 5 NA
   5. Made quite clear — □ □ □ □ □ □
2. Was the classroom instructor well prepared for each class?
   1. Never prepared — 1 2 3 4 5 NA
   5. Always prepared — □ □ □ □ □ □
3. Did the classroom instructor summarize or emphasize major points of the televised lectures?
   1. Never — 1 2 3 4 5 NA
   5. Frequently — □ □ □ □ □ □
4. To what extent did the classroom instructor work through sample problems, examples or illustrations to help clarify the material?
   1. Never — 1 2 3 4 5 NA
   5. Very frequently — □ □ □ □ □ □
5. Was the classroom instructor available either in person or by telephone to help students who had difficulty?
   1. Never available — 1 2 3 4 5 NA
   2. Actively helpful — □ □ □ □ □ □
6. What is your overall evaluation of the classroom instructor?
   1. Poor — 1 2 3 4 5 NA
   5. Excellent — □ □ □ □ □ □

B. *Instructor on Television*

1. To what extent did the television instructor use appropriate examples or illustrations to help clarify the material?
   1. Never — 1 2 3 4 5 NA
   5. Very frequently — □ □ □ □ □ □
2. Did the television instructor raise challenging questions or problems which encouraged you to think for yourself?
   1. Never — 1 2 3 4 5 NA
   5. Very frequently — □ □ □ □ □ □
3. Does the television instructor have speaking or personal traits that interfere with your learning?
   1. Constantly exhibits distracting mannerisms — 1 2 3 4 5 NA
   5. No annoying mannerisms — □ □ □ □ □ □
4. What is your overall evaluation of the television instructor?
   1. Poor — 1 2 3 4 5 NA
   5. Excellent — □ □ □ □ □ □

**Part II Modes of Presentation**

A. *Television*

1. Was the presentation of televised material organized?
   1. Congested, disorganized — 1 2 3 4 5 NA
   5. Clear, organized — □ □ □ □ □ □

*Contd...*

2. Were the televised visuals and/or demonstrations effective?
   1. Not effective at all — 1 2 3 4 5 NA
   5. Very effective — ☐ ☐ ☐ ☐ ☐ ☐
3. Were there any sound or picture difficulties during the televised presentation that interested with your learning?
   1. Constantly exhibited distracting difficulties — 1 2 3 4 5 NA
   5. No annoying difficulties — ☐ ☐ ☐ ☐ ☐ ☐
4. Did instructional television make it easier for you to take courses or acquire information during the phase of your education?
   1. Offered no particular advantage — 1 2 3 4 5 NA
   5. Very convenient — ☐ ☐ ☐ ☐ ☐ ☐
5. What is your overall evaluation of instructional television as it was applied in this course?
   1. Poor — 1 2 3 4 5 NA
   5. Excellent — ☐ ☐ ☐ ☐ ☐ ☐

B. *Printed Material*

1. How would you rate the overall value of the textbook(s)?
   1. Poor — 1 2 3 4 5 NA
   5. Excellent — ☐ ☐ ☐ ☐ ☐ ☐
2. How would you rate the overall value of the workbook?
   1. Poor — 1 2 3 4 5 NA
   5. Excellent — ☐ ☐ ☐ ☐ ☐ ☐
3. How would you rate the overall value of the supplemental material (notes, handouts, etc)?
   1. Poor — 1 2 3 4 5 NA
   5. Excellent — ☐ ☐ ☐ ☐ ☐ ☐

**Part III: Student/Instructor Dialogue**

1. Were you ever frustrated during the television presentations because you could not raise questions?
   1. Never — 1 2 3 4 5 NA
   5. Frequently — ☐ ☐ ☐ ☐ ☐ ☐
2. If you had questions during the television presentations, did you note them so as to have them answered later?
   1. Never — 1 2 3 4 5 NA
   5. Frequently — ☐ ☐ ☐ ☐ ☐ ☐
3. When tapes were replayed, did you generally review those tapes on which you had questions from the initial viewing?
   1. Never — 1 2 3 4 5 NA
   5. Frequently — ☐ ☐ ☐ ☐ ☐ ☐
4. Do you consider the discussion sessions an essential part of the course?
   1. I did not need them at all — 1 2 3 4 5 NA
   5. I could not have done without them — ☐ ☐ ☐ ☐ ☐ ☐

**Fig: 2.14** Model for a student questionnaire used to evaluate instructional TV lessons/courses scanning process is repeated (the number of pictures per second).

In the USA, TV was introduced with a 525-line picture, a standard which persists today in the America, Japan and a few other countries (such as South Korea). In the UK, TV broadcasting started with a 405-line picture, but this 'standard' was completely replaced by the end of 1984 by the 625-line standard which was introduced with the arrival of BBC2 in 1964, and which is used for all colour broadcasting.

Picture rate is governed by the need to portray motion smoothly and to eliminate flicker of the image. About 50 pictures per second are the minimum for the latter, and this proved a convenient rate for European TV set manufacturers, as it matched the frequency of the alternating-current mains supply (50 Hz, ie 50 cycles per second) which was used to 'lock' or synchronize the transmitted/received frame rates. In North America, the mains frequency is 60 Hz, so the field rate standard adopted there was 60 fields per second.

There are three major (and some minor) differences in the techniques adopted for carrying colour information within the TV signal. The 625-line/50 Hz system has two different colour signal 'standards' - PAL (most of Western Europe, Africa and Asia) and SECAM (France, much of Eastern Europe and those areas of Africa under French influence) - while the 525 line/60 Hz (North and South America, Japan, South Korea, the Caribbean) has its own colour-encoding system, NTSC. Minor variations include the system used in Brazil - 525-line/60 HZ. PAL - called PAL-M (M for modified).

If at the time of setting up a video system it is known that there will be a real need for playing recordings made on other standards (eg. an American videotape in the UK), then a point should be made of buying what are called 'tripple-standard' recorders and monitors (*both* have to be triple-standard). The recording heads are mounted on a rotating drum around which the tape is wrapped in a full or half-helical turn. The drum is spun at high speed (once for every pair of fields, ie, 25 times per second in the UK, and 30 times per second in the USA) while the tape is pulled past it at a modest 20-100 mm/s (it varies between systems). Tape consumption is thus reasonable, while writing speed is acceptably high.

Broadcast recorders use 2 in- or 1 in-wide tape on reels (though 2 in tape is rapidly going out of use); 'industrial/ educational' machines (generally) use ¾ in-wide tape in cassettes (the 'U-format', commonly referred to as 'U-matic'); and 'domestic' recorders use ½ in-wide tape, also in cassettes. The wider tape and faster writing speed of the broadcast machines give inherently better recordings than the narrower, slower tapes. The image produced is more stable, with better resolution (definition) and less 'noise' (superimposed spurious signals, such as patterning and 'busy' graininess). This becomes particularly important when tapes are copied. However, technical advances have occupied rapidly in video recording, with theresult that what would formerly have been considered 'domestic' recorders are being increasingly used in institutional settings.

A tape recorded on one type of machine may not be playable on another type of machine, even though it uses the same width tape. In the domestic ½ in market there are three common systems: VHS, Beta and V2000, the former two of Japanese origin and the latter of European origin. All three use ½ in-wide tape in cassettes, but the cassettes are of different shapes and sizes so that a VHS recorder will not playback a Beta tape, etc. Manufacturers often make ½ in tapecassettes for two or three formats, and so it is not enough to ask a supplier for, for example, 'a Fuji videocassette' or ' 3M tape'; you must be precise about your adopted format and be constantly aware of the alternatives. This is important, too when buying or hiring pre-recorded tapes or when planning to playback tapes brought along by visiting speakers. Incompatibility between the many video recording formats is one of the greatest irritations of educational and training video users.

**Monitors and Receivers**

The domestic television receiver conventionally has just one signal input connector; the aerial socket. This accepts the sound and picture through a single wire. The video and audio signals are combined on a 'carrier wave' at radio frequency (RF) for broadcasting by the transmitter. This combined RF signal must then be tuned in at the television receiver. This signal must then be 'processed' to separate the video and the audio (and both from the carrer wave) before they can be presented to the viewer as picture and sound.'

The television *monitor* accepts video and audio signals separately (sometimes video signals only). The video and audio are not combined on a carrier wave and the monitor is not equipped with electronic circuits for processing an RF signal. It is not possible to connect an aerial directly to a monitor to receive television broadcasts; a separate turner is required to do that. Monitors are the display devices normally used in broadcast and the larger industrial/educational units.

A *receiver/monitor* combines all the facilities of the first two types of display units. It can accept separate audio and video inputs but has in addition a television tuner and circuitry for processing combined RF signals, so that it can receive and display television broadcasts. The better receiver/monitors commonly provide video and audio output, too, for linking to other display units. Receiver/monitors are becoming increasingly common in the home and in education, as 'television' rapidly evolves into 'video' (Whitaker *et al.*, 1985).

Another type of monitor, an *RGB monitor*, accepts what

is called an 'RGB' input: the colour video signal is fed in as separate red, green and blue components. RGB monitors are available for use as computer display units, giving very clear and sharp graphics displays. Most RGB monitors (unless specifically for computer use) are also provided with a 'video-in' socket for connection to a camera or recorder giving a composite video output.

The major argument in favour of video or RGB monitors is that they are capable of providing better quality. Going directly from an RGB source to an RGB monitor eliminates four electronic processing stages, while video-to-video eliminates two unnecessary stages. The fewer the stages of processing, the less degradation there will be of the picture. RGB to RGB should yield the best possible picture quality, video to video slightly less good, and RF to RF worst of all (all other things being equal).

**Portable Video Recorders**

Portable recorders are usually smaller and lighter than the mains-powered equivalents of their type and format. They are available for all tape sizes, from 1 in down to ¼ in, and for all formats (U, Beta, VHS, V2000, etc). Some use the standard taape package as used by their mains-powered equivalents, but others use smaller cassettes.

Portable recorders are almost invariably powered by rechargeable batteries - each battery pack has the capacity to run the recorder (and, in most cases, the mating camera as well) for at least one of its cassettes (normally with at least 100 per cent reserve energy) but then has to be recharged. Rechargeable batteries will give reasonable service if they are *correctly looked after.* They should not be stored in an exhausted state but should be fully charged after each use (though you must follow the manufacturer's instructions on this).

Portable recorders are designed for lightness and compactness and so have no tuners/timers built in. However, a tuner pack is often available either as part of the camera-recorder kit or as an optional extra. These are mains-powered and provide the same facilities as the units built into the mains machines. In some cases the tuner acts as the mains adapter for the portable recorder and as the recharger for the battery pack.

When choosing a portable recorder, check on the features and facilities it possesses and make sure that it can be fitted with all the options that you need. Check, too, that it has the connections you need.

Two recent innovations have made the portable VCRs even more portable. First, came the *'Camcorder'* - a camera and recorder combined in one unit. This often uses a reduced size (and therefore playing time) videocassette (VHS and Beta models are available), but otherwise the equipment is not inferior to good quality domestic portable recorders. Then came the 8 mm video format, with a new, digital, recording technology, which promises to offer in this micro format a picture quality equal today's 'institutional' equipment. By the time this book is published, there will be no doubt be further developments and innovations.

**Map 2.1: Video recorder troubleshooting guide**

Observation: Some of the suggested remedies and suggestions apply only to reel-to-reel VTRs

| Problem | Possible Cause | Remedy | Explanation or Suggestion |
|---|---|---|---|
| Videotape system plays back audio but no video. | Tape recorded originally on a machine of a different format. | Find a compatible machine and use it, or duplicate tape on a usable format. | Always find out what format a borrowed tape was recorded on before scheduling it for use. |
| Snow in video. | Clogged video heads. | Clean heads with a coton swab and generous quantities of cleaning fluid. | Sometimes caused by leaving function control in still for more than two minutes. |
| | White residue on all points of tape contact. | Discard tape and clean VTR thoroughly | Bad tape in which binder adhesive has oxidized and rubbed off. Notify tape manufacturer of all numbers of tape reel. Usually, they will replace it at no charge. |
| Video, when played back, has a disruption in the image at evently-spaced intervals. | Electrical interference. | Remove power cord and reinsert in wall outlet the opposite way. | Sometimes the electrical polarity is reversed and the only remedy is to change the direction of current flow from wall outlet to VTR. |
| | VTR out of adjustment. Drive motor probably does not maintain a constant speed. | Notify proper authorities of need for technical repair. | Tape speed through a video recorder must maintain a constant speed during recording and must be played back at exactly the same speed. |
| Tape doesn't move through videotape recorder. | Back side of tape adhered to guide posts. | Remove tape, clean tape path and guide posts. Allow to dry thoroughly. | Fresh tape is often secured with a gummed tape to keep the wrap tight until use. Always cut off the first two-three feet of tape prior to use. Do not secured end with gummed tape. |
| | VTR may be colder than room temperature | Always allow VTR to warm gradually to room temperature. | A VTR that is colder than room temperature will collect moisture and cause videotape to adhere to guides and the drum on which video heads make contact with tape. |

# 3

# The History of Tele-Clubs in the World

## Difficulties Facing the Commercial and Non-commercial cinema in the villages of the Aisne

French tele-clubs were brought into existence by the difficult situation of the 16 mm small-size films in the villages of the Aisne Department. Professional operators had established several commercial circuits, but owing to the high cost of hiring films they soon found themselves faced with a dilemma: Were they to hire, cheaply, films often of poor quality, or indulge in the luxury of using better and more recent films at much greater expense which would compel them to raise the prices of their seats? Bad films and high-priced seats produced exactly the same result—attendances fell drastically.

At the same time, adult education was expanding in these country districts. As from 1945, the number of secular friendly societies, rural centres and family clubs had begun to increase rapidly in the favourable atmosphere of the liberation. Encouraged by energetic teachers, the Federation departementale des aeuvres laiques peri-et post scolaires (departmental federation for secular after school and out-of-school activities)[1] equipped a large number of rural schools with 16 mm sound-projectors. It promoted the establishment of cine-clubs, and leaders were trained for these throughout the area. A number of circuits were organized, and the Aisne became one of the best-equipped departments from the standpoint of popular culture. But although the cine-clubs, as non-commercial undertakings, were exempted from taxation, after a few years they found that they could no longer add new films to their programmes except at prohibitive prices.[2] Hence the crisis.

## Tele-Clubs, A Hopeful Experiment

The idea of utilizing community television as a means of adult education was launched in February 1950. It originated in a kind of joke made by the treasurer of the Chateau-Thierry cine-club, who concluded his annual financial report with these gloomy words : "If we are to survive, we shall have to give up the cinema and turn to television !" Television was unknown at that time in the Aisne Department, and none of those present at the meeting—not even the humorist himself—had ever seen a television programme. The Chateau-Thierry cine-club was the most prominent in a rural circuit consisting of 12 groups, which used the same films and shared a projector, and the financial position of the other 11 clubs was almost equally unsatisfactory. The annual accounts of the whole group showed a considerable deficit, giving little hope for the future of the undertaking which had been initiated with such enthusiasm only two years previously.

Looking for a way of continuing this form of popular education, which he was reluctant to give up, Mr. Roger Louis, the chief organizer, decided that his treasurer's idea of resorting to television was perhaps not a bad one. There were, however, a number of questions which would have to be answered before the new technique could be introduced to the community as a means of popular education : could television broadcasts be received in the Aisne ? were there any sets with a screen large enough to enable thirty or more people to watch at the same time? were the pictures clear enoug? what did sets cost, and how were they to be purchased?

Roger Louis wrote, on the off-chance, to Radiodiffusion-Television Francaise, asking for information on the first three of these points. The reply was both encouraging and disappointing : there were television sets with a 441 line definition,[3] which projected a fairly sharp picture measuring 1 m by 0.75 m; but RTF doubted whether they could be used in the Aisne, at a distance of about 60 miles from the transmitter. The organizer felt, however, that this information was sufficiently promising to justify further investigation of television, and a meeting with its official representatives (with whom he was entirely unacquainted). This double event took place at the Paris headquarters of Television francaise, where Roger Louis had his first glimpse of a television programme!

He was filled with enthusiasm; and though all the necessary conditions for the reception of telecasts in the Aisne were still far from present, he felt that "something simply must be done" to bring television into popular education. Back in the Aisne, he called a meeting of leaders of the cine-club in his circuit, who were infected by his enthusiasm. They decided that an experiment in reception simply must be made. But how were they to buy sets, at a price of over 100,000 francs?[4] A solution was put forward by the Peuple et Culture association, which proposed in its magazine that the public be grouped into viewers' co-operatives, a system which had already been adopted in 1946 for the purpose of theatrical performances. These co-operatives would be formed for the collective purchase of equipment, the members of the existing of cine-clubs being asked to combine to buy a television set . . . always assuming reception were possible in the district.

It remained to draw up a plan of action likely to interest television manufacturers in the idea of an experiment. The logical form for such a plan seemed to be : 1. Organization of a series of trial receptions in the villages where cine-clubs existed. 2. Public demonstrations in villages where reception was found to be possible, followed by a speech explaining the principle of the collective purchase proposed with a view to establshing a co-operative. In the light of the results achieved, this plan could be extended to other villages, and systematic action under-taken throughout the district.

For this purpose, it was essential to secure technical and financial assistance from the manufacturers and to convince them thata the venture was likely to prove a worth-while commercial proposition. This was not easy. One manufacturer however, after long hesitation, yielded to the persistence of Roger Louis and agreed to supply the necessary equipment and to meet the cost of the experiment---though he was convinced beforehand that it would be an utter failure. As luck would have it—or, as the technicians declared, by a miracle—reception proved possible, if not always excellent, in many of the villages where the tests were made. All that remained was to see how the purchasers' co-operative would work out. The village of Nogentel, which had already distinguished itself by the number and variety of its achievements in the field of popular education, was chosen as the guinea-pig for this purpose. On the first night, over 120 people crowded into a classroom intended for no more than 30 children.

## Two Trial Villages

After Nogentel came Etampes, a village near Chateau-Thierry. Here again the first attempt was completely successful. The question now was, which of the two villages would be the first to buy a large-screen television set and open its tele-club? Friendly rivalry arose between them. Membership of both the former cine-clubs had been mixed, consisting partly of local inhabitants and partly of townpeople. All of them were eager to get their tele-club started. But the railway-workers and the employees of the co-operatives were the most numerous, and also the most active in propaganda. The stage reached by the subscription-list was discussed every day in the engine-sheds and workshops.

In order to show, in a way that appealed to the imagination, how the money was coming in, Nogentel constructed a thermometer and Etampes a dial, made of wood and cardboard and marked out in thousands of francs. These were set up outside the school in each village, so that people could watch the total mounting day by day. All classes of the population shared in this community effort—though the highest proportion of subscribers came from the least wealthy section. It took no more than a week to raise the 150,000 frs. needed for the purchase.[5]

## Growth of Tele-Clubs

Selected to represent a wide variety of conditions (capability of the teacher, size and mentality of the population, wealth of the village, housing conditions, reception, etc.), 20 villages were then chosen for a repetition of the experiment, so that the development of public interest in television and its programmes might be studied over a given period (one year).

In each of these villages the same procedure was adopted: a general meeting, installation of a receiving set in the school, speech (by an organizer from outside the village)[6] explaining the system of collective purchase, free admission for all comers to the first three programmes, entrance fee for subsequent programmes, distribution of leaflets, use of the local press for publicity. Despite the great variety of conditions governing the experiment, the results were in nearly all cases identical. The time taken to raise the required amount varied from five days to a month, according to the village. There was only one failure, and this was largely due to a series of mishaps — the set did not work well, the programmes were unsuitable, etc.

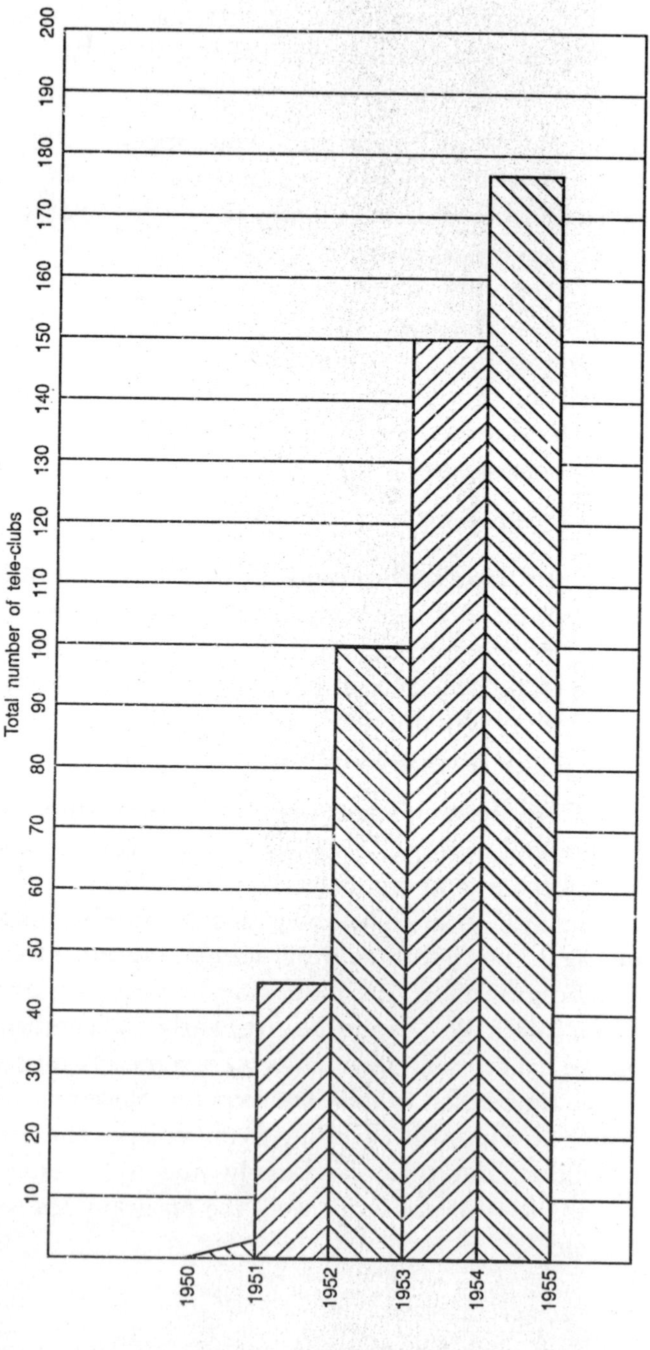


**Graph 1:** Growth of Rural Tele-Clubs

The movement spread rapidly. By the beginning of 1952, 43 clubs had been founded and were giving regular programmes, while 40 receiving sets, provided by the manufacturer as a "permanent loan" to help the experiment forward, were used with a view to the opening of further clubs.

In 1954, some 180 tele-clubs in about ten departments were giving regular programmes. But requests for the creation of new clubs were still more numerous; and the limit of potential expansion is not yet in sight. By the end of 1955 over 17 million people in France will be able to watch French television if they wish.

There are, however, certain obstacles to this increase in the number of clubs. Since they are an entirely new development in adult education, they need to be introduced to the public, with an explanation of their purpose and method. At this stage of expansion, there is a need for national organizers to undertake the tasks carried out by Roger Louis at the beginnign of the experiment — he himself has been fully occupied, during the past two years, by his new responsibilities as a producer. In order to ensure that numerous school and after-school educationists will follow in his footsteps, a permanent system of information and organization is urgently needed. But the educationist's ignorance of or prejudice against television is not easy to overcome.

It would be a good thing to have the support of a new organization — one which, while benefiting from the best results hitherto achieved in the fields of adult education, would not be hampered by administrative red-tape or old, fashioned teaching methods. A Federal of Cultural Television was founded on 18 March 1952, but did not survive, having to struggle against the apathy or hostility of the big adult educational associations. It has now given birth to a new association, Television et Culture, sponsored by a young and vigorous movement whose purpose is to apply new methods of teaching of popular education.

Educators must also be trained in the use of television as an educational medium; an initial seminar on "practical teaching" in tele-clubs was scheduled for the end of 1954. Manufacturers, too, should make their financial and advertising resources available for the development of a big collective television movement. This would be a farsighted policy. A country like France, with only an average standard of living, cannot provide a big enough market on the basis of "family sets" alone. At the beginning, the manufacturers undertook technical research to enable a 441-line definition to be projected on to a large screen, and perfected the apparatus required for collective viewing. But they do not seem to have expended so great an effort on the 819-line definition. It is to be hoped they will soon resume research and construction to facilitate collective as well as home viewing. The former is not commercially to be despised; the Inspectorate-General of Popular Education at the Ministry of Education has already announced plans for equipping 150 experimental tele-clubs in 1955 in the chief adult education institutions and associations.

### The Membership of Tele-Clubs

It might be thought that the members of our village tele-clubs would all come from one particular social class. Our survey has, however, shown that the most different types of people attend. Television has proved so attractive that each telecast draws audiences from all classes alike. As we shall see when we come to "Etat d'urgence", communication between groups with conflicting interests is not always easy, but at least they all come — whereas in the old-established village associations, such as the firemen's society or the municipal band, social taboos are much more in evidence. Here, by way of illustration are some of the categories represented in the tele-clubs: at Viffort, 27 small farmers, 6 farm labourers; at

Montfaucon, 15 small farmers, 13 large farmers, 3 farm labourers; at Dammard, the 15 most regular viewers include 4 large farmers and 8 farm labourers; while at the Nogentel tele-club, whose members are not all occupied in agriculture, the 23 most regular participants in the debates include 4 small farmers, 1 farm labourer, 8 workmen and 3 teachers.

Attendance at many of the adult education groups is frequently by no means representative of village society as a whole. In the tele-clubs, things are very different. Their membership is not indeed an exact reflection of the local population. Young people between 15 and 25 provide a higher proportion than the other age groups; and the men came more than the women, who are often kept at home in the evening by housework. Also, even in villages with less than 600 inhabitants, membership among industrial workers and, still more, farm labourers is proportionately lower than among office-workers or large farmers. At Montfaucon only 10 per cent of the population are large farmers, but they account for 25 per cent of tele-club membership. At Chatillon, a market-town with 600 inhabitants, the high proportion of the office-workers is most evident: they form 6 per cent of the total population, but 29 per cent of tele-club membership.

Generally speaking, however, all ages and professions and both sexes, are fully represented in our rural tele-clubs. As regards the different social and professional categories, there is hardly ever a difference of more than 20 per cent between their representation in the village and in the tele-club—which shows that most tele-clubs contain a typical cross-section of the whole community. At Montfaucon, small farmers represent 43 per cent of the village population and 43 per cent of club membership; at Viffort the figure is 42 per cent of population and 45 per cent of club membership. At Chatillon there are 23 per cent skilled workmen in the village and 25 per cent in the tele-club.

It might also have been feared that the clubs, while well attended during the winter, would be neglected in favour of other pursuits during the summer months. Attendance does, indeed, fall off by between 5 per cent and 10 per cent in the summer, owing to the claims of outdoor work; but although people come a little less regularly, they do come. The villagers would protest if the clubs closed down when the season of work in the field came round. Viewers at one of the regular tele-club performances were asked, in April; "How many times a week do you come to the tele-club?" The replies are given in Table 3.1.

**Table 3.1**

| Weekly attendance | Winter | Summer |
|---|---|---|
| | % | % |
| 4 or more visits | 7 | 10 |
| 3 or more visits | 29 | 22 |
| 2 or more visits | 28 | 21 |
| 1 or more visits | 20 | 18 |
| less than once a week | 2.2 | 8 |
| no reply | 13.8 | 21 |

Do regular viewers come more or less automatically to the club? If so, is there perhaps a danger that television may tend to standardize leisure-time habits? Or that the attraction of 40 hours of telecasts per week may upset the natural balance of the workers' recreations?

What our survey shows is the very vaied nature of the audience. The above table, showing summer and winter attendance, was compiled chiefly from the replies of regular viewers, but in actual fact those who come less than once a week make up far more than 2.2 per cent or 8 per cent of the total. For the audiences do not consist entirely of "regular clients". Many people drop in by chance. This makes for a changing public, difficult to sum up. For instance at Dammard, a village with a number of large farms, the schoolmaster estimates that 65 of the 80 viewers come once a week or less. At Nogentel, where the population consists of farm and office workers in about equal proportions, audiences average about 30; but the day a locally-made film was shown, over 100 viewers came. When some important event is televised, audiences are sometimes five times as large as for an ordinary programme; this was the case at Etampes when the coronation of the Queen of England was shown. In short, there is in all the villages a wide gap between the figures for regular viewing and for occasional attendance. Again at Nogentel, the local team estimates that 15 per cent of the population come under the former heading, 40 per cent under the latter.

What are the principal types of club televiewers? First, there are the *occasional viewers*. These are the most numerous. They come in particular circumstances, or on special occasions, when some family or public event is taking place. A relative or friend comes on a visit, and is brought to "see the television". Or the papers announce that a president is to be elected or a queen crowned, and that "the ceremony will be televised". In this category we may include the intermittent viewers who comes only at very irregular intervals.

The *ordinary viewers* fall into three categories. The "regulars", who come to the club on an average at least once or twice a week, for "their" programme—theatre, variety or outside telecast, as the case may be. Some of them have "their" day—Wednesday, Saturday or Sunday. According to our attendance survey, confirmed by the educationists, 55 per cent of the ordinary viewers are "regulars". Then come the "steadies", who visit the tele-club, on an average, twice or three times a week. They come for the sake of the club—as much to meet their fellow-members as to watch the programme. They make up about 35 per cent of the ordinary viewers.

Finally there are what might be called the "enthusiasts"—those who come three or four times a week, see all or nearly all the programmes, and even visit the club outside the programme hours. Many of these are unmarried people, or young married couples. They feel at home at the tele-club, whose community atmosphere supplements the family circle or provides a substitute for it. It is they who chiefly support and help to run the clubs. They amount to between 10 and 15 per cent of the ordinary viewers.

The general success of the tele-clubs is all the more noteworthy in that material circumstances are not much in their favour. A large proportion of the villagers cannot attend, because they would have too far to walk home in the dark, along lanes which are often muddy or snowy. Only 7 per cent of present viewers live more than a kilometre away from the club. Yet Montfaucon consists of 10 hamlets and Viffort of 7, a number of which are several kilometres away from the club. If the country schools had school buses, they could bring parents and children together, and club membership would show a further considerable increase. But such innovations, though badly needed, are still far distant, and the French tele-clubs realize that they must go ahead without waiting for them.

In short, all our observations and reflections warrant the conclusion that the tele-club is a form of recreation which is finding a natural place in village life. It is not reserved for any particular social circle, nor is membership confined to a handful of fanatics. It attracts a widely varied audience, and each member fits the club activities into his personal programme of recreation. Many people come only at very irregular intervals, to celebrate some event of personal, family or general interest. For others, the club becomes their favourite spare-time haunt. Some people come regularly to a particular programme, some make it the occasion for an "evening out", and some attend in order to meet their friends or join in group activities. Thus the tele-club as a social institution offers very various possibilities, adaptable to the manifold needs of a small village.

## Equipment of the Clubs

### *Premises*

The tele-club's appeal to the public is certainly not due to the comfort it provides. The cinema and the theatre are supposed to owe their success in great measure to well-padded seats and eye-catching decoration; but most tele-clubs are housed in school classrooms. In France, as in other countries, village schools differ considerably is size and appearance, usually they are not large, consisting of only one or two classrooms. In small villages the building usually dates from the period 1881-85, when primary education became free and compulsory. Villages which suffered damage in World Wars I or II have more modern buildings. The are a few cases, but only a few, where the tele-club operates on other premises, more suitable for research—such as the main hall of the Rural Club at Dammard.

A classroom is stamped with the personality of the teacher who presides there. If he has a feeling for decoration, knows how to use his influence with the municipal council, and can stimulate the children's imagination, the room is bright and cheerful. The oldest of the wooden benches on which the audience sits have been replaced by modern chairs, and the benches themselves are arranged with a certain informality. The iron stove has been somehow concealed. The walls are adorned with engraving, colour reproductions and children's drawings. But many teachers, excellent in other ways, have neither the time, the resources nor perhaps the taste for such improvements. In that event the classrooms have remained unchanged since the days when the parents or even the grandparents of the present occupants went to school there, and provide no comfort for the body or pleasure for the eye. There aer not enough school benches to seat the entire audience at a "full house", so that backless benches, putting a great strain on the viewers' muscles, have to be fetched to eke them out. Fuel is expensive; and the custom established in certain villages, where the viewers bring the teacher an extra supply of wood for the tele-club, is not everywhere observed. Where it is not, the fire lit to warm the afternoon classes is kept up until the beginning of the programme and gradually dies out during the evening, so that the debate at the end is conducted in defiance of the rapidly-falling temperature. And on Thursday, the weekly holiday, no fire is lit at all. Few tele-clubs indeed attract by the comfort of their premises. The old school buildings were not planned to accommodate radio and television. Acoustics are often bad and, as all the seats are on the same level, the view from the back rows in a packed house leaves much to be desired.

But the audience duly squeezes on the cramped old benches which shave their knees. The spectators are apt to sort themselves into groups—here a flock of children; there a cluster of old ladies, several local winegrowers, or lads about to leave for their military service who are "chipping" the compact cluster of girls. All of them have their favourite seats. All of them talk, laugh, stamp their feet or eatcall, and even during the telecast there is never complete silence, except at particularly tense moments. Most of the time the programme goes on the accompaniment of noisy comment, whispering, exclamations, stifled squeals, and children's laughter. In short, everyone feels at home.

In many cases greater comfort might certainly be provided. Here too the tele-clubs are doing good work by calling attention to the need for the improving the school buildings and classrooms.[7] Admittedly the unpretentious surroundings contribute to the "atmosphere" of certain telecasts, helping viewers to feel themselves linked to the outside world without being obliged to "dress up". But the skill shown in adapting to new ends what was already inadequate for its original purpose should not constitute an excuse for ignoring requirements upon whose satisfaction the future development of the French village is largely dependent. The introduction of primary education made it necessary to build a school in every French commune: the expansion of recreational facilities now calls for the provision of a communal house of culture, which would provide accommodation for a tele-club, a 16 mm cinema, a library, an assembly hall and so forth. An enquiry such as our points directly to the need for a plan for the extension and modernization of cultural equipment in France, to be drawn up with an eye to the requirements not only of schools but of after-school education as well.

Our enquiry has also revealed the social function of the best teachers. These public educationists are not merely schoolmasters; they are also leaders of rural community. Despite their uncomfortable premises and the meagre grants, they succeed, by dint of competence, energy and self-sacrifice, in continuing their educational work outside school hours. They uphold the prestige of the non-denominational schools. Respecting every type of belief, they assure the continuing influence of the school among the many country labourers whose official education ceased when they were 14 or even younger. Their work among young people and adults serves to continue the struggle against ignorance and prejudice—factors that impede individual development and hold the villages back. Teachers are probably in no country more active than in France. It is to them that rural tele-clubs owe their "flying start", just as it was they who fostered the thousands of out-of-school and after-school associations that have arisen in our villages and small towns.

### *Reception Equipment*

Most of the tele-clubs considered in our survey are at present equipped with projection sets using a medium-sized screen (1 m x1.20 m). Only one, that at Viffort, which is still in the experimental stage, uses a direct view set of the domestic type. A few already have 819-line receivers; of these, only one—St. Aubin—is in our main district, while three—Boulaye-Mivoie, Coudray St. Germain and Aux Marais—are in auxiliary localities.

The great majority, however, are still using 441-line receivers. This is not due to a preference for that as against the other definition. When the first clubs were opened in the Aisne, the 441-line transmitter was the only one powerful enough to make reception possible at a distance of 60 miles from Paris (the 819-line transmitter was stiff in the experimental stage). Moreover, large-screen receivers—"for projection on a separate screen", as it is called—were not then available for any other definition. Most tele-clubs were therefore originally equipped with 441-line receivers. This type of apparatus has, however, a number of drawbacks:

1. The picture tends to be blurred, and the large screen, which magnifies any flaws, makes this all the more tiring to the eye.
2. A "line transformer" has to be used at the transmitting end, to convert the 819-line into a 441-line definition, and this lowers the quality of the reception even more.
3. There are frequent breakdowns at the transmitting end, since the 441-line transmitter is to be abolished in 1958 and little or no maintenance work is now done on it.
4. Owing to the wave-length which is used, the telecasts are very liable to interference from cars, high-tension cables, engines, etc.

For all these reasons, the tele-clubs are now trying to obtain 819 line receivers—which, thanks to the technical improvements recently introduced into high-definition equipment, can now provide satisfactory reception in districts which were formerly too far away from the transmitting station.

One problem remains to be solved. The 819-line projection receivers are far more expensive to buy and to operate than the 441-line ones. Very few manufacturers have begun making them; and the new optical system used in projection, though it has greater possibilities (the size of the picture can be varied), is more costly and more fragile. Moreover, the cathode tubes employed do not last long. It still remains to investigate the possibility of an 819-line receiver more suitable for use in the tele-clubs. Manufacturers have not yet, in this respect, undertaken the research they have devoted to the promotion of domestic television.

## The Operation of the Club

### *Finance Organization*

Most television receivers have been bought with funds raised collectively by the local people. In some cases the municipal authorities have made a grant towards the purchase—at Villers-Cotterets, for instance, the municipality had a classroom specially fitted up for use by the tele-club. Leading members of a community have sometimes made exceptionally generous contributions to its tele-club, although they themselves never visit it. Part of the expenses have frequently been advanced by older cultural associations, such as the school friendly society or the municipal band.

Most tele-clubs require their members to pay entrance fees, in order to cover expenses, pay off purchasing costs, finance the later purchase of an 819-line receiver, or provide for other cultural activities such as excursions, buying of books, etc. On the average, the cost of the set is paid off in two years. This type of financial organization bears further witness to the spirit of co-operation prevailing in the tele-clubs.

### Days and Hours of Reception

The choice of days for reception restricts and affects programme selection.

The first thing to bear in mind when fixing club-days is the season, which influences the work, and the leisure-hours, of country-people far more than it does those of town-dwellers. The experience of a number of local teams (Venteuil, Montfaucon, Chatillon) goes to show that after Easter there is a sharp fall in attendance at tele-clubs among those who work the land. The best period, whether for collective reception or for telecasts intended more particularly for countryfolk, seems to be from the end of the autumn work to about 15 March.[8] These considerations apply with less force to the non-farming sections of the public, although the factory workers nearly all have family gardens and are thus involved to some extent in the seasonal activities of the farmer. Of course there are always "fans" and people less absorbed by work on the land, who come to the club tele-casts in spring and summer. Old people come less often in winter because of the cold, but they attend more frequently in summer, that is why over-all attendance decreases by no more than 10 per cent. But during the warm months there is a perceptible drop in attendance among those who are working.

The days of reception are fixed to a great extent to fit in with the week's work. Satuday evening, Sunday evening and Wednesday evening are by far the best times, and were advocated by over 100 of the 200 local people who replied to the enquiry made as part of our survey; only 25 people voted for Monday, which took fourth place on the list. The least favoured days are not so clearly indicated. The survey heard some simple but forcible observations illustrating the influence of farm-work on leisure. "All days are difficult, because we have to get up every morning at 6 O'clock, to milk the cow." Saturday is the best day, however, "because we can rest on

Sunday" and "because we can bring the children, who have no school next day". Sunday evening is favoured too, because "Sundays are different from other days; we go out". And Wednesday is a good day "because it cuts the week in two, and because we can bring the children, the same as on Saturdays".[9] Monday is the worst day, because "we're resting after getting tired on Sunday", or because "we have to do the work we didn't bother with on Sunday". Farm-work similarly affects the choice of hours for the programmes. A great majority of the persons questioned said they wouldlike these to begin at 8 p.m. in winter and 8.30 in summer, and end at 11 p.m. (67 out of 180 replies).

A fair minority (48 out of the 180) preferred the winter programmes to end at 10.30 p.m. Here again, all the reasons given are concordant. "In winter we eat at six o'clock or half-past, and if there's long to wait we just go to bed." "In the summer, work goes on till late" said one farmer "so in the country it is better for the summary programmes to begin late." "Quite a lot of people are held up by work in their gardens" said a factory worker. "All the progarmmes have something interesting about them, but I don't think they should go on beyond 11 O'clock" said a craftsman. And a farmer's wife wound up by saying "Winter or summer, we get up at the same time, and that means early".

### *Announcement of Telecasts*

While the days for telecasts are picked chiefly so as to fit in with habits of work, the announcement of the programmes follows local customs. For although newspapers are now read more in country districts, not many viewers learn of the tele-club programmes from a daily or weekly paper. Even the wireless is seldom consulted for this information, though there is a set in almost every home (only 13 per cent of the persons question listened to television announcements on the radio). Of the viewers who replied to our questions 46 per cent said they knew of the programmes from the notice which the leader of each tele-club put up at the club-door (a very rough-and-ready procedure, incidentally, more often than not, the items are simply written in chalk on a blackboard). On important occasions the schoolchildren copy the list on to slips of paper which they take round to the various houses, or else—as at Chatillon or at La Chapelle-sur-Chezy—the announcement is made by the local policeman, who acts as town crier.

This shows the influence that can be exerted by a good club-leader who has gained the villagers' confidence. It shows, too, that the tele-club, though using one of the most up-to-date communication media, has fitted perfectly into village life, and that its activities, like those of all spontaneously-formed country groups, are largely governed by local customs.

### *Viewers' Reactions during Telecasts*

In order to understand the way the audience reacts during telecasts, we must remember the informal atmosphere of the "auditorium" which we have already described. Some people arrive early, to get the best seats--the few chairs which are available here and there as a change from the school benches, or a place near the stove— but, generally speaking, the viewers have their recognized positions: the old people near the screen, the young ones at the back where it is dark, the children in front where an eye can be kept on them. There is also a tendency for people to settle in groups, according to their social category: whether they are labourers, small farmers, big farmers or belong to some non-agricultural calling, they like to keep together in their own particular corner, and to give free vent to their opinions—which they often do in audible tones, much more readily than in a cinema or even a cine-club. This attitude is not confined to collective viewing in country districts, but is also to be observed at public telecasts in towns. Tele-club meetings are lively and even at times noisy.

The noise is of two kinds, both of which denote keen interest. It may express approval: during an adventure film such as "Lost in the Jungle", shouts and exclamations are heard from the audience as it wataches the treasure-hunt, the heroes creeping forward through the tall grass where danger lurks at every step, or the battle between the "good" and "bad" characters. Another example was provided by the first showing of a very popular variety programme at the Villers-Cotterets tele-club, when the leader noted that "very few individual rfemakrs were head during the tele-cast, only loud laughter after the jokes and 'gags'. At the beginning I had had to ask the audience not to get excited; there were 58 people in the little room".

But noise many equally express disapproval: it then takes the form of ironical comments, protests, or even cat calls. To remain silent without being asked to do so may be a sign of good manners. "Sometimes I need only walk about the room", writes one leader, "and the noise stops at once". Silence may also indicate concentrated attention. The organizer of a wine-growers' tele-club remarks, with reference to the first three "Etat 'd'urgence" telecasts, that "during variety shows, and sometimes even during films, audible comments—sometimes coarse or sarcastic—may be heard from time to time. But at these telecasts there was almost complete silence, which denoted very close attention".

Smoking is allowed, and some leaders say that cigarettes are definite indications of approval or disapproval. "Judging by the small number of cigarette-ends found in the classroom and by the silence that prevailed during the telecast" wrote the Cramaille club leader on the first-showing of "Etat d'urgence", "this programme pleased viewers very much. When they don't enjoy a show there are many more cigarette-ends, for the same number of spectators". The audience thus makes itself felt as a particularly strong contribution to the atmosphere of a tele-club, the spectators remaining aware of themselves and of their neighbours, whom they know well. Even when a feature film is being telecast, the tele-club does not engender that sense of entranced isolation almost "hypnotic", into which an audience is plunged in the cinema where there is no communication—even silent—between neighbours. In this respect the reactions of tele-club viewers are more like those of a theatre audience; the constant and active awareness of companionship is part of the attraction that these broadcasts have for the spectators.

### *Discussions After Telecasts*

The tele-clubs all began merely as groups assembled for collective viewing. When the programme ended, at about 11 O'clock, the audience went straight home to bed. Any discussion was sporadic; the teacher, afraid of tiring and discouraging the specators, as a rule made no attempt to organize it as a regular feature. When those in charge of the survey suggested to the leaders that they might ask their clubmembers to discuss the "Etat d'urgence" broadcasts, many of them wondered whether the country-people, usually so taciturn and suspicious, would venture to speak—whether any type of discussion would prove possible, apart fromthe spontaneous expression of opinions which takes place in a friend's house, in the marketplace or a cafe. In most of the clubs this was the first time spectators had ever been asked to join in a real debate, to answer questions and give their views in public, in front of their friends, neighbours, wives and children. Yet, here again, the results exceeded the highest expepctations. "Which shows" adds one leader "that it is just a matter of finding the right subject." In other words, the lack of discussion was due chiefly to timidity on the part of leaders and audiences alike. The leaders had had no opportunity of studyign the teaching methods by which such debates should be guided. It had not even occurred to them that their own experience needed to be supplemented by a study of educational methods applicable to tele-clubs. Moreover, since none of the French television programmes touched on matters affecting the work or social life of countryfolk, they had so far had no opportunity of initiating discussion on any subject connected with eveyday life in rural districts.

Some leaders cannot always prevent a discussion from trailing off into disconnected chatter which follows no plan, reaches no conclusions, and towards midnight just fades out. Others—more numerous—come up against the opposite difficulty. Accustomed, as schoolteachers, to hold forth on their own, they talk far too much, and anticipate the reactions and replies of their group. A teacher's response is nearly always more prompt than a farmer's; a skilled educationist will therefore take care to fit the pace of the discussion to the mentality of the audience, not to his own. Even the way in which questions are put may rob the replies of their spontaneity. Respect for the teacher is such that few people will venture to differ from him, if he badly expresses his opinion before ascertaining theirs. Neither will it do to put the questions in such a way that they must be answered by a mere yes or no—"Are you in favour of such-and-such a thing?" For here the reply will simply be a mechanical one. Besides, the reasons for a choice are much more interesting than the choice itself, and public explanation of them is of greater educational value, silence it obliges the speaker to observe, form an opinion and present his arguments.

Given favourable circumstances, however, discussion really does stimulate the audience. The expression of ideas is no longer reserved for a bold minority, always the same, who tend to monopolize the debate; it spreads to the majority, or at least to a substantial proportion of the spectators. There is then a possibility that after the debate, after the discussions which continue during the following days—whenever the ordinary circumstances of work and leisure permit—new attitudes may emerge. Tele-casts, as widely varied in character as a piece of scientific reporting and the presentation of an artistic master-piece, may point the way to a form of cultural development that meets the needs and satisfies the aspirations of each individual and each group. Discussion may help viewers to gain a better understanding of their surroundings; may awaken their desire to cultivate their minds, and enable them to develop their gift for self-expression.

The form of the debate will vary, of course, according to the quality and subject of the telecast—whether it be a film, a variety show, a play or an outside broadcast. The principles by which the most successful leaders and their assistants are guided may, however, be summed up as follows:

1. Help the audience to formulate the impressions they have actually felt but cannot at first put clearly into words. The leader must be careful not to pass too quickly to final judgments and general ideas, because then the most talkative and best educated will "put off" the others, those who keep quiet but think all the same; and the latter, feeling embarrassed and humiliated, will go away and never come back. The least-educated must be helped and guided with special attention and sympathy, though encouragement must never take the form of suggestion or be given in a patronizing tone.
2. Steer forward the audience's reflections on the broadcast in a natural, gradual way: list and classify their impressions and afterwards compare these with other impressions resulting in other circumstances from other telecasts—finally assessing or if possible measuring them, using a scale of judgments commensurate with the ways of thought of the audience concerned, such as: exceptional, very good, good, average, bad, very bad.

3. Discussions develp the participants' critical faculties and their powers of self-expression.

4. Last but not least, exceptional skill will be required if these debates and discussions are to have any practical effect on everyday behaviour, whether in work, recreation, home life or the activities of the local community.[10] In this way an amusing and well-conducted discussion may constitute a veritable mental training for tele-club members.

Later, when dealing with "Etat d'urgence" broadcasts, we shall consider the problem of the frequency and nature of members participation in these discussions. But it can already be said that the leaders' statements almost all agree in this—despite the fact that differences of temperament exist between the populations of the different villages and between the social structures of the various tele-clubs—that viewers who were regarded as hopelessly shy have plucked up courage to speak and have developed their powers of expression. Thanks to their newly acquired boldness, they have begun to take a greater share in the general affairs of the tele-club. This has enhanced the vitality of the group as a whole, and increased the number of active members.

## Importance of Tele-Clubs

### *Television and Cinema*

As we have seen, the French tele-clubs owe their inception to the crisis of the 16 mm commercial and non-commercial cinema. After they had been operataing for four years, we felt that it would be interesting to try to discover how tele-club audiences regarded the cinema as compared with television. It might perhaps have been thought that tele-viewers would look upon the tele-club as an attempt to make a virtue of necessity, and as something inferior, to the cine-club. But no less than 73 per cent of those questioned express the opinion that it is better for their association to work with television than with the cinema; 24 per cent are unable to decide; but their hesitation is quite natural, for most of them are members of tele-clubs such as those at Venteuil and Chatillon, where reception has constantly suffered from interference, the causes of which we have already mentioned. The most important point to stress is that even in these unlucky villages, despite these drawbacks, only 3 per cent of replies were uncompromisingly in favour of the cinema.

Still more important is, we feel, the estimate of the advantages and drawbacks which the audiences find in cinema or television respectively. The two great qualities which television is considered to possess are: Its programmes ("Programmes are wider and more varied . . . television covers a tremendous field . . . "). Its operating costs ("The tele-clubs are less expensive to run"). These two advantages are mentioned by twice as many people as those who advance the advantages connected with the cinema (77 votes to 31).

The two chief advantages of the cinema, on the other hand, may be summed up in two sentences: the cinema shows a clearer picture, less during to the eye; the cinema has a large screen.

Its two chief merits, therefore, are of a purely technical nature.

The televiewers thus show that they are quite able to weigh the cultural and financial advantages of group television—even with the 441-line definition—against the technical advantages of the cinema. Despite present technical shortcomings, tele-club audiences, after four years' experience, have developed a strong sense of the possibilities which this medium offers for their entertainment or cultural development. They feel that its potentialities are boundless, compared not only with those of the cinema, but with those of any other means hitherto available for widening the horizon of daily life in the villages. "Television covers a tremendous field . . ." The tele-club is at once an information centre, a window on the outside world, a source of knowledge on all kinds of practical subjects, a place where readings can be given, and a theatrical auditorium, concert-hall or cinema.

### *Domestic and Group Television*

Before concluding these remarks on the importance of tele-clubs, we should consider whether these clubs, which show a tendency to expand even further than the cine-clubs, do not constitute a merely transient phenomenon, soon to be superseded by domestic television. Or whether, on the contrary, they reflect an economic situation which may persist for a long time, and satisfy certain permanent needs and aspirations in popular education. These are key problems which affect the direction to be followed by television in its educational and general policy, and by adult education as a whole.

Three direct and simple questions were put to viewers.

**Question 1.** "Would you like to have a television set in your own home one day?"

Out of 225 persons questioned, 198 replied: 20 per cent of them said no, 68 per cent yes. Most of the negative replies came from small farmers burdened with work. Their reasons were as follows (in order of frequency): 1. The fear that television might steal time from work, for which the whole day is not too much. 2. Refusal to spend so much money on a luxury. "It's too expensive." 3. Some people, not only small farmers but workmen and office workers as well—especially the younger ones—prefer group viewing. It gives them a chance, while watching the telecasts, to escape from their family circle and meet friends of their own age. "I prefer the tele-club." But the great majority of persons questioned dream of having their own television set one day.

This statement requires some amplification. To begin with regular attendance at the tele-club usually makes short work of the prejudices which still cause certain sections of the public to hestitate about buying a set. This observation is all the more significant when we remember that one of the arguments most frequently put forward by opponents of television is that "it isn't good enough yet, watching strains one's eyes". As we have seen, several tele-clubs still have 441-line sets, and therefore receive a poor-quality picture; breakdowns are also far more frequent than with the 819-line equipment. Yet despite these disadvantages a large majority of the people who attend collective telecasts are in favour of television.

On this point there is no noticeable difference between the reactions of the various social classes; the agricultural and non-agricultural workers express the same wishes. Television seems to exert its attraction irrespective of social distinctions, at any rate within the tele-club public itself.

The 68 per cent who responded favourably to the idea of one day buying a private set may be classified according to the reasons they gave: 1. It is a "home entertainment" to be switched on or off at will. "It's a home variety show." It's like having one's own cinema." 2. Much less numerous are replies which refer to the unpleasantness of going out in the cold, of walking, sometimes for long distances, in all sorts of weather, along muddy lanes. This reason is however often given in replies from elderly people. "In winter it's too cold to go out." 3. A few replies mention the rather uncomfortable conditions in most of the classrooms where the tele-clubs operate, as compared with cinema, etc. "The chairs aren't so hard at home". "It's more comfortable at home".

At Coudray St. Germer, five farmers have bought or ordered television sets since the tele-club was founded in 1953.[11]

Does this mean that the only function of the tele-clubs is to help to spread individual and family viewing? That result would in itself be valuable, in a country where more than 36,000 out of 38,000 communes are too small to have their own television shop.

**Question 2.** "If you were to find yourself with an extra 150,000 francs in hand next year, would you buy a television set?

Of the 225 persons questioned, 195 replied, 34 per cent saying yes and 53 per cent no. A majority of those who would be prepared to buy a set were employed otherwise than in agriculture (a significant point); whereas among those who would not make such a purchase even if they had an unexpected balance on hand, there was a clear majority of agriculturists, and chiefly of small farmers.

We felt it would be interesting to supplement this question by another which would help us to discover the place occupied by a television set on the lists of purchases contemplated by individual members of club audiences.

**Question 2(a).** "If not, what would you buy instead of, or sooner than, a television set?"

Replies, in order of frequency:

1. Means of transport (33 per cent): motor-cycle, car, motor-scooter.
2. Modern household equipment (27 per cent): washing-machine, "household equipment", refrigerator, central heating, shower-bath.
3. Basic household equipment (23 per cent): repairs to the house, "interior alterations", bedroom furniture, "furniture, so as to get married", dining-room furniture, linen, "something for my wife", etc.

4. Miscellaneous (17 per cent): farm equipment, "moving into a house" paying off debts, "travelling in Europe".

The above table has the advantage of showing exactly what the majority of our televiewers feel they need more urgently than a television set. The conclusion which emerges is that the decision to buy such a set is governed by the general living standard of the household. It may therefore be expected that in France, and more still in countries with a yet lower standard of living, the tele-club will long continue to provide a majority of people with their only chance of enjoying telecasts. If we are to believe what the economists forecast regarding the improvement in living standards,[12] it is unlikely that the average French household will possess a television set even in 1970. The purchase of a set is considered to have its place in the section of family expenditure which it is customary to enter under "miscellaneous"—money spent on luxuries or recreations. And this section is governed by a law which was long ago discovered by the economists: the sum allocated to "miscellaneous" expenditure cannot be increased until the section "food", "clothing", "housing" and "health" have received about as much as they can absorb. We may therefore safely assert that group viewing in its various forms, will long remain, in the majority of countries, the only means of bringing television within reach of the general public, and especially of the country public. But does the tele-club merfly satisfy an economic necessity?

**Question 3.** "If you had a television set at home, would you still like going to the club?"

Of the 174 replies, 25 per cent said no and 75 per cent yes. The value of the replies is subject to the same limits as that of the question: we have no definite evidence to show whether the members of a tele-club would really continue attending the group programmes once they had their own sets. Those who already own private sets do not seem to come any longer, but the number of such private owners is as yet very small.

It is also possible that the wish to "please" the leader had some share in determining the replies, since these called for a great effort of imagination from people who cannot at present even contemplate such expenditure. However, the fact that the replies were annoymous was some guarantee of sincerity; and further proof that this question was taken seriously was, we feel, provided by the fact that the replies did not yield the 5 to 10 per cent ironical comments usually called forth by this type of survey in France (there were no such comments, in fact).

The 25 per cent of negative answers came: from small farmers; from small employees. The reason most frequently given was a devotion to home life: "Then we would be able to watch and listen quietly at home." A policeman explains that "Then I shall be able to get at home all the entertainment I get from the tele-club". In only one instance did the answer seem to be prompted by hostility or failure of self-adaptation to tele-club life; "Because the tele-club isn't nice." Among the 75 per cent of favourable replies, those from workers, both agricultural and non-agricultural were proportionately the most numerous, but the actual majority was made by the small farmers and wine-growers.

What are the grounds for continuing the tele-club even after the individual households have been equipped with receiving sets? Information on this point is gained from replies to a subsidiary question, "When and why would you continue to visit the tele-club?" The following, in order to preference, are the reasons given:

1. Because of the debates. "To discuss interesting programmes."
2. To take part in meetings. "So as not to be alone", "So

as to get together with friends and work-mates" (reply from a wine-grower).

3. As a reason for an outing. "So as to get out", especially on Sunday afternoon or evening.
4. For the pleasure of watching a performance. "Because it's like going to a show", or "To get the cinema atmosphere now and then" (a clerk).
5. For various reasons (the least numerous). "To see the programmes when my own set is out of order"; "From a wish to support the school cultural association"; "To help the children's friendly society" (to which the tele-club receipts are given); or sometimes, as in the case of an SNCF[13] fitter, "Whenever the tele-club needs me".

## Conclusions

It will be realized from all the foregoing that the rural tele-club is a new type of adult education institution. Having usually come into existence as a co-operative, formed for the group purchase of a receiving set, it is an association in the most precise meaning of the word. It meets a social need, and is fully representative of all categories of the local population. It acts as an incentive to the purchase of private sets. The spectators come to it not only to enjoy the programmes but for the sake of other group activities as well.

This new type of group organization seems to have a greater power of attraction than certain older associations. In country districts it seems to exert a stronger pull than the cine-club. Everywhere it is reaching new sections of the people, and in cases where it is operated as part of an established out-of-school or after-school association it has stimulated interest in the latter. Its cultural potentialities are considerable, but these cannot be fully developed until premises have been made more comfortable and leaders given more thorough and specialized training. However, the tele-club already provides a setting conducive to social intercourse and general self-expression by its friendly unconstrained atmosphere and the nature of the subjects debated there. It can help to remedy the loneliness which often afflicts country people. It shows Paris productions to the countryfolk and offers an effective means of widening the horizons of village life.

So sudden an expansion of the village outlook raises many problems which must be solved if the daily life of the individual is not to be thrown out of gear, and if there is to be a genuine, and not merely apparent integration of country life into modern civilization. It is still too early, to reply to these questions. We must consider the French television programmes in greater detail and discover which, to judge by response from the tele-clubs, are the most popular programmes and what cultural possibilities they offer.

## References

1. In France, in addition to the official services of the Ministry of Education, important associations, approved by that Ministry, have been set up to co-ordinate after-school activities, provide teachers with the necessary materials and train them for the work. Apart from the Confederation francaise des (aeuvres perl- et post-scolaires, we may mention the Federation Francalse ds Foyers rureux, the Federation Francaise des Maisons de Jeunes et de la Culture, and People et Culture, an educational movement interested in the development of tele-clubs in country districts.

2. One difficulty is that the number of 16 mm films available to non-commercial circuits is comparatively small—partly because commercial distributors are uninterested in, or even hostile to, this line of business, and partly because the associations cannot afford to have 16 mm copies made.

3. 441-819 definition. Like the screen of a photograph reproduced in a newspaper, which is made up of a number of black dots of varying sizes, the television screen is made up of lines of varying light intensity. These lines cover the screen in a continuous sequence from top to bottom, and the "definition" refers to the number of lines which make up the entire television image.

French television began its broadcasts in 1944 with a 441-line definition. This was increased in 1948 to the higher definition of 819 lines, and receivers with this higher definitions came on the market some time after that date. To satisfy owners of 441-line sets, French television continues to broadcast on both definitions. The 441-line broadcasts will be discontinued in 1958, by which time owners of low-definition sets are expected to have replaced or converted their receivers.

4. Weights, measures and monetary values have not been converted in the text into their anglo-american equivalents, except for kilometres which are expressed in miles. For the convenience of the reader we here give the equivalents for the French values mentioned in the text:

   100 French francs equal 28.50 cents and 2/-.

   1 hectare equals 2.471 acres.

   1 litre equals 1.057 U.S. quarts and 0.880 British quarats.

   1 kilogram equals 2.205 pounds.

5. For instance, the following table shows the subscribers in one of the two villages, classified according to their professions (It should be noted that the population of this village consists mainly of factory and office workers employed in the neighbouring town):

| Profession | Number | Contribution (francs) |
|---|---|---|
| Small pensioners and people with small private means | 4 | 13,000 |
| Farm workers | 9 | 20,000 |
| Factory workers and civil servants | 19 | 47,000 |
| Small farmers | 16 | 29,000 |
| Medium farmers | 5 | 10,000 |
| Large farmers | 8 | 20,000 |
| School | | 30,000 |
| Total | 61 | 169,000 |

6. There were two reasons for this: (a) A teacher is often reluctant to ask the public to put up money, whatever the purpose. He feels it is like begging. (b) An organizer brought from the town makes

a greater impression on country people than the teacher they know and see every day—whatever the latter's merits.

7. Appendix VIII, General table showing acquisitions or improvements [...].

8. In countries where the seasons do not fall at the same junctures as in France, this period should be shifted to suit local conditions.

9. In France the primary schools are closed on Thursdays.

10. See Appendix IV: Plan and guide for discussion of the various types of telecast.

11. The same thing has happened in other villages where the tele-club has often been the indirect cause of such purchases.

12. La Civilisation de 1970, by J. Fourastie. Paris, Presses universitaires, 1954.

13. French national railways.

# 4

# The Problem of Distance Education through Television

What are we to understand by the "cultural possibilities" of television broadcasts? A didactic view of educational television is held in some quarters—an inacceptable point of view because not taking account of all the subjects and techniques available for the education of the public through television. We chose another starting point. Televiewing is first and foremost a leisure-time occupation: the extent to which it can be used for cultural purposes, and the bounds to be set to such use, must therefore be determined by reference to the main purposes of leisure. Of these there are three: to bring relaxation after the fatigues of every-day work; to provide entertainment, and take the mind off that work for a short while; and to help to develop the personality, by showing people how to cope more satisfactorily with the problems of their daily lives. These closely inter-related functions constitute a response to certain fundamental needs. A weekly programme should allow scope for all of them. There should be some measure of each in every evening's telecast; otherwise the audience will be fatigued or bored. We will now consider in all the various types of telecast included in one week's or one evening's programme, see which are the most popular, and conclude by analysing the possibilities they offer for an educational use of television in the widest sense of the term.

Such a use implies that the programmes must, as a whole, be such as to induce what we have called "active attitudes" in the spectators. A wide variety of methods may contribute to this education by television—the demonstration of a process or recipe, the systematic provision of information, the illustration of some important problem by means of artistic techniques, the description of some great discovery or the presentation of a masterpiece. We are thus adopting a very elastic interpretation of television's cultural possibilities.

A study of the attitudes adopted by tele-club audiences towards such programmes is important. For these audiences are in no way selective; consisting chiefly of factory workers and small farmers, and being completely representative of a country such as France. The foremost purpose of popular education is undoubtedly to raise the cultural level of this type of public (mopre than 85 per cent of whose members have had only a primary education) among whom, moreover, the future purchasers of television sets are likely to be found, when the price is eventually reduced to meet their pockets. Thus, owing to its social structure, the tele-club public constitutes the public of the future for television. Furthermore, it is grouped in clubs, whose members attend primarily for entertainment, but which also offer them a change of atmosphere—the opportunity for discussions—and help in developing their personalities. These people probably reveal, by their attitudes, a cultural level slightly higher than that of members of the corresponding social categories who do not belong to such associations. The level reached in the tele-clubs may therefore set a standard of comparison for any organizer who wishes to please a wide public and at the same time seeks to raise its cultural standards.

But how are we to decide what is the cultural level to which one must address oneself? Audience mail tells us only the reaction of those few who are in the habit of writing: but hardly 6 per cent of televiewers in France write to

Radiodiffusion-Television. Public opinion polls indicate only the average opinion in the different social categories. And it would be rash to rely on the opinions of the critics, who have all had a secondary education and have a "Parisian" culture.

## Popularity of Different Programmes with Televiewers

As already explained, the tele-clubs receive programmes normally on Wednesdays, Saturdays and Sundays. We have confined our survey to the telecasts received on those evenings—with the one exception of "Trente-six chandelles" (thirty-six candles), a fortnightly broadcast which attracts a substantial audience, although given on Mondays. All these productions, regularly viewed in our tele-clubs, add up to a total of about 12 hours out of the 40 hours' weekly activity of Television francaise—in other words, to about 30 per cent of the programmes. They cover all the chief types: variety, films, plays, literary programmes, practical subjects, news reportages, documentaries . . . . It may be said that the items generally received in our tele-clubs provide typical, though incomplete, samples of the programmes as a whole.

Certain of these typical programmes are presented through pictures and comments in the illustrated pages at the head of this section, and the viewers' opinions of these programmes are analysed in the following pages:

We shall not deal here with the special type of "documentary" represented by "Etat d'urgence", as we shall be giving later on (Part Three) a detailed analysis of this series, which was devoted to the main current problems of rural life.

*Number of those who apaproved or disapproved—average approval or disapproval, for the public as a whole.* We began by trying to find out how many people liked a particular programme and how many disliked it. For, summary as this division may seem, it corresponds to the way in which most opinions are expressed in the tele-clubs themselves.

We found that the three highest marks; 6, 5 and 4,[1] expressed clear approval, and that disapproval really began with mark 3. We, therefore grouped together the three highest marks, and again the three lowest, in order to discover the total number of "approvers" and "disapprovers" respectively. We assessed the strength of both reactions by taking an average of the marks which were "for" and of those which were "against".

Abstention in respect of programmes which are regularly received is probably most often equivalent to disapproval. The most definite example of this was the case of "Lectures pour tous". This was the only programme which called forth much more dislike than approval, and as to which, in addition, an unusual number of people abstained from replying.

*Variations in expressions of approval according to employment, sex and age.* We began by calculating averages because they gave the best reflection of the referendum system in the tele-clubs and of the teachers' ways of thinking. However, as most programmes were awarded strong or even very strong approval, it was not easy to make any closer analysis of the varying reactions among the main categories of spectator. It was therefore necessary to devise some more sensitive method of recording, assessing and comparing the different trends revealed by the experiment.

We consequently decided to convert the marks of the questionnaire into indices instead of averages. The figures thus obtained will not give a direct picture to the reader, but they serve to indicate certain relative differences between the trends of the various groups.[2] We can then apply the theory of probability to these differences as revealed within our sample, in order to discover in what cases they have general validity, with less than a 10 per cent risk of error (significant differences) or less than 5 per cent (highly significant differences).

We confined ourselves to studying the indices of approval because it was only by comparing these that we could arrive at interesting conclusion, capable of statistical expression, regarding opinion among tele-club audiences—which as we have already said, is on the whole favourable to the telecasts.

### *Variety Programmes*

These gained the highest marks of all: 78 to 92.5 per cent of televiewers expressed very strong approval of the music hall and circus programmes, and of "Trente-six chandelles". Greater enthusiasm for the circus was shown by farm labourers and other workers, and particularly by small farmers (a highly significant difference), than by non-manual workers.

The same observation applies to men and women between 25 and 34 years old, who are keener on horses and acrobats than are the members of the age-groups immediately below and above. It would perhaps be an over simplification to attribute this marked preference for circus items on the part of our public to a mere hankering after superficial enjoyment. We shall refer to this again later.

### *Films*

The feature films shown on Sundays tie with "Trente-six chandelles" as regards percentage and average of approval; about 80 per cent of the replies express a liking for these programmes. In fact there is less disapproval shown for the feature films than for most of the vaiety programmes, though many people complain that they are old releases. As for the sequences from recent films, given in "A vous de juger", they are approved by about 60 per cent, although unsophisticated audiences usually dislike extracts and incomplete works.

What about documentaries, generally reputed to be tedious? The French documentaries, with travellers to present and explain them, are approved by over 60 per cent of televiewers, with an average of 4.5 marks. The series of composite documentaries on animal life was, indeed, approved by as many viewers, and marked as highly, as the Sunday evening feature films!

Films are more popular with farm labourers and other workers than with small farmers. Documentaries about animals appeal more to women than to men; but there is no reason to regard any of these differences as significant, except in so far as non-manual workers show a marked predilection for such documentaries (highly significant difference). These first results are already enough to give some ideas of the vast possibilities for the use of the cinema in television—whether feature films, extracts from films, or certain documentaries or composite documentaries. Later on, however, we shall be giving a more detailed analysis of the many possibilities offered by films. Much is to be inferred from the fact that an ordinary documentary, with no plot or "trimmings", can prove as attractive to televiewers as a feature film or a variety programme of such established popularity as "Trente-six chandelles".

### *Plays*

As everyone knows, the growing success of the cinema has been causing great difficulties for the theatre during the past twenty years or so. In France theatrical activity is almost entirely confined to Paris, and has no deep roots among the general public—despite the pertinacious efforts of a few distinguished producers during the last few years. However, more than 60 per cent of televiewers express strong approval (4.67 marks) of studio-produced plays, while only 7 per cent dislike them. The theatre seems to appeal to women slightly more than to men, but all age-groups show much the same attitude, though manual workers are less enthusiastic than non-manual workers (a significant difference). Approval is as

Graph 1. PROGRAMMES: PERCENTAGE OF THOSE APPROVING AND DISAPPROVING; AVERAGE OF THOSE APPROVING AND DISAPPROVING

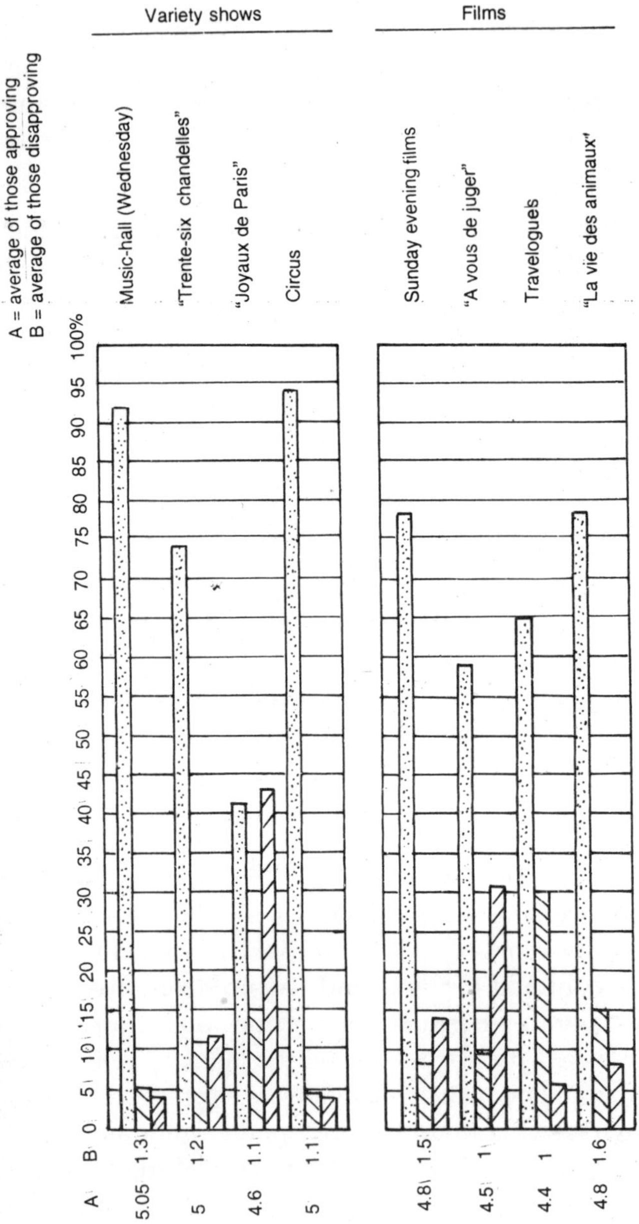

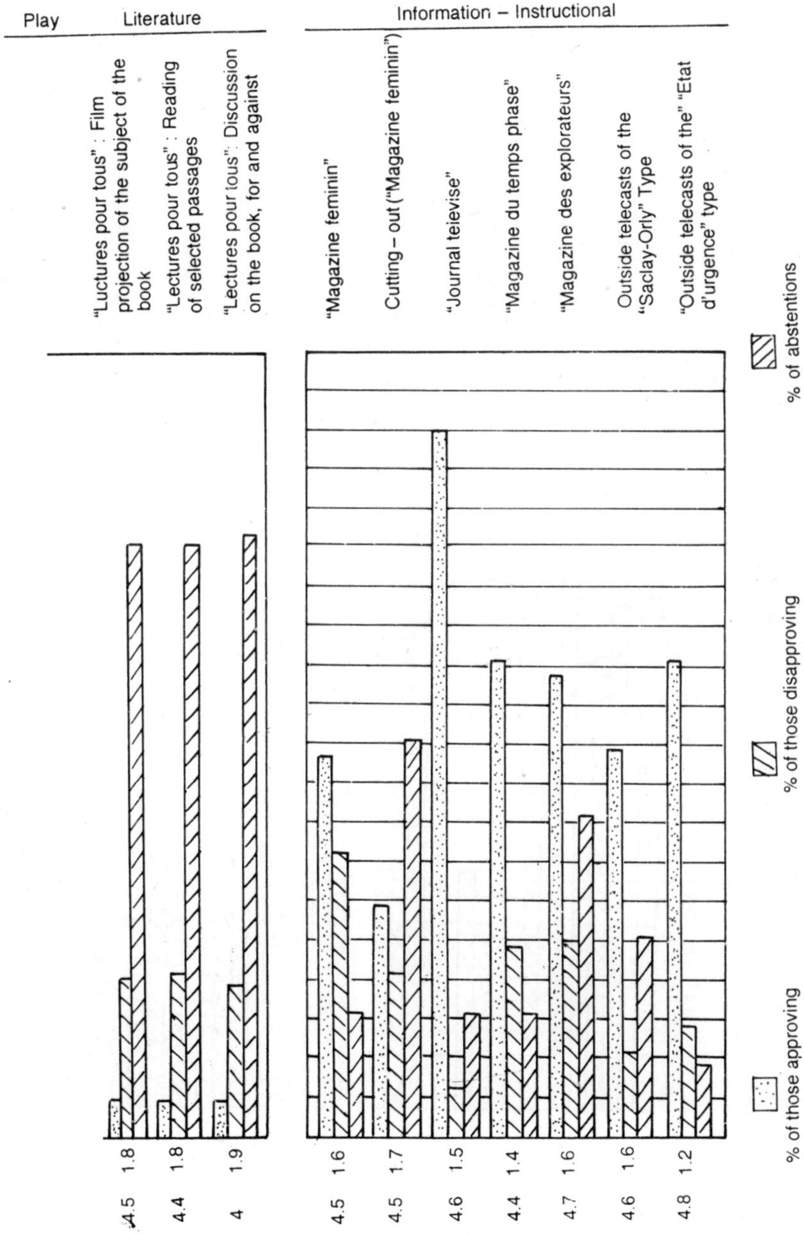
Play
Literature
Information – Instructional
"Luctures pour tous" : Film projection of the subject of the book
"Lectures pour tous" : Reading of selected passages
"Lectures pour tous": Discussion on the book, for and against
"Magazine feminin"
Cutting – out ("Magazine feminin")
"Journal televise"
"Magazine du temps phase"
"Magazine des explorateurs"
Outside telecasts of the "Saclay-Orly" Type
"Outside telecasts of the" "Etat d'urgence" type
4.5 1.8
4.4 1.8
4 1.9
4.5 1.6
4.5 1.7
4.6 1.5
4.4 1.4
4.7 1.6
4.6 1.6
4.8 1.2
% of those approving
% of those disapproving
% of abstentions

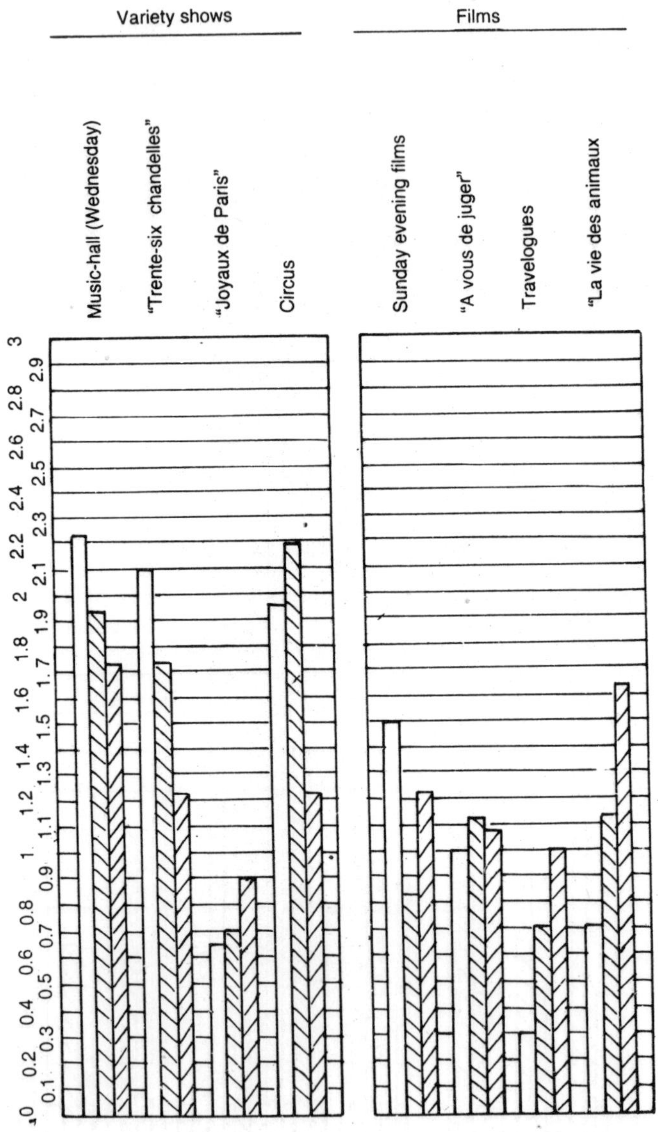


Graph 2. INDICES OF APPROVAL ACCORDING TO OCCUPATION

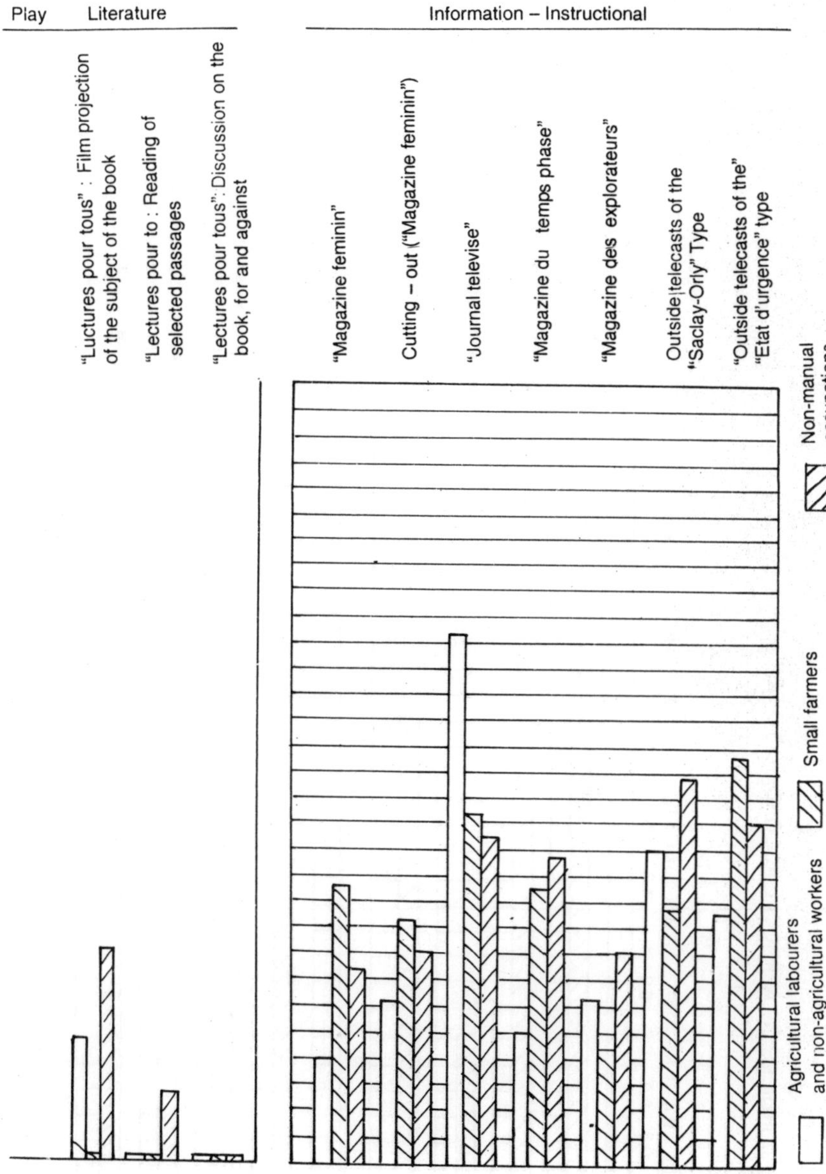
Play
Literature
Information – Instructional
"Luctures pour tous" : Film projection of the subject of the book
"Lectures pour to : Reading of selected passages
"Lectures pour tous": Discussion on the book, for and against
"Magazine feminin"
Cutting – out ("Magazine feminin")
"Journal televise"
"Magazine du temps phase"
"Magazine des explorateurs"
Outside telecasts of the "Saclay-Orly" Type
"Outside telecasts of the" "Etat d'urgence" type
Agricultural labourers and non-agricultural workers
Small farmers
Non-manual occupations

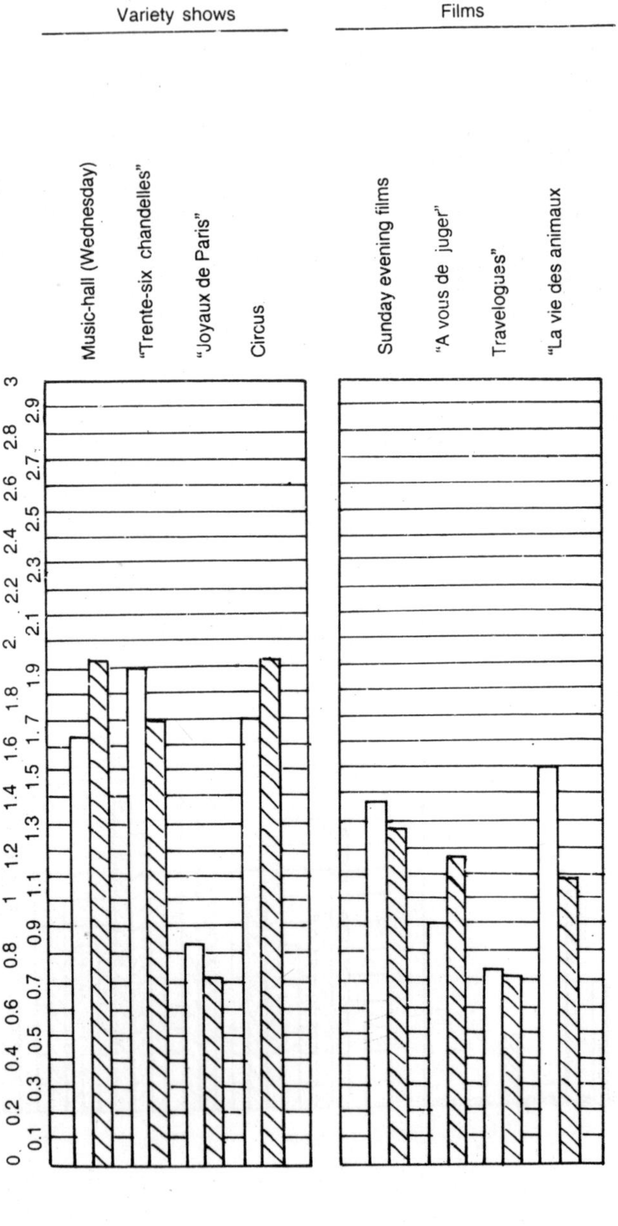


Graph 3. INDICES OF APPROVAL ACCORDING TO SEX

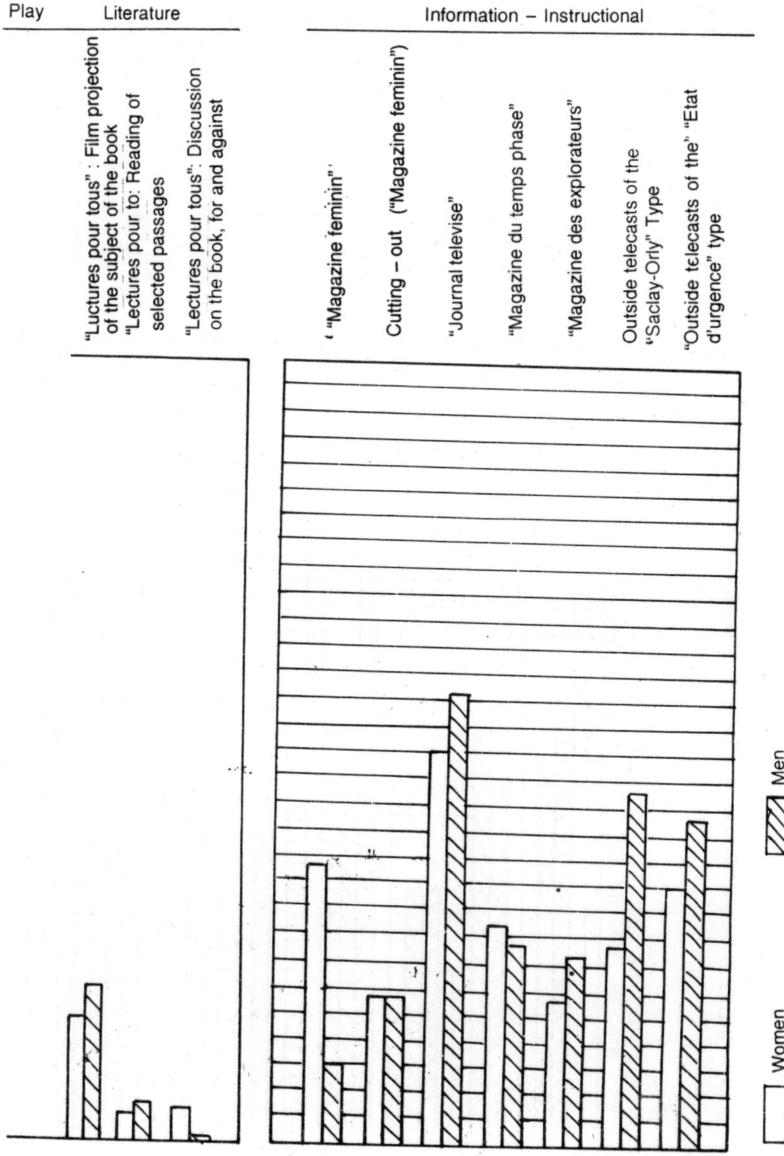
Play
Literature
Information – Instructional
"Luctures pour tous" : Film projection of the subject of the book
"Lectures pour to: Reading of selected passages
"Lectures pour tous": Discussion on the book, for and against
"Magazine feminin"
Cutting – out ("Magazine feminin")
"Journal televise"
"Magazine du temps phase"
"Magazine des explorateurs"
Outside telecasts of the "Saclay-Orly" Type
"Outside telecasts of the" "Etat d'urgence" type
Women
Men

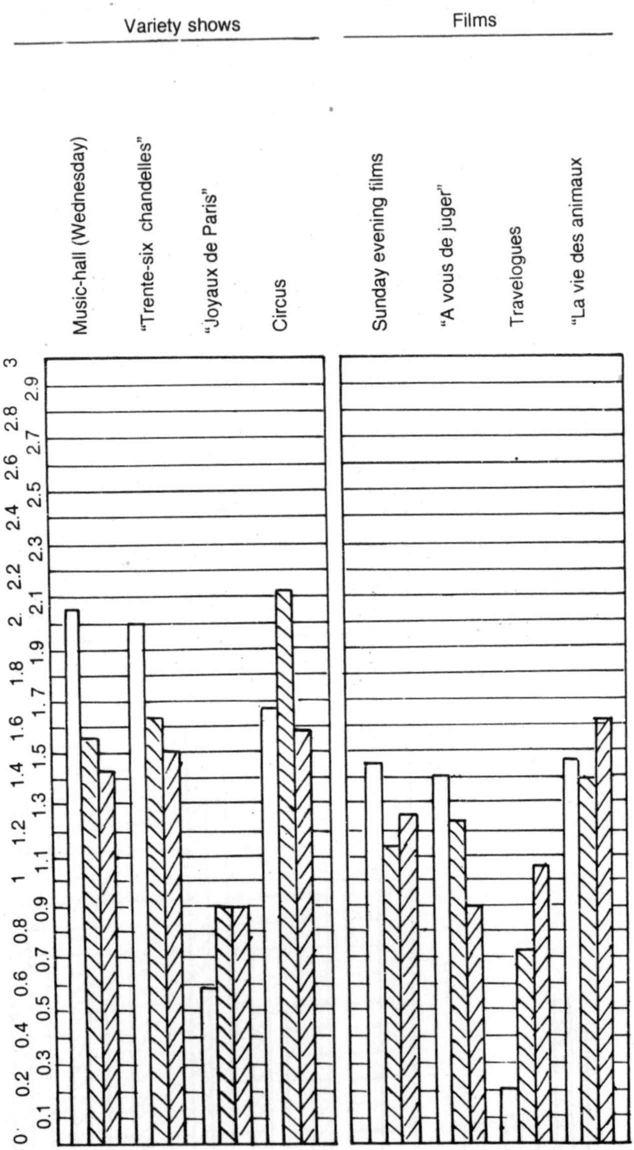


Graph 4. INDICES OF APPROVAL ACCORDING TO AGE GROUP

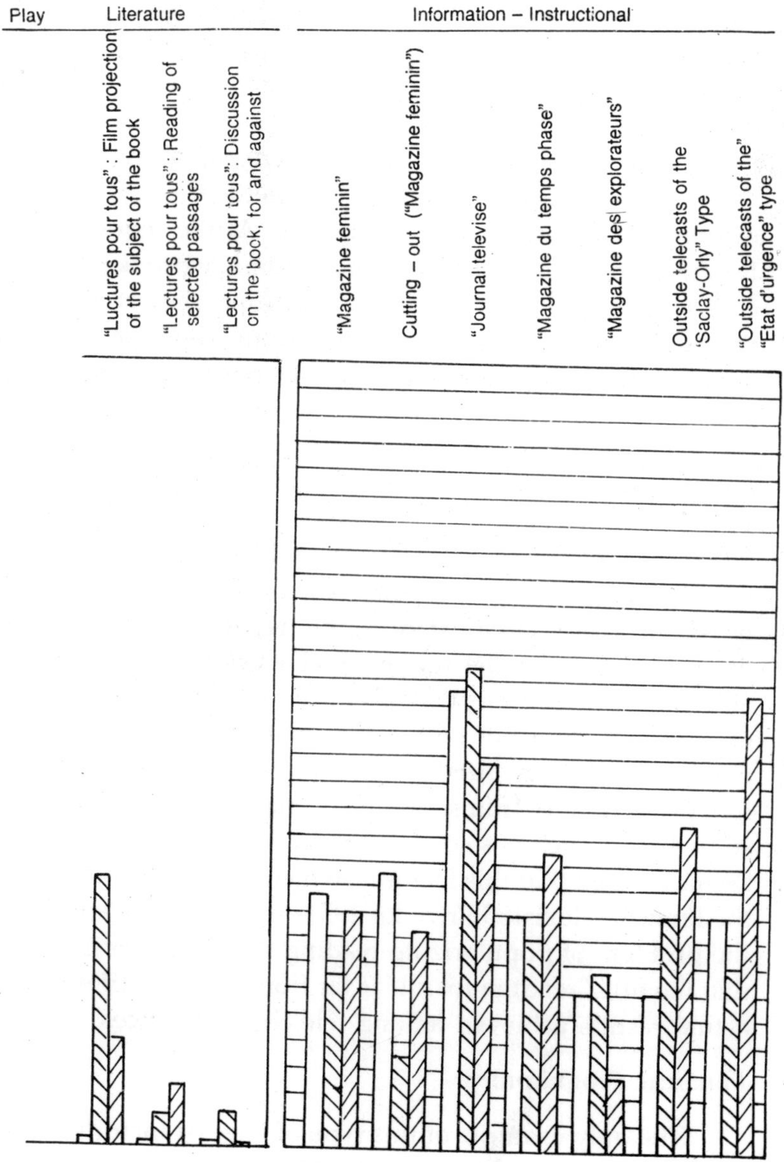
Play
Literature
Information – Instructional
"Luctures pour tous" : Film projection of the subject of the book
"Lectures pour tous" : Reading of selected passages
"Lectures pour tous": Discussion on the book, for and against
"Magazine feminin"
Cutting – out ("Magazine feminin")
"Journal televise"
"Magazine du temps phase"
"Magazine des explorateurs"
Outside telecasts of the 'Saclay-Orly" Type
"Outside telecasts of the" "Etat d'urgence" type
age 21-25
age 26-39
age 40 and over

high, however, among small farmers as among non-manual workers.

### *Literary Programmes*

These signs of strong approval are replaced, when we come to the chief literary feature, "Lectures pour tous", by evidence of almost unanimous dislike. At the request of the Programme Director of Television francaise, we took particular care with our study of opinion regarding this programme, mentioning in our questionnaire all the separate methods adopted by the producers of "Lectures poutous"—discussion with the author, projection of a film on the same subject as the book, regarding out loud of a number of selected passages, or organization of a debate "for or against" . . . . Only between 4 per cent and 8 per cent of the viewers liked this programme, while over 20 per cent disliked it; and, as already explained, the exceptionally high proportion of those who did not reply must, in these circumstances, be regarded as indicating disapproval. Even the non-manual workers were not keen about this programme; they produced in fact the lowest index of approval. And not one of the small farmers or workmen liked it. The few favourable opinions expressed all referred to the projection of films on the same subject as a book—something which is seldom done in this programme. It thus seems evident that this feature—which has just been awarded the French Television Prize for 1954—has by no means solved the problem of popularizing reading through television, and that the title "reading for all" is far from being justified by the actual results achieved among tele-club audiences.

### *Practical Programmes*

The only example of this type of telecast included in the regular tele-club schedule is "Le Magazine Feminin", whose merits seem to be keenly disputed, with 48 per cent of opinion in favour and 36 per cent against; it is naturally more popular with women than with men. Only 29 per cent of viewers like the cutting-out lesson, whose appeal is too limited, while 20 per cent dislike it and over 50 per cent give no reply. Here again, as with "Lectures pour tous", the great number of abstentions indicates a certain aversion, due to the same causes and confirmed by verbal evidence. Moreover, unlike the magazine as a whole, this item is no more popular with women than with men. It is somewhat puzzling to find that these programmes, concerned with household problems, receive such a tepid welcome from the women member of the tele-clubs.

### *News, Outside Broadcasts*

The "Journal televise", one of the favourite programmes, received very strong approval, comparable to that of the variety programmes, from 85 per cent of viewers. Workmen are the staunchest supporters of this daily review of current events, the non-manual workers being much less keen about it (highly significant difference). On the other hand, the review of past events, the "Magazine du temps passe", appeals less to the workmen than to the small farmers and non-manual workers (significant difference). The majority of our public, however, likes this review (61 per cent with an average of 5 marks, as against only 23 per cent of disapproval with an average of 1.5 marks). It might be well to take greater advantage of this keen interest in actual happenings. By carrying it further and deeper, programmes of this kind might add to the public's knowledge of history and geography.

The journal is, as it were, a series of outside broadcasts in brief. How do audiences respond, generally speaking, to full-length outside telecasts? Their attitude varies: a first investigation shows that reports by explorers on distant countries, deserts or polar regions ("Magażine des Exploreateurs") are not outstandingly popular. True, nearly 60 per cent of televiewers express approval of them; but 26 per cent dislike them. In this respect the non-manual workers, workmen and small farmers are more or less alike in their attitude, whether among the young people or among adults of under 40. The people over 40 years old are the strongest in their dislike.

Documentaries on social themes such as "Etat d'urgence", on the other hand, receive stronger approval and less disapproval—14 per cent as against 26 per cent. The index of approval is almost as high for women as for men, though the chief supporters are the men of over 40 (significant difference). These telecasts seem to be particularly favoured by the small farmers, though no marked difference can be perceived between their response and that of the workmen and non-manual workers. It would seem, therefore, that this type of outside telecast, devoted to a social theme, is likely to interest everybody.

As for outside telecasts which introduce viewers to a large airport such as Orly, or to an atomic laboratory such as that at Saclay, 47 per cent express strong approval, and only 11 per cent disapprove. Bearing in mind, however, that 60 per cent of viewers expressed strong approval of "Etat d'urgence" while only 14 per cent disliked it, we might be led to conclude that audiences prefer reports of this latter type; this would be confirmed by the difference between the index figures (1.22 as against 0.69). There is nothing absolute, about this conclusion. All that is clear at present is that televiewers take a general interest in outside telecasts, with a strong preference for reports on current events and a special interest in those dealing with social problems, such as "Etat d'urgence".

Such are our first impressions of the tastes of the tele-club members and the manner in which those tastes vary according to social category. While variety programmes are "first favourite", certain other features are very nearly as popular. Interest in these latter is not confined to professional people or to men and women who have reached a higher level of education, but is shared to some extent by all club members, irrespective of occupation, age or sex. We will now proceed to a more detailed analysis of these judgments. In order to ascertain the cultural possibilities of the most successful among the various types of programmes.

## Analysis of the Cultural Possibilities of the Most Popular Programmes

To do this, we had to make a further enquiry and put questions of greater difficulty to the televiewers. How were such questions to be worded, in order to keep within the members' vocabulary and range of ideas? How could we make sure of obtaining replies which would satisfy the varied and complex requirements of the organizer and the teacher?

We will simply give, below, the list of questions asked during this stage of our survey; as will be seen, it gives detail of the points already mentioned in the methodological introduction:[3]

1. To clarify the possibilities of certain types of programme, we began by asking the spectators which features they regarded as the most successful and which the least successful. Pleasant and unpleasant memories indicate that a feature has made a deep impression on the viewer's feelings.

2. Another indication of the effect produced by a series is to be noted from the changes in the spectators' attitude towards it as the weeks of its telecasting go by. Some programmes are not liked at first, but win approval as time goes on; and the contrary may also happen.

3. The purpose of a cultural programme is not merely to please the spectators, but to improve their taste, add to their knowledge, awaken new ideas in their minds and show them new ways of doing things. Hence our

third question—which programme have, according to viewers, really brought about changes of this kind?

4. There are other signs of educational effectiveness, which relate not to the past but to the future. The wish to see some feature again often shows that it has awakened no mere passing interest, but a lastaing enjoyment which will help its content to be assimilated. Unfortunately owing to the vogue of "the latest thing", the craze for being "up to date" and flitting from one subject to another, the television service often hesitates to repeat a feature. We asked tele-club spectators whether there was any programme they would like to see again—and if so, which?

5. We next asked them whether they had any particular wishes regading further programmes, not in a general way, but with a view to promoting the purposes for which leisure time is intended—recreation, amusement, information, instruction, extension of general culture.

6. Finally, it is helpful to an educator to know what viewers expect from the various types of programme (roles of the programmes). But if this question had been put directly, it would have been unlikely to elicit many replies. We put it indirectly, in what seemed to us to be the most suitable form.

It was to be expected that there would be comparatively few answers to these questions, all of which were difficult, and that they would not lend themselves to full statistical analysis. The comparatively numerous abstentions cannot always be regarded as indicating disapproval or indifference, as they did in the case of the literary feature already mentioned. Only 144 people out of 225 were able to mention any film they remembered, though 213 had given marks to the film programmes as a whole. So it is evident that in this case the number of abstentions was due chiefly to the difficulty of the question and the length of the questionnaires. This is a natural reaction, especially as, the period being the middle of April, it was not always possible to have a sufficiently long talk with the persons questioned before they wrote out their replies (lack of time, an inconvenient time of year, an official census taking place at the same moment, etc.). The ideal would have been to do everything by verbal enquiry, spending if necessary seveal consecutive months in the villages.

However, even the comparatively few answers we received in the short time available to us yielded results more revealing than those usually gained from a public opinion poll, and more interesting than those of the empirical examination which may be made by the educationist in the course of his professional work. We reduced the risk of hasty generalizations by ignoring the replies when there were less than 10 to any single question, by systematically cross-checking all the answers. We used only such replies as contributed to a profitable analysis of the cultural possibilities of each type of programme. The only aim of this qualitative enquiry was to prepare hypotheses for future quantitative enquiries and to suggest certain lines which educational action might follow for the time being. The conclusions we reached by comparing and cross-checking the replies to all these questions[4] were as follows:

### *Variety Programmes*

It might have been expected that in an adult education association variety programmes would gradually lose their appeal. But this does not seem to be the case. We found 14 instances where there was a decline of interest, but in 32 cases the contrary had happened with regard to "Trente-six chandedles" ("it's not to stupid as it used to be") and the circus programme ("I used to think it was just for children" said one farmer).

The pleasant memories left by variety programmes seem, however, to be rather vague. They relate, never to a particular feature, as in the case of the theatrical and film programmes, but to the type of entertainment itself. Variety is not mentioned by any televiewers who is trying to remember which features may have influenced his tastes, ideas, etc. And variety programmes are the only ones which the audience considers as being meant solely to provide "rest and recreation". So even those who enjoy them are apparently well aware of their limitations. A further interesting observation was made in connection with the wish for new "rest and recreation" programmes. Most people took this to be an enquiry as to which of the existing programmes they would like to see more of. And here, variety items were mentioned only three times, as against 19 requests for films (chiefly comic ones). It does not look, therefore as though tele-club audiences want more variety programmes, and this impression was often confirmed in the course of conversations. In any case there is no reason to suppose that they look upon variety items as the chief purpose of television. In our opinion only one main point remains to be clarified—what underlying need gives rise to this strong and widespread taste for programmes whose limitations are, it seems, apparent even to the viewers themselves?

### *Films*

Our enquiry led to very different conclusions in respect of films, full-length and "shorts" alike. In the first place, feature films, like variety, leave far more pleasant memories (108) than unpleasant ones (34). But film memories are more individualized—the reference is seldom to a type of film or to an author, and nearly always to a particular title. Oral enquiry confirmed this conclusion and showed, further, that among all television programmes it is the films—their subjects, plots, acting and stars—which viewers seem to remember best.

Which films have left the best impression behind them? On the whole the masterpieces. Remembering the number of indifferent films shown in public cinemas in France (of the 2,000 films released in France since 1947, about 90 per cent have been standard products of no real value), one is astonished that the unsophisticated tele-club audiences should reveal such sound taste. Of the 17 films mentioned between 26 and 8 times, only two or three are not masterpieces, and even they are not bad: those most frequently mentioned were, in order of frequency. "La Bataille du Rail", "Rendez-vous de Juillet", "Manon", "Jour de Fete" and "La Symphonie Pastorale".

Realistic films make up a definite majority of those which are favourably remembered (realistic films are mentioned 246 times by 61 per cent of the public, and non-realistic films 157 times by 53 per cent of the public). Workmen, both agricultural and non-agricultural, are particularly fond of realistic films, followed closely by the small farmers and, at a distance, by the non-manual workers (significant difference); 61 per cent of workmen chose realistic films, as against 48 per cent of small farmers and 25 per cent of non-manual workers. And these realistic films are either satires on everyday life, such as "Les Vacances de M. Hulot", psychosocial studies, such as "Claudine a l'Ecole", or social studies like "L'Ecole Buissonniere", "La Bataille du Rail" and "Rendez-vous de Juillet". These films not only tend to improve the taste of the audience but offer great possibilities for social education and the extension of general culture. One wonders, however, whether full advantage is at present taken of these possibilities when these films are introduced and commented upon in the tele-clubs.

We further noted that this liking for good films is apparently durable. Not only do they arouse little opposition (4 per cent), but they are never mentioned among the programmes in respect of which there has been a variation in viewer appreciation, whether in a favourable or unfavourable sense. The cinema thus appears to be well established in the esteem of televiewers—no longer subject to fluctuations of popularity.

It is amusing to note some of the repercussions of films on daily life. The cinema was already known to influence spectators' behaviour, ideas and store of knowledge. But what is less generally realized is that, in tele-clubs, films seem to do more than anything else to promote a taste for reading—much more than a specialized literary programme such as "Lectures pour tous". The only replies to the question "Have any programmes led you to read books?" referred to theatre and cinema plots—"Clochemerle", "Fabiola" or "Le Silence de la Mer".

Finding that feature films made such a lasting impression on the memory and on daily life, we naturally wondered whether the televiewers would like to see them again. The response was clear—95 per cent of them would like to see again the films they had enjoyed at the tele-club, the cine-club, or in a public cinema. It is perhaps a mistake to suppose that an important film should be shown only once. Its influence would be enhanced by a second showing. In any case, there is a keen and widespread desire to see certain films again—136 titles were mentioned 336 times, almost the same figure as for the "most pleasant memory".

It is interesting, too, to discover that the televiewers have very sound taste: they never ask for a re-showing of televised novelettes or minor films, only for masterpieces. This confirms what we found as to the programmes which left the most pleasant recollections. Another the quite different fact also emerges—the four films most often mentioned include two pieces of social satire, "Don Camillo" and "Les Vacances de M. Hulot", and a psychological and comic trilogy by Marcel

Pagnol, "Marius - Fanny - Cesar". The desire for a second viewing of comic films with aesthetic and human interest is confirmed by the televiewers' requests concerning programmes "for rest and recreation". As already explained, variety programmes were mentioned only three times in this connexion, whereas there were 19 mentions of films, including 11 comic films.

The cinema is always the first item to be mentioned in the replies to all questions concerning the purpose of telecasts: entertainment is sought from various types of film, but chiefly from comedies; information and general knowledge are sought from travel shorts on foreign countries; and films receive 24 mentions, as a way to familiarize viewers with famous works, as against 10 for plays and only 6 for literary works. It would therefore seem that, of all types of artistic masterpiece, those of the cinema are by far the most popular with tele-spectators.

***Plays***

It is becoming clear that television is helping to reawaken an interest in the theatre among an unsophisticated public. The provincial public knows little about the theatre, and is therefore unable to formulate requests for new plays. There is much less desire for the retransmission of plays than for that of films (12 mentions as against 136). Yet the liking for plays seems to be steadily increasing among tele-club audiences; so the Saturday evening theatrical programmes must be having a definite effect on their taste. Not one of those questioned liked the theatre less than before, while seven liked it more; the written replies themselves were too few for any observation to be based on them, but they were confirmed verbally by the leaders of certain tele-clubs. The leader of the Nesles club even went so far as to say that "televiewers first discovered the cinema at their tele-clubs, and then the theatre". In the replies to the general questionnaire, too we find remarks such as "I've found out what the theatre is like" (a farmer); "The theatre is something quite new for us, and we could only have got to know it through television" (another farmer); "I understand plays better now" (a farm labourer); "I thought I preferred the cinema to the theatre, but now I never miss a Saturday play" (a young country schoolmaster).

Not all the plays given on television have been chosen with an eye to the susceptibilities of country folk; hence the unfavourable impressions left by some of them, which were too frivolous or too subtle—such as *Ce qu'a dit le vent d'Est* (15 times) and *L'invitation au chateau* by Anouilh (10 times). Even *Liliom,* though an excellent play, is mentioned six times as a disagreeable because of its subject, whose immorality was more readily perceived than its humour. Yet 91 people mentioned pleasant and 25 both pleasant and unpleasant memories, while only 3 received nothing but had impressions. *Litiom* itself is mentioned nine times among the pleasant memories. The five plays most often mentioned include a great work by Paul Claudel, *L'Annonce faite a Marie* (10 mentions); while the play which heads the list, with 43 mentions is *Volpone,* one of the masterpieces which the great producer charles Dullin rescued from oblivion during his career. And the majority of those who enjoyed *Volpone* are small farmers and workmen.

### Literary and Musical Programmes

As regards literary programmes, further enquiry made no change in the unfavourable attitudes we have already described, but even confirmed it in several respects. It is true that some people say they disliked this feature at first, but have grown to like it better. Yet among those in favour of dropping certain programmes, 15 mention "Lectures pour tous", which comes second, after a very "highbrow" game called "Pieces a conviction" (16 mentions). Probably therefore, this type of programme appeals only to a very limited number of French people—those whom a secondary education has left with a taste for present day literary life or for games based on learned allusions. Artistic programmes which present engravings, pictures or statues seem to make no impact whatever upon the tele-club audiences, for they are never once mentioned in the replies. Music, whether classical or light, seems, on the other hand, to please them better; and we were able to obtain verbal confirmation of the wish expressed by 15 televiewers, who thought that more television time should be given to this type of programme.

### *Practical Programmes*

Though opinions vary greatly, there can be no doubt that the "Magazine feminin" is the favourite practical programme with tele-club audiences. In response to the question "What do you choose, or would you choose, to add to your practical knowledge?" domestic features received 60 votes, as against 17 for "Le club des inventeurs", a programme dealing with small technical inventions. But most of the replies (53 out of a total of 57!) called for the introduction of a type of programme which has so far been little developed on French television— programmes which give an idea of different occupations and professions. This overwhelming majority indicates a latent need among tele-club members.

### *Information and Instruction*

The opinions expressed about news telecasts showed that our public takes a keen interest in the principal review of current events, the "Journal televise". The strength and extent of this interest in what is going on becomes even more apparent when we consider the "most pleasant memories" left by news programmes and outside telecasts.

Most popular of all, with 92 approving mentions, was the coronation of the Queen of England. We were told that on that day some of the tele-clubs—that at Etampes, for instance—had an audience five times the usual size. Only 20 people mentioned the telecast of P.resident Coty's election. But the 14 expressions of "unpleasant memories" referring to the election of the President are probably all to the credit of this type of programme. For though certain viewers declared that the telecast from the Palais de Versailles ranked as their least pleasant memory, it was not because the programme itself bored them—very much the opposite! They would have liked the election to "go with more of a swing". They remembered it unfavourably because of the Assembly's difficulty in making up a majority—eight days of voting and bargaining! This interpretation is based not merely on the reasons given for disliking the long drawn out presidential election, but upon the cross-checking of the wishes expressed for the future: of the 52 suggestions for the improvement of public affairs programmes, 31 (the majority) bear on news and 12 call specifically for the direct televising of debates in the National Assembly. Nowadays, when it is so often asserted that the man in the street takes no interst in public affairs, it is particularly important to note a trend in the tele-clubs that favours the use of television as a means of encouraging public interest in the functioning of democrataic institutions.

Next to the coronation of the Queen of England, the memory most frequently recalled is that of the report on the "Tour de France" (45 mentions). Foreigners can scarcely imagine the enthusiasm aroused by this, the chief bicycle-race of the year. It is said that more than 15 million French people have gone out of their way at least once in their lives "to watch the Tour de France go by", which makes it easy to understand why the televised report was so eagerly followed. Apart from this, 77 replies mentioned other sports features, expecially: all-in wrestling matches; the six-day cycle race; boxing matches. Sporting events have a wide appeal, and many who did not share this taste have developed it thanks to television. But has full advantage been taken on the educational possibilities offered by these features?

Turning to the "most pleasant memories", we find confirmation of the televiewers' interest in the "Journal televise" as a whole, to which refernce has already been made. It was this series which provided 37 people with their favourite recollection in the field of television reporting. We found confirmation, too, of the satisfactory approval indices obtained by outside broadcasts on social subjects (36 mentions of the tour of Orly Airport, and 27 of "Etat d'urgence"). "Etat d'urgence" is referred to 9 times among the programmes aimed at increasing knowledge (rural problem), and takes third place on this list. However, among series whose popularity declined as they went on, "Etat d'urgence" is mentioned 13 times (as against 14 mentions of "Trente-six Chandelles"). Later on we shall discuss certain defects in this production, which may account for the fact that some televiewers tired of it.

Another point of interest to any educationist who wishes to add to his audiences' general knowledge by means of television is our viewers' feeling that the telecasts have increased their knowledge of geography more than anything else. "I've seen things I had never seen before—the sea, the Alpine meadows" writes a farm labourer, while a small farmer remarks, rather curiously "I've discovered that the Finns have faces like ours—I thought they had faces like Chinese". Of the 58 people who replied, 31 say they have learnt more geography, while 18 mention "scientific knowledge". Reporting, with or without a film, seems to be the best means of conveying knowledge of this kind, which is often fairly detailed. Our audiences like live telecasts. They also like the telecinema. These distinctions, while useful to specialists, do not always mean very much to the ordinary spectator, as we shall see more clearly when we come to the opinions expressed about "Etat d'urgence". For the moment we must not forget that we have confined ourselves to describing and commenting upon the tele-club members' answers to certain difficult questions, which will help us to gain a clearer view of the cultural possibilities of the various types of telecast and to draw some provisional conclusions as to the right direction for future programmes. We will therefore conclude this second part of our survey with a few practical suggestions which may serve as hypotheses on which to base future experimental telecasts, aimed at encouraging active attitudes among the general public.

**Suggestions**

Our enquiry into the reactions of rural tele-club audiences to the programmes of Television francaise showed us, in the first place, the potential extent of television's contribution to culture. Certain purely didactic claims on behalf of "educational television", reveal an ignorance of the needs of our village manual workers in regard to leisure time occupation. It should be borne in mind that even the organized tele-club public, guided by skilled educationists and with over four years' experience of television, still prefers variety programmes—in other words, sheer entertainment—to anything else.

Before taking up arms against such "shallow taste", it would be well to consider which of the worker's needs is reflected in this fondness for recreational programmes. As we have seen, the tele-club has become an established feature in the life of the community; group viewing adapts itself well to local habits and the demands of everyday work. And it is the needs and obligations of daily life that account for the general popularity of recreational programmes. It is these programmes which best fulfil the two chief functions of leisure, to which we have already referred. In the first place, they provide relaxation: "The programmes are very suitable for their purpose, which is to amuse without tiring" says a farmer's wife; and a workman explains "I like the Wednesday music hall programme very much, because it gets rid of the mid-week tired feeling". Unlike lectures or big films, they do not require concentration, or even sustained attention. "They are lively, because they're varied"; "They have rhythm". The turns are short; they follow in quick succession; there is always something new, and often surprising, to catch the attention.

In the second place, these programmes provide diversion. "It does everyone good to have a change of ideas." Farm work is strenuous, produce is not selling well, so people look to the tele-club to cheer and amuse them. "When I come to watch television it's to cheer myself up, and these variety programmes are very gay" says one workman. After *Volpone,* the play which left the best memories was *Le Don d'Adele,* a good comedy. Of the suggestions for new features, 44 ask for something cheerful, and only 17 for something serious. Of the four big films which televiewers would most like to see again, three are comedies. And the audiences' liking for all-in wrestling is due not so much to its violence, which few people find really convincing as to the fact that it is acrobatic and funny at the same time. "It's good circus stuff" says one viewer. It is this general wish for something funny which prompts a farmer to say that "television is too serious".

Televiewers like to be made to laugh, but they also like to be made to dream. They have a great eagerness to see marvellous sights, "such as one never sees in our kind of life". They are grateful to the variety programmes for "bringing within our reach entertainments that we seldom see (circus) or never see at all (music hall)", as a farm labourer says. Farm people are particularly fond of the circus, perhaps because it shows them animals—horses and dogs—working in a way that is quite extraordinay, in contrast to the ordinary work they do on a farm. The keenest circus viewers are men of 25 to 39—possibly because, in bringing their small children to the show, they revive their own childhood memories, detached from everyday concerns. Countless people who are starved of luxury or beauty look upon the music hall shows as a consolation for their unhappiness and an embodiment of their dreams.

But to the judge from the answer most frequently given, it is the stars who are great attraction of the variety programmes. "I like these programmes", says someone "because they give one a chance to see the singers who are heard on the radio", or as someone else puts it, "It's like meeting the big stars one's always hearing about". Each televiewers has his or her "own" stars, the personification of individual desires or ideals. These semi-mythical personages serve to embody dreams of power, beauty or adventure which cannot be satisfied in real life. It is all the easier for televiewers to feel they are sharing in the stars' lives, since some of the variety programmes (such as "Trente-six chandelles") show the performers with no script or set part to play: "you see them close-to", they are "friendly"—rather as though you had met them in the street or invited them to dinner. The "interviewer" himself asks them questions on topical subjects or problems in everyday language. They answer in the same manner: each member of the audience feels as though television had brought Michele Morgan or Jean Gabin to his own home. It is the "exotic" brought to your doorstep.

In these circumstances, are we justified in speaking of the "cultural possibilities" of television? Despite its limitations, our enquiry into the cultural potentialities of the tele-clubs enables us to answer this question in the affirmative. As we have seen, even the limitations of the variety programmes were quite apparent to the televiewers, who show an almost equal interest in programmes with great cultural possibilities: programmes which can build up personality are just as likely to win acceptance as are the purely recreational features. Television can make leisure time into an opportunity for culture.

The attempt to promote group education by means of television, regarded in the widest sense and adapted to the workers' leisure hours, should not be confined to a small number of features, but should underlie the greater part of the programmes. It should surely be possible to give greater culture value even to the variety items, without diminishing their charm.

The general taste for comedy, whose strength we have already indicated, might be further satisfied by programmes in which parody, satire and humour were exercised in regard to a wide range of subjects taken from private or social life. Humorous writers, actors and journalists undertake to make their public laugh every week, or even every day: what is to prevent television from doing the same thing in its own way, with a permanent comic feature? To think while they laugh is an old tradition among ordinary people everywhere.

A further example is provided by the popularity of performing horses, wild beast acts, and song or dance numbers. Small farmers and workmen are extremely alive to the quality of good "work". One of them writes: "I like the circus and the Wednesday music hall best, because they show us people and animals actually at work". It seems likely that greater advantage could be taken of this interest in work, through programmes showing backstage views of cabaret, music hall or circus life, with the athletes, acrobats, tamers or performers at work and being interviewed about their working methods and style of life, their childhood, their past careers, the problems confronting them in the ring or on the stage, the way the audience can play its part, etc. Interest in stars might thus lead to the acquiring of a living culture.

What cultural possibilities are offered by the remaining programmes? The practical programmes are intended to help people reflect on everyday tasks so as to enable them to carry them out with more pleasure or greater efficiency. "Magazine feminin" does not seem to have achieved this aim. Televiewers shows a marked difference of opinion about it. They do not, however, object to the actual type of feature. Some have said they would like these practical programmes extended to include technology and craftsmanship. "I'd like the practical programmes to show something about my job." Though the enquiry did not point to any very definite conclusions, we gathered, from what the tele-club leaders said, that it would be advisable to lengthen and vary the list of subjects dealt with in a "magazine". It should cover the problems of household and family life—the children's education, the arrangement of an apartment, how to buy toys or build up a record library. Cooking and cutting-out do not interest enough televiewers (less than 5 per cent in our enquiry), and many people find them boring. Do they produce no effect at all? That does not seem to be the case. But the fact chiefly stressed by everyone who claimed to have gained practical information from the cooking or cutting-out demonstrations was that "It gives you ideas", as a farmer's wife put it. What tele-club members expect from this particular "magazine" is not detailed instructions, but general advice on household matters. The "magazine" should serve as a permanent adviser; and more of its time should be devoted to the day-to-day routine of a typical family, with advice from well-known stars and interviews with women from various walks of life—the chief problems by which the family is confronted being discused in an intelligent conversational style.

But, it may be asked, must the "magazine" necessarily give detailed practical advice? It might do so now and then, but in the ordinary way it should simply awaken the women's interest in the subjects it deals with, and tell them how to find out more. It would be sufficient to set up an enquiry service or to give some addresses, or perhaps to introduce a few books, with comments. The women could buy these books and learn to get the best out of them. This would probably widen the appeal of the "magazine", and it might come to play both a practical and cultural part in family life.

Group education also seeks to acquaint the public with masterpieces of art and literature. Television has unprecedented facilities for solving this problem. Tele-club experience suggests that the masterpieces which appeal most to viewers are those produced by the cinema. Some technicians feel that the small screen requires productions made to fit it. We agree. Television will gradually develop a style of its own. But it would be a mistake to reduce the ratio of films in television. Our televiewers are explicit on this point—they enjoy seeing good films, and would like to see them a second time.

The masterpieces of the cinema can do much to educate public taste. Through television, which for many people acts as "home cinema", they can awaken a feeling for beauty and stimulate thought about important problems. If full advantage is to be taken of these possibilities, the groups must be given more encouragement to think for themselves. On the French television service, films are presented in a way which, though generally brilliant, is too complicated and too "precious" to capture the televiewer's attention. The language used is too refined; the ideas expressed are too far removed from the lives of workmen and small farmers. It might be possible to lead off the discussion in the clubs after the viewing by a short televised debate between professional critics and people from various walks of life.

Fuller use might be made of our audiences' fondness for films in awakening their interest in other art forms—painting, music, literature—by discussions highlighting certain aspects of the film itself, or the literary or other sources from which it originated—providing, of course, that these discussions are conducted in language which is clear, precise, and understandable by all.

Introduction to literature through television cannot be confined to telecasts about the latest novels. These, as we have seen, are quite "lost" on our club audiences. In France the problem of extending reading among the public is tremendous, and television could probably be a great help in solving it. We have emphasized our viewers' interest in topical events. Attempts to encourage reading should make full use of this. The topical appeal of a book does not necessarily lie in its literary aspects. For 90 per cent of the population it stems from something quite different—from current political, social or human considerations. Any very successful film starts a fashion for the classic or modern book on which its plot was based. A political trial may double the number of readers of some modern book. The sudden opening-up of a new country, may prompt people to read some great book which deals with it, and so forth. Television must set about preparing features which present literary works from this highly topical point of view.

Speaking more generally, the reading habit should be inculcated, not merely on the basis of one particular feature, but with the help of every programme which gives pleasure and has cultural possibilities. It will be remembered that, in a public opinion poll recently conducted by the BBC, 63 per cent of televiewers said they were reading less than before. In the tele-clubs, where the educator's influence makes itself felt, the trend is muclfless negative. A certain type of programme can, however, be a danger to private reading. It is for the producers to encourage individual enthusiasm for books, by their method of presentation, their commentaries, and the particulars they give. The right lines are indicated by the experiment in reading among children, conducted at Seattle, which we described in the Introduction. To encourage reading should be a permanent concern with all good producers and directors.

There are various ways of introducing a great literary

work on television. But the growing popularity of televised plays and the drawing power of "stars" suggest that more use should be made of straightforward reading and dramatization of books, the reading to be done by well-known stars of the theatre or cinema. We think, too, that discussions between the author and the leaders of a few public reading clubs, guided by a chairman with an unaffected way of speaking, might do much to spread reading through television.

Another problem which our tele-clubs are challenging the television service to approach much more boldly is that of the extension of general knowledge. Most children leave school at the age of 14; but the citizen of a present-day democracy needs to increase his knowledge all the time. How can this need be satisfied without boring him? News telecasts could perhaps be extended and made more exhaustive, to form a basis for the acquisition of fresh knowledge. The "Journal televise" is one of the most popular features and the chief criticisms made of it, apart from accusations of prejudice or triviality, are that "it is not full enough", or that "it's a pity we usually get only the Paris news". This "journal" might be longer and more instructive—its descriptions might be more detailed, its information more precise, its statistics more numerous, its subject-matter and the problems it describes more closely related to their period and surroundings.

One workman said, rather charmingly, that he liked the "Journal televise" "because it's about my *own* times". This feature might include a greater number of informative items, presented in its usual way, thanks to more numerous diagrams, more detailed commentaries and longer interviews. It would thus help to give the general public an insight into our own times, through the presentation of some particular event. By making use of films, sketches, maps, interviews, etc., the "journal" might provide the indispensable "background" for the building up of knowledge. Unfortunately, in their wish to please (whom?), the "journal" commentators sometimes feel impelled to be rapid, superficial, sparkling—to fire off paradoxes or indulge in subtleties. These are quite the wrong tactics when addressing an unsophisticated audience.

The same course of action would be even more appropriate to the reporting of great events. The coronation of the Queen of England left very vivid memories. Why not follow up this display of interest by a programme devoted to the great moments in the history of the British Empire and its chief economic, social and cultural features, illustrated in a really varied and lively manner?

Democracies often lament the public ignorance about civic questions. Might not a better use be made of the momentary interest awakened among the public by certain events, such as elections? These would provide an opportunity for telecasts describing the development, operation and significance of the various public institutions. It might perhaps be well to appoint a permanent advisory body of historians, geographers, ethnographers and sociologists, to supply television producers and directors at any time with information which would help them to place current events in their proper chronological and spatial setting.

Such an institution might be of service even for telecasts which seem, at first glance, to have very little relation to current events. Let us consider sport, for example. The season of the cycle "Tour de France" is about the only time of year when the French public takes any interest in the country's geography. Would it not be desirable and possible to introduce a series of programmes lasting throughout the tour and constituting a "geographical tour de France", in which the towns and provinces through which the cyclists pass would be presented to the huge public that comes to watch champions like Louison Bobet and Fausto Coppi? In a more general way, reports on topical events in the field of sport, whether cycling, football, wrestling or athletics, might provide glimpses of the different peoples, provinces and lands while describing their champions and sports teams. The excitement worked up in connexion with commercialized sport, which so often acts as an opiate for the public, could thus be turned to account for the spread of worth-while knowledge. Sports writers have already blazed the trail, but television has so far shown little readiness to follow them.

We must once again emphasize the outstanding importance attached by tele-club audiences to the knowledge of geography. Surely the interest aroused by travel stories and travel documentaries could be put to better use? Telecasts could, for instance, prepare people for holidays in certain districts or provinces—the Riviera, Brittanay, the Alps. Or they could deal with the general problems confronting those parts of the country, stimulating the desire to investigate them by reading monographs, biographies, descriptions, novels or essays.

Television francaise has perhaps not made the most of the tele-club audiences' interest in geography. It should be possible to use this popular subject as introduction to the methodical study of other branches of knowledge, whose theory and terminology appear more complex. Using this approach, knowledge can be easily acquired, by a kind of intelligent journey of exploration through nature and human society. The research-worker looks at things from a standpoint not far removed from that of the spectator eager to learn more about his surroundings or about the world he dreams of entering. This angle is receiving more and more attention in present day education, which devotes an ever-increasing amount of time to "background studies". And geography covers all other fields of knowledge, or at least touches them at certain points; physical geography serves as an introduction to geology, physics and chemistry; economic geography leads to political economy, and biological geography to the medical sciences; while cultural geography paves the way to the study of manners and customs, etc. Modern geography, considered in its wiest sense (ecology), is often closely related to ethnography, sociology and anthropology. The far-ranging and disconnected interests which have often been said to detract from the value of geographers as scientific research-workers are an asset where introduction to science is involved. That is why geography might be used as a stepping-stone to amost all the other sciences.

The televising of composite films built up around one element in nature—animal life—has already shown what might be achieved by the composite treatment—on humorous, dramatic or poetic lines—of other elements in nature or human society.

An introduction to physics through the exploration of a particular setting has been demonstrated by outside telecasts such as the visit to the atomic laboratory at Saclay. Though tele-club audiences express general approval of this type of programme, they severely criticized the method, commentary and structure of this particular programme, declaring that "one couldn't really get the hang of it", "it was too long", etc. The same comments were made about the "scientific telecasts" in which an expert is interviewed about the principles underlying his discoveries, rather than about their results. In our opinion, the backbone of any scientific teaching through television should be supplied by a description of the practical applications of the particular science in question.

Such an approach might serve as an effective introduction to the lives, achievements and theories of scientists. Between the programme which consists meely of a difficult, tedious lecture, unbearable to the average viewer, and the superficial report with no educational value, there may be room for composite features in which cinema and "live" television, pictures and words, stories and ideas, comments and interviews, explanations and suggestions for reading combine to acquaint the general public with highly complicated problems. It now remains for us to investigate a programme of this kind, consisting of the 13 telecasts which made up "Etat d'urgence" and whose aim was to interest rural tele-club audience in an important problem involving rural economy, sociology and policy. We must repeat that we regad the results of this supplementary enquiry into the cultural possibilities of important telecasts merely as hypotheses to be verified by further surveys in the near future. Our practical suggestions, too, are submitted only as hints for the general trend of programmes which will have to be tested by experiment, as we tried to do with "Etat d'urgence".

## References

1. Instructions to the televiewers were "Mark the following programmes from 1 to 6; if there are any you have never seen, or do not know well enough, put an x against them". 6 means exceptional approval (outstanding); 5 strong approval (very good); 4 approval (good); 3 uncertainty (neither approval or disapproval) (average); 2 disapproval; 1 strong disapproval.

2. Notes on Methods, Calculation of the positive and negative indices of programme appraisal.

3. See p. 25.

4. See Appendix V, Tables based on questions concering the cultural possibilities of telecasts.

# 5

# The Programmes

## Background

### *1952 : The First Attempt*

Less than a year after the formation of the first tele-clubs, the leaders of the movement realized that they would have to widen the field of their activities. It was not enough to encourage the opening of tele-clubs and then operate them and "conduct" their meetings; it was also necessary to induce Television francaise to provide programmes more suited to the popular education movement to which this new type of club owed its origin.

As early as 1950 Television francaise was asking the tele-clubs to send in periodical notes on the programmes received, as a supplement to the information gained from audience mail and from the critics. When, forwards the end of 1951, the leaders of the movement asked for progrmmes to meet their requirements, their request was favourably received. As a result, Television francaise, in August 1952, offered to organize a series of regular telecasts which, though available to all viewers, would be intended primarily for tele-clubs.

The television authorities, however, wanted to devote these programmes to specifically rural problems, whereas the tele-club leaders would have preferred something designed to meet the needs of popular ducation in its widest sense.

This was a new type of series, inasmuch as its intention was to draw up programmes with the organized tele-club public definitely in mind. But from another point of view it constituted an even bolder innovation. The series was to be produced, not by a television expert, but by an active worker in the field of popular education. This was Boger Louis, the founder of tele-clubs in France, who had had long experience of evening meetings and study circles, cine-clubs and reading clubs. He knew nothing of how a television programme was "put on", but he knew how to awaken the immediate interest of an unsophisticated audience in a general problem, a subject of study or an art.

From October 1952 to June 1953, for the first time in the history of Television francaise, an organization formed for group viewing had a programme specially planned for it—"La vie a la campagne" (life in the country). But the Programme Department was not over bold. It refused to alter the day and hour of other features to make room for "La vie a la campagne" during the usual tele-club hours. It pur the programme at noon on Sundays, and later at 6 p.m. on Sundays, neither of which times was really suitable. At those hours there is no one in the tele-club; and these programmes, theoretically intended for them, were hardly received at all except by home viewers. The authorities allowed only 5,000 frs. per telecast to meet expenses. This covered no more than 1 or 2 minutes of "live" transmission; the producer had to fill in the rest of the time with whatever documentary films he could manage to borrow! The programme depended for its existence on film lending libraries. Preparations often consisted merely of a hunt for films available on free loan. And as, from the outset, the producer was given very insufficient time for preparation, he was in a state of constant uncertainty. The trouble was that this series was regarded at what is called an "educational" programme. It was therefore doomed to be "run on a shoestring", in accordance with the infortunate view—far too widely held in the majority of television services—that while it is natural to spend large sums on entertaining the public with variety shows, it would be a wicked waste to spend even one-tenth the amount in an attempt to teach or spread culture among that same public through so-called "educational" telecasts. For lack of funds, the programme invariably followed the same course; a film would be introduced by the tele-club leader, and then run through, after which there would be a discussion, more or less unscripted, between the leader and the girl TV announcer—the latter playing the part of an ignorant but wellmeaning townswoman. Sometimes someone would be interviewed; and suggestions would be made to the viewers to continue the discussion among themselves, and to write to the television giving their own ideas.

This feature was, however, lucky in two ways. For one thing, one of the girl announcers on the Television francaise agreed to help Roger Louis without receiving a fee; and for another thing—still more important—as the discussion, contrary to the established custom in television, did not follow a written script, it had a sincerity and simplicity which the audience was quick to appreciate.

As these programmes were not reaching the tele-clubs, Roger Louis felt that his chief aim should be to give town viewers an idea of the tele-club movement and of living conditions in the country. He used television as a means of linking town and country, and tried to convey a better understanding of the conditions of rural life as compared with those of industrial and town populations.

It is impossible to give a complete list of the subject dealt with in the programmes, which were given monthly from October 1952 to July 1953, but we will mention some or them by way of example:

*Forests*: wild life.

*Drainage*: the collective effort made by one village toset up a drainage system.

*The first step*: story of the individual efforts of one smallholder to improve his holding.

*Alpine meadows*: life of the mountain dwellers in the Alps. Peaceful countryside: argument between a young Parisian and his brother on the subject of modernization.

*Town and country life*: an attempt to compare the ways of life of townspeople and countryfolk. Explanation of their attitudes towards each other.

*Farmworkers and miners*: an attempt to compare the working lives of the miner and the farmworker.

*Countryfolk and the war*: attempt to investigate the attitude of countryfolk towards the war and the problems with which it confronted them (from the standpoint of the accusations brought against them by town-dwellers).

*Family life*: the life of a town family, seen in the light of the statistics issued by the Institut National de la Statistique et des Etudes economiques (survey of the marketing and utilization of agricultural produce).

Viewers' letters showed a very favourable racation. This was so much the case that, before the end of the series, the Television francaise made a further grant, so that it became possible to hire commercial films, and even to make one film about the creation of the Nogentel tele-club. Was this success due to the subject-matter of the telecasts, whose aim was to rid townspeople of their prejudices regarding countryfolk, or to the sincerity displayed by the organizer? However that may be, the tele-club movement thus succeeded, for the first time, in directly introducing its own particular problems and style into telecasts. The television authorities felt encouraged to follow up their initiative.

## *Origin of the "Etat D'urgence" Series of Telecasts*

In 1953 Television francaise was able to arrange a further series of telecasts in co-operation with the tele-clubs—this time with considerably larger funds, thanks to help from Unesco. It will be remembered that Unesco had decided to conduct, in one of its Member States, an experiment in the use of television for adult education in rural areas. France offered the co-operation of its television service in implementing this project. Under the agreements concluded between Television francaise and Unesco, the former met all the ordinary expenses of producing this series, and undertook to transmit it at an hour convenient to tele-club viewers.[1] Unesco was responsible for the extra expenditure which enabled the producing team to extend its range to an area exceeding that which is normally accessible to television.[2] Unesco also provided facilities for making a scientific check of the results of these programmes.

## Principle and Planning of the Telecasts

A number of considerations influenced the choice of a subject for the series of telecasts. In the first place, the programmes had to be of special interest to countryfolk in the departments where tele-clubs existed; yet they had also to interest town viewers, for there was only one television network in France and all features had therefore to be arranged so as to please a sufficiently high proportion of a viewing public. Moreover, the programmes had to have a definite educational purpose, with measurable results. And finally they had, as far as possible, to make use of all the technical resources of production.

After much discussion between Roger Louis and the responsible officials of Unesco's Mass Communication Department, who were helped by advice from experts attached to the French Ministry of Agriculture, it was decided that the general purpose of the series should be to demonstrate the vital problems confronting French agriculture and the need to solve them by introducing modern methods. The series was to provide new ideas which would prompt new activity. It therefore bore no resemblance either to the purely informative programmes like the "Vie a la campagine" series—aimed solely at acquainting townsfolk with the problems facing country-dwellers—or to the strictly educational type of programme.

Throughout the preparation of the series, and even after it was launched, there was considerable controversy about its general trend. Programmes intended for one particular category of viewers might bore the others. This difficulty became evident during the actual telecasts. When Roger Louis spoke directly to tele-club members, the Programme Department of Television francaise objected, fearing that town viewers would switch off. But when he spoke to the audience in general, it was found that response in the tele-club was less spontaneous and that it was difficult, afterwards, to induce their members to discuss the subject of the programme.[3]

In order to lay down the general line of the series, the producer and the Unesco specialists therefore asked themselves: "What is the common denominator of wine-grower and farmer, workman and engineer, the town family and the country family? How can we deliver our message to a particular section of our audience without boring the others?"

The solution was to describe all the problems within the framework of "true stories". Everybody takes a certain interest in their neighbours' private lives, and through this interest the viewers could be given a grasp of the main general problems affecting their own existence.

It was consequently decided that, in nearly all the programmes, the main features of the problem would be set forth as part of the story of a present-day Frenchman. In many cases the man himself came to the studio. Thus, for instance, viewers were introduced to Mr. Lecomte, whose son had joined the army and left him, at an advanced age, to work his farm by himself; and thus, too, they sided for or against the small farmer and the industrialist who came to discuss the vital question of credit. Whether the subject was re-allocation of land, co-operation, the flow of young people to the towns, or woman's life in the country, it was always the tale of personal experience which made the greatest impression.

**Problems of Rural Life**

But what were the problems at issue? This could not be discovered in Paris. An inspector from the Ministry of Agriculture advised Roger Louis to go and study them on the spot.

This investigation led much farther than had been anticipated. The aim was to find subjects for the telecasts, by travelling about in country districts in search of places where a vital problem was obviously calling for solution. Landscape, setting, situation and participants in the telecast had to be found—all in the districts, and if possible in the actual villages, where the tele-clubs were operating. The organizer hoped that this would increase the impact of his programmes and stimulate the club members.

The investigation took three weeks. In three districts—Tardenois, Brie and Champagne—Roger Louis put his question "What's wrong in your part of the world?" to members of both sexes, representing a wide range of occupations, age-groups, financial and social positions, and cultural levels. He questioned teachers sand parish priests, veterinary surgeons and doctors, shopkeepers and managers of co-operatives. And in particular he tried, by spending a great deal of time with big farmers, farm labourers and small farmers, to discern the main features of the unsatisfactory situation prevailing in rural districts.

In the Tardenois the big farmers grow sugar-beet on farms that cover from 200 to 1,000 hectares[4] or even more. They are prosperous, and have carried standardization and mechanization to the furthest possible extent. Output is high. But they are wondering what is the best size for a large-scale undertaking—200, 500 or 1,000 hectares? They complain that competition knows no restraint, that the market lacks all organization. They are not always sure of selling their crop. Many declare that the work is becoming more and more difficult, owing to the shortage of qualified workers; they feel that the flow of population from country to town will have unfortunate repercussions, and are worried about the social unrest which sets up a barrier between them and their workers.

The farm labourers, for their part, complain of their low wages and their housing conditions, which are frequently squalid. Most of them earn considerably less than 20,000 francs a month. They do not get the paid holidays or the free time which factory workers enjoy, and are often marooned on wide stretches of land where no entertainment is available. They are "organized" but have no powerful trade unions like those of the town workman; and they are more "resigned" in outlook. The proportion of Frenchmen among them is steadily declining, and those that remain are regarded by many people as the dregs of society. The best of them make for the towns, and the investigators did not meet a single "exile" who was homesick for his village. On the contrary, all those who leave take every opportunity of urging their friends to do the same.

The small farmers have other subjects of complaint. There are over 3 million of them in all, with farms of less than 20 hectares; and they represent a great variety of types. To consider only the district of the tele-clubs, the problems which exist in wine-growing regions such as Chatillon and Venteuil are not the same as those found in "mixed crop" areas such as Montfaucon and Viffort. Nearly all the farms in the wine-growing district have their own tractor and their own sulphating machine for treating the vines. The yield is good and the standard of living higher than elsewhere. But all these small wine-growers are at the mercy of the big champagne firms. They have modern equipment, but often do not know how to use it to the best advantage. A considerable effort in the way of co-operation has indeed been made; but individualism coupled with the tendency to "get into a groove", has kept the vineyards too small (many of them are less than 2 or 3 hectares); prices are therefore high, and this restricts the market.

But it is in the Brie district, with its mixed crops and cattle-beeding, that the situation of the small farmers is the worst of all. Their buildings, tools and methods are old-fashioned and out of date; yields are very inadequate, and the produce is hard to sell, being greatly over-priced. In such circumstances, the small farmers tend to withdraw into themselves, cutting down their output and leaving land untilled. They do not dare to borrow money for modernization purposes. They work themselves to death, to achieve a standard of living which in many cases is very low. Even the wealthy among them have often grown avaricious, for fear of what the morrow may bring. The young men are heartily sick of the work, and the girls are ready to leave for the town at the first opportunity. Thus the villages are being drained of their population

### *A Few Figures*

They travelling town-dweller thinks of the countryside as a place for a holiday or a Sunday outing; whereas for many countryfolk it has become uninhabitable. Here are some typical examples of the discomfort that prevails.

The villages in which our tele-clubs are situated are not buried in the depths of Auvergne or Finistere; they are within 60 miles of Paris. Three of them are on the outskirts of a country town, Chateau-Thierry. Yet 65 per cent[5] of the public affected by our investigation have no running water. Of the 21.5 million people who live in country districts in France, only 9 million have running water. One housewife out of two has at her disposal a primitive wash-house with no real shelter, and 95 per cent of this public have no communal drainage system. Facilities for recreation are also scanty. Although these villages have gifted organizers, 70 per cent of them still have no village hall and 65 per cent are without a sports ground.

Are the houses more attractive than the villages as a whole? Most of them are at least 100 years old. Those of our tele-club members are no exception to this rule. Less than half of them have been brought up to date. The housewife has to fetch water from the public fountain or horsetrough. More than half the people have no water laid on at all. "A tap above the sink" is something to dream about. Electric cookers are rare, to be found in hardly one in five homes we are discussing. Wood is frequently used for heating, as it costs less than electricity or coal. Only one person out of two uses butane gas for cooking. Central heating is a luxury beyond the reach of 90 per cent of our public. Ninety-five people out of 100 own wireless sets, but hardly 15 per cent have main drainage in their houses. And 85 per cent have no washing-machine of their own.

The chief reason for this shortage of equipment in village and home is the low yield of crops, stock-breeding and agricultural work in general. Of the small farmers among our audiences, more than half work by rule of thumb and keep no accounts. The swing-plough has been abolished, and the vast majority of small farmers have all-mental wheel ploughs; but only 12 per cent have tractors. It seems likely that many of the others cannot afford to buy one, though it would increase their output and consequently their income.

Another point is that the land is probably too sub-divided, the holdings are too scattered. Why do the farmers hesitate to suggest re-allocation—the re-grouping of the small plots? In the Aisne only 80 communes out of 400 have had their land re-allocated—and the Aisne is an enterprising and exceptionally advanced department. Only 6 per cent of the farmers we are considering have a re-allocation commission at their disposal. If up-to-date machinery is too expensive to buy, the small farmers might perhaps club together to gain the benefit of it. Some of our tele-club viewers belong to the co-operative movement and most of them are members of a buyer's or purchasers' co-operative, but less than 20 per cent enjoy the advantages of a machine-hiring co-operative. As for the collective ownership of household equipment, such as washing-machines, this is practically unknown. All these examples serve to illustrate the alarming situation noted by the producer.

**The Final Plan**

Once back in Paris, Roger Louis and the Unesco officials discussed matters thoroughly with the Ministry of Agriculture, the Ministry of Education, the organizers of after-school courses and representataives of the Commissariat General au Plan de Modernisation (General Commissariat for Planned Modernization), the Direction de I'Equipment du Territoire (Directorate of Territorial Equipment) and the agricultural trade unions, before drawing up the final plan for the telecasts.

The districts concerned being so poverty-stricken, the producer decided that the experimental series should deal first and foremost with the problem of the poorest farms, which are also the most numerous, and should be addressed primarily to small farmers. The chief aim should be to hasten their realization of the need for modernization and to suggest some possibilities for improvement, despite the difficulty resulting from the present dispersed state of landownership.

The series of telecasts was intended to show that such an effort was practicable, provided modernization of equipment went hand in hand with the use of agricultural credit, the re-allocation of rural property, increased co-operation and better conditions for women and young people. To stress the seriousness of this problem for small farmers and for the nation as a whole, the producer decided to call the series "Etat d'urgence".

The arguments to be expressed in the thirteen telecasts were centred on four principal points:

*Presentation of the facts* (telecasts 1 and 2). Description of the present-day life of the countryfolk in the district selected. What makes it almost intolerable not only to them but to all who are dependent upon agricultural output. Something must be done. But what? And hew? Suggestion of a possible solution of the resultant problem, as part of a desirable and logical development the motorization, or rather modernization of the farms and the adaptation this would entail.

*Consideration of the problems and their possible solutions* (telecasts 3 to 9, inclusive). There are obstacles: the question of credit, the widely-dispersed holdings, the individualistic attitude of the small owner-farmers. Some solutions have been found, others are still to seek. The importance of a community spirit. Is there a glut of produce?

*Consequences of this development on the human level* (telecasts 10, 11 and 12). Need for development on the human as well as the technical level. Motorization and mechanization have no value unless accompanied by a far-reaching change in the way of life and outlook of the people; role of women and young people.

*The first step must be taken* (telecast 13). This trend of development, which progressively transforms agriculture from a way of life into an occupation, calls for preliminary education. Schools of agriculture and after-school training courses exist, or can be instituted.

Although the telecasts in their final form did not absolutely adhere to this plan, owing to the numerous technical difficulties which arose as they went on, the main line laid down was carefully followed.

The subject-matter of each of the 13 telecasts was deliberately kept fairly general, so that each had its own interest and was more or less independent of the others. Viewers could thus enjoy any telecast in the series without necessarily having seen them all.

Every feature was required to abide by the following principles, which were based on experience gained in popular education : (a) it must be planned with a view to group reception, to be followed by discussion of the problems it raised; (b) it must deal with subjects of immediate interest to the districts where the experiment was to take place; (c) it must be confined to a limited number of subjects, in order to simplify analysis of the results achieved; (d) it must, whenever possible, make use of illustrations or examples drawn from the district itself; (e) it must, so far as possible, encourage or supplement some local activity already undertaken, in such a way that the practical effect of the telecasts would be easy to assess.

## Stages in Carrying Out the Plan

### *The Production of Films*

The programmes were to consist, in varying proportions, of films and "live" telecasts from the studio. According to the original plan, the 13 telecasts were to include a total of about two and a half hours of film time. The first step in the preparations consisted of making these films, after choosing locations for them.

The production team consisted of five members—a director, a producer who was also the head cameraman, a continuity-girl, a cameraman who was also assistant producer, and an assistant electrician.[6] The working atmosphere was friendly and practical: every member of the team willingly undertook several tasks, and all took turns in helping whichever one among them was the best qualified for any particular job.

At the very outset a problem arose which put the team to the test, before it had had time to get into real working condition. The filmed portion, illustrating the talks, had been planned in the form of "stories", introducing characters, who were thus required to play a part and build up a dramatic "interpretation". The human aspect was regarded as more important that the technical; but at the beginning there was a difference of opinion. The director felt that the parts should be played by professional actors, since only they, he considered, would know what to do in front of the camera and be able to give a natural performance. The producer argued that the stories to be told, and which the films would illustrate, were not fictions, and that the real people concerned must be brought in, so as to secure the requisite natural atmosphere. He thought that real countryfolk alone would give the desired impression of authenticity, without which a country audience would be left unmoved.

Both sides vigorously defended their respective points of view. Finally it was decided that the search for a locality should be accompanied by a search for suitable peasant performers. If these could not be found, there would still be time to call in professionals.

All the illustrative films were to be made in the southern part of the Aisne and Marnte departments; where there were many tele-clubs, whose leaders gave extremely helpful information about which of the country people should be sought out, and introduced the team to the traditionally aloof and mistrustful local communities.

Despite these introductions, and the fact that most of the countryfolk visited by the team were regular viewers and thus took an interest in the scheme, considerable diplomacy was needed to persuade them to appear in films; and still more was required before they would allow the cameraman to film their farms—especially "inside". Not only did they fear loss of time and inconvenience, but they felt a kind of embarrassment at the idea of "showing everybody" the setting of their private lives. They disliked intensely the thought that other countryfolk would be appraising and criticizing their domestic arrangements. "You'll make fun of us", "You want to show how backward we are"—or, on the contrary. "The others will say we're stuck up"—such were remarks that the team heard daily. The task of persuasion was particularly difficult when it came to inducing a family of countryfolk, whose technical methods and style of living were more than usually backward, to reveal to the camera the most typical examples of those methods. Nobody likes to be held up as an example of "how not to behave".

The process of reconnitring the ground consisted, in fact, almost entirely of long discussions. After a week of such contacts, the team became convinced that the policy of using countryfolk as actors was the right one; so this made it possible to settle more or less definitely where the different items were to be filmed.

The preparation of the actual scripts was then undertaken, in the light of the suggestions gleaned during the "tour of inspection"; further important changes were made in the general project, and the "shooting" began.[7]

Practical experience showed at once that the decision to use "impromptu" actors was a good one. When the first shots were made the director carefully explained to the countryfolk, step by step, what they were to do, imitating the facial expressions and the attitudes they were to adopt. But it very soon became apparent that all these precautions were quite superfluous. A short explanation at the beginning was quite enough, and the temporary actor then improvised his part with disconcerting ease, without a single false note and without ever "piling it on".

"The best actors in the world could never manage that!" declared the director, when he realized with stupefaction that hardly any of the scenes shot would need "retakes".

Still more astonishing was the fact that he sometimes suggested an attitude while shooting was in progress, and the suggestions were obeyed, without the camera recording the slightest sign of hesitation or artificiality, the briefest ill-timed glance.

Helped by exceptionally good weather, the filming was completed in very favourable circumstances. One example may be enough to give an idea of the local people's actively sympathetic attitude towards the film team. During the reconstruction of the opening of a tele-club in the village of Nogentel, for a film to be used in the telecast on "the community spirit", 80 of the village people submitted to being filmed from 8 p.m. to 2 a.m. (though most of them had to be at work very early next morning) and, in the dazzling light of the projectors, patiently went over and over a single short crowd scene which was difficult to get exactly right—and this, of course, with no payment whatsoever.

In this connexion it should be mentioned that in every case the producer had the greatest difficulty in persuading these impromptu actors, who had lost one and quite frequently several days' work, that it was entirely natural for the Television to compensate them and that they had thoroughly deserved this.

The filming was done in two separate periods, and completed at the end of December.

But the films had been shot "silent". So once back in Paris it remained not only to cut them, but also to add the sound track.

In the first telecast, a film was to be presented by a countryman who was the author of the story and acted in it as well. The recording of his commentary was attended by circumstances which are worth describing.

This Mr. Demarck—a wine-grower at Grouttes, a little village in the south of the Aisne—had been asked to write the commentary for his own story, as related in the film. But the commentary, when written down and read back by its author, seemed "all wrong" in some puzzling way. Even the actual sound was disagreeable. M. Demarck's characteristically rugged voice, which the producer was bent on using, sounded artificial, and the words completely without individuality.

After several unsuccessful attempts, the producer wrote a different text—with no better luck.

On the verge of giving up the method of "the story told by its author", the organizers then said to Mr. Demarck, as a last hope; "Try to imagine you're telling your story to a pal . . . keep pace with the picture, but if you can't manage that don't worry . . . just carry on!"

"What about my paper?"
"Put it in your pocket and forget it !"
"Ready? . . . Go ahead !"

We then from behind the glass partition, watched the unique sight of a peasant alone in front of the microphone, gesticulating and grimacing as he told his story—now being shown on the screen—to an imaginary friend. It went on for

20 minutes, by the end of which time Mr. Demarck, without a page of script, had recorded a faultless commentary with no over-running. The sound engineer had never known anything like it before !

### *Preparing the "Live" Telecasts*

To find people who could take part in the discussions to be televised direct from the studio was even more difficult than to find countryfolk who could illustrate their own lives before a film camera. The producer had to solve two problems: he must find people all of whom were capable of putting their views clearly in words that the public could understand, and some of whom were ready to come out in public against widely-accepted solutions such as the re-allocation of land, or co-operation. A few examples taken from the producer's notes will serve to illustrate these problems:

"For the third telecast, on redit, we had to find four representative participants—two industrialists, and two peasants (one small and one big farmer). The debate on such a subject was bound to be lively, and we had to make sure that it would not degenerate into a fist fight in front of the camera. The participants had to be carefully selected, but there were only two days left ...

"We called a scratch meeting of industrialists in the television offices gave them a subject and started them discussing it. The discussion was closely followed by the producer and the director, who watched every detail of the participants' behaviour, manner of talking, etc. By the end of the discussion two people had definitely come to the fore; they were asked to take part in the programme two days later, and accepted. The two peasants still had to be found. The producer spent the day before the telecast driving about the Aisne countryside looking for two men who could hold their own in an argument with vocal and well-informed industrialists. With the help of local rumour, which gave clues as to who could stand their ground in these circumstances, he brought back with him in the evening two farmers whom he had relentlessly snatched from their peaceful homes...

"Rehearsals began on the morning of the day for which the programme was fixed, and took on from the very start a heated tone which had to be restrained and yet encouraged. The participants were certainly in no danger of 'drying up' that evening !"

The country people's reluctance to give vent in public to views which might seem old-fashioned is shown in the following note on the difficulties met with while preparing the fourth telecast, on the re-allocation of land:

"About 50 per cent of farm folk are uncompromisingly hostile to the present method of re-allocating land, while 50 per cent fiercely defend it.

"But while the supporters bring sound arguments in support of their views, the opponents justify their attitude by almost exclusively personal considerations. (I'd have liked that piece of ground, but they didn't give it to me.... My neighbour got the best of it, etc. . . .)

"Even while making the film to illustrate the difficulties encountered in connexion with the re-allocation process, the producer was obliged to co-ordinate the criticisms which various participants made in an undertone, and try to give them a general application.

"The 'live' part of the programme was to consist partly of a discussion between a peasant who approved of re-allocation a peasant who disapproved, and a technical expert.

"Despite a thorough search, it proved impossible to find an opponent who had sound arguments to put forward, as the peasants who were notorious for their violent opposition to re-allocation refused, one after the other, to come before the camera and explain their views, for fear of seeming 'reactionary'.

"The balance of the programme was thus endangered.

"We could, of course, have 'invented' a worth-while opponent by asking an actor to take the part and using a written script; but the producer was against this, as a matter of principle.

"Rehearsals took place, therefore, without an opposer; but a new difficulty arose when the technical expert was found to have an impressive flow of speech.

"The producer asked him to explain in a few words the technical aspect of re-allocation, whereupon he began a long discourse which dealt merely with the preliminary work he had to complete before embarking on the actual re-allocation.

"His speech, though very interesting, was of course much too long. On the other hand, he had that rare quality, a striking 'television personality', and this had at all costs to be taken advantage of.

"The whole of the day immediately preceding that of the telecast was spent in trying to stem the flood of oratory of a man whose command of his subject was quite exceptional, but who was yearning to display it in the minutest detail. When the evening performance came along, the producer had his work cut out to prevent the discussion from becoming a mere monologue.

"It is quite understandable that specialists, justifiably proud of their fine achievements, should want to describe these as fully as possible. This confronts the producer with one of the most important problems which can arise in composing a cultural programme: the expert is indispensable, but his technicalities may easily prove too much for nontechnical viewers to swallow. It still remains to work out a suitable type of telecast for the general public and to perfect it by degrees, so that the audiences and the well-intentioned experts can learn as they go along."

This telecast made a considerable stir in several teleclubs, where people accused Roger Louis of being a "propagandist" and preventing the opponents of re-allocation from gaining a hearing. Fortunately, this was the only case where it was not found possible to give the opposition view; for in the only other telecast (no. 6, on co-operatives) where no representative of the opposing party could be found, one of the participants agreed to serve as "devil's advocate". Accordingly, this countryman, though he himself approved of co-operation, put forward the arguments he had often heard from neighbours. He was familiar with these criticisms because he was accustomed to refuting them; but for once he used them without contradicting them.

"Rehearsals were held, and this man acquitted himself perfectly. We had been forced to depart from the principle we had so far been able to maintain—that of leaving each participant to say what he really thought; but we had avoided bringing in a professional actor. Even if the spokesman of those hostile to co-operation did not share their opinion, he at least knew that there were some serious grounds for holding it. The drawback was that his friends and neighbours might see him defending views they knew he did not share, and the inconsistency would perhaps make not only this sixth telecast, but the series as a whole, seem less convincing to them."

Professional actor or peasant-actor? Experience has supplied a clear answer to this question. No one could present the life of the peasant better than himself; even when it came to putting forward other people's views, the non-professional who knew his subject inside out carried more conviction than a professional actor could ever have done.

## Subjects of the 13 Telecasts

Here is the list of the 13 telecasts which made up the "Etat d'urgence" series, as actually given:

1. Thursday 7 January: "What I saw among you".
2. Thursday 14 January : "Moucherelle farm" (motorization on a large farm).
3. Thursday 21 January : "Credit".
4. Thursday 28 January : "Partition and ownership" (Land reallocation).
5. Thursday 4 February : "The community spirit".
6. Thursday 11 February : "Co-operation no. I".
7. Thursday 18 February : "Co-operation no. II".
8. Wednesday 24 February : "Co-operation abroad".
9. Wednesday 3 March : "Over-production?".
10. Wednesday 10 March : "Women in the country".
11. Wednesday 17 March : "The country homestead".
12. Wednesday 24 March : "The story of Bernard" (rural youth).
13. Wednesday 31 March : "Summing up".

In order to understand the results achieved by "Etat d'urgence" in the tele-clubs, the reader must be made acquainted with these 13 telecasts. Our intention is to convey, as faithfully as possible, the essence of the ideas, style and technique employed in each of them. We shall not analyuse their content according to the rules established by psycho-sociologists such as Berelson. The purpose of the following description is different, and more limited. Its chief aim is to give some idea of the impressions left by "Etat d'urgence" as a series.

## FIRST TELECAST

### "What I Saw Among You"

| *Technique used* | *Contents* |
|---|---|
| *Direct* Commentary by the producer and leader, & Roger Louis | Explanation of the title and brief account of the whole problem of agriculture. Two objects are shown to drive this problem home—a close-up of a *food ration card* to take viewers back to the period not so long ago when France did not have enough to eat, and a *bank note* to show that food is still rationed, but in another way. Town and country folk alike have to find out together why French agriculture is not meeting everyone's needs and why farmers themselves are no longer "getting enough" out of agriculture. The aim of this series is to investigate what is wrong with French agriculture. |
| *Telefilm* in the village of Viffort in the Aisne department. | The lovely countryside as seen by the passing tourist. But let us have a closer look. Here is Viffort with its 227 inhabitants—a "dying" village. No water laid on; the villagers draw water at the fountain. The only shop in the village is a musty old place which hardly anyone visits. |
| | The newest piece of building is the 1914-18 war memorial. The children playing their games dart about among houses that look as if they are about to collapse. They go into the old twelfth-century church, now practically in ruins and play the old harmonium. They take to their heels at the sudden noise and echo. |
| | The population is rapidly dwindling. Why? The village is scattered, work has few prospects, and the roads are bad. The village |

is made up of 17 hamlets spread over a distance of some 10 miles.

View of a farm, owned by "Pere Lecomte"- 30 hectares,[8] 4 horses, 10 cows. For 30 years Mrs. Lecomte has been getting up every morning to milk the cows. It is a dull life with little family companionship, taken up with looking after the animals, ploughing, unrelieved work. In the evenings Mr. Lecomte goes to sleep over his newspaper. He is single-handed. His son has left the farm to become a soldier in North Africa; here, life was too hard. Mr. Lecomte is now going to sell his farm. And all this is happening 50 miles from Paris.

*Direct*
Commentary by the producer. Discussion between the producer and Mr. Lecomte.

Life on the land is indeed hard. Ten hours' work every day. Why did Mr. Lecomte's boy leave home. The father himself is going to tell you. "This is a made-up story. Mr. Lecomte is here behind me.

We have just seen Mr. Lecomte on his own farm. Here he is in the studio. His boy wanted to buy a *tractor* to make work easier. But the tractor would have cost too much. Mr. Lecomte couldn't afford one, yet that would have been the only means keeping his son on the land.

A third person speaks, Mr. Demarck, a peasant who has managed to buy a tractor.

The new speaker is thoroughly won over to the advantages of *mechanization*. "I'm a firm believer in mechanization." But it also has its dangers as drawbacks.

*Telefilm*
Mr. Demarck's tractor (filmed in the village of Crouttes, Aisne).

Mr. Demarck clubbed together with friends to be a tractor. The neighbours were sceptical and curious. "They're all perfectly right; but so am I? The new owner is anxious about whether the tractor will manage to get up his steeply-sloping fields. It does so successfully but all sorts of problems arise—handling of the machine, spare parts etc. One day the tractor breaks down and has to be haul back by horses.

The tractor is only a beginning. It is unsuitable for small plots of land, and thus raises the problem of the *re-allocation of land.* And if horses are dispensed with altogether the manure supply is cut off. Can artaificial *fertilizers* replace natural manure?

Then again, there is the question of paying off the capital expenditure involved. It is better to club together—which raises the question of *co-operation.*

Mr. Demarck can afford such expense because he has vineyards in addition to his other fields. Wine pays better. The advantages of *several crops* "Wasn't I right?"

Return to the direct discussion Mr. Louis, Mr. Lecomte and Mr. Demarck.

Mechanization is only one aspect of *modernization;* taken by itself, it presents serious dangers. Modernization requires not only confidence but also a plan of action and, above all, suitable *vocational training* for farmers. It creates financial probiems that can be solved only by co-operation.

But Mr. Demarck's children have remained on the farm.

Direct Roger Louis talks to his audience to his audience

Tele-club audiences are invited to discuss together the problems raised by the telecast.

## SECOND TELECAST

## "Moucherelle Farm" (Motorization on a Large Farm)

Direct production by Roger Louis. Features from Medieval Book

Let us begin by looking back into the past to try and find an answer to the question raised in the first programme.

History shows us that the development of farm tools is part of a more general evolution.

For a very long time these tools remained unchanged and then suddenly, within a lifetime—that of your grandfather or your father—peasants abandoned the scythe for the paper-blinder.

Telefilm, the Musee des Arts, Meders.

Yet machines too have their own history. A few types of machinery used before the machine age (viewers are urged to visit the museum).

Direct by R. Louis

Peasants are wrong when they say: "There is no reason why I should change my methods; my father and grandfather managed all right with what they had." Their fathers did have to adapt themselves to new conditions. The present generation must be likewise by changing over from the horse to the tractor.

Yet mechanization, though unavoidable, involved an extensive readjustment of working methods.

Is such adjustment possible ? Here is something that happened in our own Department of the Aisne on Moucherelle Farm. The farmer is called Mr. Leguillette, and he has worked this farm for twenty-five years.

Telefilm Visit to Moucherelle farm

We see the farmer in his office, on the telephone and watch the cows being machine-milked. Me. Leguillette takes us over his farm—230 hectares are in one block, carrying 180 animals. The farm was bought in 1923. It was gradually reorganized and improved, through the use of all resources in the cause of modernisation. Purchase of the first tractors. Successes and setbacks. By experimentations a solution is found to the problems that are constantly arising. Mr. Leguillette now has 25 million francs worth of machinery. The sons are doing advanced vocational study.

| | |
|---|---|
| The telefilm is interspersed with views of the farm as it was and as it is | The homes of the farm-hands have also been improved. Mr. Leguillette's life has been completed changed; mechanization has brought him comfort and prosperity which have made it comparable with that of a city industrialist. |
| | Many problems of course still remain, especially that of setting the children up in life. Mr. Leguillette is obliged to raise loans which he is not always suit of being able to repay. |
| Direct R. Louis talks to his audience | Naturally, Mr. Leguillette's situation cannot is compared with that of the small farmers. With his 90 acres he can hardly be called a peasant. But what he has achieved on a large scale can surely be attempted by you smaller peasants, on your own level. |
| | What are the obstacles? They will be considered in the following programmes, but meanwhile there is no denying that modernization is a question of life or death for the whole of French agriculture. |

## THIRD TELECAST

### "Credit"

| | |
|---|---|
| Direct Introduction by R. Louis | Justification of the series title. It is an urgent matter to modernize agriculture. The first obstacle in the way is the financial problem. Modernization means mechanization and that is costly. Small farmers haven't enough assets for the purpose. |

| | |
|---|---|
| Direct | A round-table discussion between two industrialists, a big farmer, a small farmer and R. Louis. In order to modernize a small farm, an average of 5 million francs is needed. What can be obtained through agricultural credit, since such a sum is beyond the means of the small farmer ? |
| Telefilm Extracts from a film an agricultural credit | Le Credit Agricole (agricultural credit), which, operates as a mutual aid society, grants farmers long-term loans at very advantageous rates; but there is a limit to the amount of money available. Only some of the requests can be met. |
| Direct Assumption of the discussion | An industrialist finds these advantages unfair. He too, would like to be able to borrow on equally favourable terms. He has difficulty in understanding why the peasants hesitate to avail themselves of the facilities thus offered them.<br><br>However, farmers run risks unknown in other walks of life—dependence on atmospheric conditions, and a long wait for "return".<br><br>The discussion becomes heated. "Wait a minute" says the small farmer, "do those industrialists really look as if they were hard dlone by ?" It is clear enough, however, that industry needs a prosperous agriculture. But misunderstanding and ill-feeling have gradually built up a barrier between townsmen and countryfolk. The small farmer, in a fury, shouts at his interlocutors: "If we small farmers are ruined, so will you be too!" |
| Direct R. Lousi, conclusions | The leader sums up the discussion. Small farmers cannot alone, at their level, solve the general problem involved in the |

modernization of French agriculture which requires thousands of millions of francs. They should, however, now take the first step, so far as they themselves are concerned, by endeavouring to make better use of their resources and the credit facilities available to them. R. Louis asks viewers the question that a peasanta economist, Arthaud, put in one of his books:[9] "Is it better to save up for a whole lifetime in order to buy one two extra hectares to be worked with the same old-fashioned tools, or to try to gradually improve what one already has and modernize one's farm, however small it may be ?"

## FOURTH TELECAST

### "Partition and Ownership"

Direct R. Louis gives a few facts. He shows the cadastral survey of a commune where there has been no re-allocation of land. Views of the places where the facts related occurred. Interview with an agricultural engineer responsible for land reallocation in the Aisne Department

The second obstacle to the modernization of small farms is the splitting-up of properties.

A few examples illustrate the urgent need for the re-allocation of land, as well as its difficulties.

France is divided into 150 million units of land which is worked by 3 million farmers. This makes an average of 50 units per farmer. But the land is not all of the same value; peasants are jealous of one another; and the re-allocation of land is a costly business (4,500 francs per hectare), apart from which it takes time (an average of four years per village). At present, land has been re-allocated in only 1,800 communes out of a total of 38,000 and at this rate it would take 100 years to complete the process. After which one would have to begin all over again.

| | |
|---|---|
| Telefilm La Chapelle-sur-Chezy | Land is being re-allocated in a village, La Chapellasur-Chezy. The cadastral survey is projected on the screen. We then go to the town hall, where a heated discussion between those concerned is in progress. One farmer, after a violent outburst goes off in a huff. In an interview, he dwells on the drawbacks of the solutions proposed. The school is thrown onto the screen; the children there will one day say whether today's measures were "worth while" or not. |
| Direct Conclusions by R. Louis | Should farms or properties be regrouped ? This is a serious problem. But if nothing is done, the smaller farmers will be swallowed up by the bigger ones. This is already happening in some areas. You small farmers must think over this question and discuss it among yourselves. |

## FIFTH TELECAST

### "The Community Spirit"

| | |
|---|---|
| Direct R. Louis | The programme on the re-allocation of land has brought in a large mail for the producer. Not all the correspondents agree with the remedies posed, but all recognize the disastrous consequences of the splitting-up of land and concede that the greatest obstacle to all possible solutions is the absence of any real community spirit in the village.<br><br>The development of our villages is greatly hampered by individualism; yet it is not hard to revive the community spirit. Tele-clubs themselves are an example : television sets are very costly but, by clubbing together, the inhabitants of many villages have purchased a set for their joint benefit. |

| | |
|---|---|
| Telefilm | Founding of the Nogentel tele-club, an example of community effort.<br>Could not the effort that these country folk have made in regard to television also be applied to the solution of other problems ? |
| Direct Discussion | An official of the Ministry of Agriculture comes and talks about community organization in many mountain villages where natural hardships (climate) have accustomed the peasants to practise constant mutual aid. |
| Direct R. Louis | In conclusion, we see that present-day economic conditions will bring home to peasants in other parts of France the fact that they can no longer "manage" except by actively co-operating with one another. |

## SIXTH TELECAST

### "Co-operation No. 1"

| | |
|---|---|
| Direct R Louis—discussion of a few letters from viewers | The telecast on the community spirit has also produced letters from many viewers. Some of them agree with us; others accuse the "Etat d'urgence" series of making propaganda in favour of co-operatives. The interest aroused by the films and discussions of the previous telecast encourages the producer to continue along the same lines. |
| Telefilm Extract from a film on the Alpine pasturing system | The community spirit has always made itself felt, eventually, in the economic sphere. One of the best illustrations of this fact is the Alpine pasturing system, practised in certain mountain districts ever since the middle ages and already referred to in the previous telecast. The inhabitants bring their herds together to be driven onto the uplands. One bull is enough for all. |

Direct R. Louis

The community spirit is a way of life. In our regions it is reflected, with varying success, in the co-operative system. What do peasants think of their co-operatives ? Are they imbued with the community spirit ? Two farmers come and discuss the question. The first is vehement in his criticism of co-operatives—these, he says, have now become too large and impersonal; each member is only a number, and the director can never be seen ; the co-operatives have reached inhuman dimensions.

You are in fact—the other objects—criticizing the co-operatives for being too successful. If our co-operatives are to have any effect on the agricultural market, surely they must be large and powerful ?

Of course—comes the reply—but co-operatives are longer reflect the will of their members, who have no real influences on the Director, and do not even receive the refunds to which they are entitled.

Telefilm

One of the farmers then speaks of the situation prevailing before the development of co-operatives when farmers had to make long journeys and the smaller farmers were unable to stand up to highly organized middle men. The small farmer former carried his produce by railway himself, and wasted time and money.

Direct

The discussion is continued in the presence of the director of a large dairy co-operative, who replies to criticism. At present, co-operatives have to make substantial investments so as to keep in the forefront of progress. The dairy directed by the speaker

| | |
|---|---|
| | started with a capital of 12 million francs and later had to invest over 100 million in various kinds of equipment. Through co-operation, producers control part of the processing of their products and reduce the profit made by middlemen at their expense. Finally if members of co-operatives are not satisfied with their organization, they should voice their opinions at the general meetings. They are the masters. |
| Telefilm | Visit to the Dairy Co-operative at Chateau-Thierry, which handles 25,000 litres of milk a day. |
| Direct | The discussion is resumed. Many farmers fear the tendency shown by certain co-operatives to become unwieldy. Nevertheless, with all its faults, the co-operative remains the only really effective remedy for most of the economic problems encountered by farmers. |
| | R. Louis sums up the discussion. The co-operative is necessary. But has it become too large ? Should farmers revert to smaller units. This question will be discussed by the tele-clubs. |

## SEVENTH TELECAST

### "Co-operation No. II"

| | |
|---|---|
| Direct R. Louis | After the criticism levelled at the principle of co-operation, we shall trace the history of a co-operative which, over the thirty years of its existence, has lost none of its community spirit. |
| Telefilm | History of the *Wine Producers' Co-operative of Mailly-Champagne*, founded in 1924 when |

there was a disastrous slump in sales. It managed to hold its own, thanks to the united efforts of its members and their dogged perseverance. It now ensures the annual sale of 150,000 bottles of Champagne.

Direct

The director of the Mailly-Champagne Co-operative is shown in the studio alongside Roger Louis and enlivens the history just recounted with a few personal reminiscences.

Discussion

He is joined by the representative of the Federation nationale de la cooperation agricole (National Federation for Agricultural Co-operation), a city industrialist, and a senior official of the Ministry of Agriculture.

The industrialist complains bitterly of certain co-operatives' competitiveness with private industry. They do not sell any cheaper to the consumer, and do not pay any more to the producer. Most of them, therefore, are useless.

The defenders of co-operatives retort that even if they do not pay any more to producers (which is often true) their mere presence is a guarantee against exorbitant prices. They act as price-regulators of the market, and are a positive factor in modernization and progress. Their telecast, like the third (dealing with agricultural credit), gave rise to heated discussion in the tele-clubs. Some farmers with a deep-rooted dislike for the towns followed the discussions between their representatives and the spokesmen of industry as if they were verbal pitched battles, or at any rate serious sports events.

## EIGHTH TELECAST

### "Co-operation Abroad"

| | |
|---|---|
| Direct Introduction by R. Louis | Co-operation is a world-wide phenomenon. Co-operatives in the different countries have a total membership amounting to several hundred millions. How are they administered outside France ? The question may be of interest to French peasant who will see from pictures of other lands hold their colleagues there have set about solving their problems. |
| Telefilm | A documentary on co-operation in India. Re-allocation of land, agricultural credit, mechanization. This far off country faces the same problems at France, but on a very much larger scale. The government is encouraging the growth of co-operatives, but the country will need outside help.<br><br>Next comes a film on co-operation in Denmark—a country famous for its co-operatives, which have built up the prosperity of Danish agriculture. Each peasant belongs to a good half-dozen co-operatives associations. This is a fine example of success.<br><br>Finally, a third film shows how Canadian fishermen survived the economic depression by setting up their own fish-canning co-operative. |
| Direct | One of the founders of the International Co-operative Alliance draws the inferences from this rapid survey of co-operation throughout the world. Despite differences in local conditions, French farmers can learn much from their colleagues abroad, as regards the spirit that should imbue their association and the legal and economic aspects of the problem. |

## NINTH TELECAST

### "Over-production?"

The whole programme is direct

R. Louis raises the problem of the over-production dreaded by the peasants. He reminds viewers of certain pre-war periods when wheat was "thrown away" while millions of human beings were starving to death. Is the same story to be repeated ? Can there be any fear of over-production while three-fifths of the world's population are underfed ? On the other hand, French farmers have difficulty in marketing their produce, and it is at this very juncture that the General Commissariat for Planned Modernization advocates a 20 per cent increase of agricultural production in France.

Discussion

Several persons gather round R. Louis to talk over this problem together—one of the most influential leaders of French agricultural trade unionism, a farmer who at the same time is a writer and an economist, a representative of the General Commissariat for Planned Moernization, and the President of a Departmental Chamber of Agriculture.

The farmer opens the discussion. He can't understand what is going on. "We are told to produce more, and the more we produce the less we get for it. Yesterday I destroyed 3,000 kilograms of carros that I couldn't sell."

But while producers are faced with these difficulties, France imports 100 milliard francs worth of agricultural produce a year. Our imports must be reduced, we must increase our exports and, above all, we must adapt our production to the markets available. The population of France is increasing and Europe would be only too glad to purchase in francs the produce that now has to be paid for in a dollars. We must produce more; but our products must often be better, more varied and, above all, cheaper.

Farmers have difficulty in following this reasoning, which involves considerable familiarity with national and international economic affairs. Here we come to the problem of vocational training. But in any case, while the community is entitled to ask for a fresh effort from agriculture, while it can and must ask for more, better, cheaper and—occasionally other produce, it should in return protect the farmer against the risks involved in this process of adjustment, which he cannot shoulder alone. The government asks the farmer for higher output, he must guarantee him the sale of his produce at stable minimum price.

## TENTH TELECAST

### "Women in the Country"

Direct R. Louis presents the problem

In each of the previous telecasts reference, and often frequent refernce has been made to the situation country-women. It would be pointless to try the modernize French agriculture without improving the lot of countrywomen, who are bound like slaves to wearisome work, the use of outdated equipment and a badly organized timetable. It is hardly surprising that most girls' one ambition nowadays is to leave their father's farm, "where life is too hard".

Discussion

Roger Louis gathers round him for this discussion an agricultural domestic science teacher, a city housewife, a peasant girl from

| | |
|---|---|
| | the Tarn Department and a peasant housewife from the Aisne. But the discussion is preceded by a film showing how all too many countrywomen have to live today. |
| Telefilm | The life of a farmer's wife in Vendieres (Aisne). "Everyone is always hungry, animals and people alike; there is no end to it all." No running water, and a muddy courtyard. The daughter wants to marry a man frcm the city. |
| Direct | The discussion continues.—Couldn't the farmer's wife organize her work better ? For instance, she could stop her hens from laying in any old place; the use of the various buildings could be better planned. But proper organization is a thing that has to be learnt. |
| Telefilm The agricultural domestic science school of Dilly (Aisne) | An agricultural domestic science school, showing its pupils, what they do, what they learn and the methods used. |
| Direct R. Louis, then assumption of a discussion | But when girls leave the school where they have spent a year learning to use all modern aids for the housewife, how will they react when they return to their own homes, where equipment is lacking and they have to take up their old round of work? |
| | They will have a struggle and will have to exert their influence on their surroundings, gradually persuading their parents or husbands of the advantages to be reaped from small investments and some measure of reorganisation. |
| Telefilm | A film, showing a home that the farmer's wife has planner methodically, will bear out this statement. |

Direct assumption of a discussion

The peasant girl from the Tarn protests that this over-simplifies the problem. "If may father could afford to buy a tractor, I wouldn't need to help with the ploughing any more—that's the hardest thing for a woman—and I could devote my time to the household." But apart from money questions, old folk don't like having their habits changed. "Despite everything I say to him, my father still persists in drying his maize in the kitchen."

All too often the men are content to pity the women (if needed they go so far) and do nothing to ease their burden. Perhaps the only way out is for girls to refuse to marry farmers until the latter can bring themselves to spend some of their money in improving the lot of countrywomen.

But the State too, cannot disclaim responsibility. Once all homes have running water in the kitchen many of the women's troubles will be over.

In short, men and women, families and communities, must realize the importance of the problem and bring some imagination and understanding to it. That is one of the keys to the destiny of French agriculture.

## ELEVENTH TELECAST

### "The Country Homestead"

Direct Presentation by R. Louis

The problem of the homestead is directly bound up with that of countrywomen. It has many different aspects and is one of the key factors in modernization. In this telecst there will not be time to deal with more than the technical aspects of the problem to the exclusion of its financial and human aspects. In any case, all we can do is to set a discussion going.

Discussion. Showing of photos and sketches

Two architects responsible for reconstruction, and an expert on the organization of agricultural work have come to the studio with R. Louis this evening. They will explain, with the help of photos and sketches, a new approach to the problem of the country homestead and farm buildings in areas when the war destroyed everything and made it necessary to begin all over again.

The chief aim in all this work is to simplify every task, and to save time by eliminating all unnecessary effort. Buildings and their use are planned more rationally through a process of regrouping and standardization.

In order to have a standard for comparison, the time spent by farmworkers in moving from one place to another was measured before and after reorganization, and it was found that for every 16 hours so spent before reorganization only 10 hours were spent after it, i.e. there was a saving six hours.

Much of this reorganization could be carried on even in areas that have suffered no destruction. For instance, if buildings were linked up by concrete paths, goods could be transferred between them more easily.

Here again, however, we come up against the problem of funds. A law concerning country homesteads provides for subsidies on a 50/50 basis for persons wishing to modernize their properties. But although 20,000 requests have already been met, demand far exceeds the possibilities of satisfying it. It has been possible to carry out barely a tenth of the operations required.

Farmers could, of course themselves make a fresh effort. But they would then need: suitable training and information; more substantial financial support.

## TWELFTH TELECAST

### "The Story of Bernard" (Rural Youth)

Telefilm

Bernard, the son of a small farmer, has come back from the army where he lived another kind of life. The future held out for him in the village does not appeal to him. For 18 months he has chewed over the insult always hurled at him in his regiment : "You're just a clod-hopper". Bernard wants to be his own master, to join up with a friend in Paris, to stroll along the houlevards with pretty girls. He wants to be off—and the film shows his last afternoon in the village. He is walking towards a mirage—six miles to the station. Why is he going ?

Direct discussion

Roger Louis, a young farm labour, a representative of the Catholic Young Farmers' Club, the mayor of a small commune in the Seine-et-Oise Department and the Director of Agricultural Training in the Ministry of Agriculture are going to try to explain the position.

Bernard is leaving because he is not earning a living; because working conditions are unbearable. There are tens of thousands of Bernards whose one ambition is to "get away". It is the best and most energetic young men who do it. Bernard is bored in his village, where there is no entertainment. And he is not free; his father pays him nothing and keeps him in subjection. In the town he hopes for more rapid promotion. Every year 60,000 young people leave the country for the town. Within the space of a few decades 600,000 have left a single province, Brittany.

What can be done about this drift to the towns ? To begin with, recreation should be organized and more comfortable conditions provided; roads should be improved, and water laid on; a "country centre" should be set up for recreation, educational activities and television. But young people, for their part should understand that leaving the country usually gets them nowhere. They should try to club together, to do something in their own village, set up their own sports or study centres, and ask for assistance; they should never "give up". Funds are available, but there is a tremendous demand for them. If they begin on their own, the municipality will often follow and give them support. They have to prove their worth.

Then there is the question of vocational training. Young people in the country learn their work on the spot—by watching how things are done, without any theoretical training, without being able to make any comparisons and broaden their experience. The authorities should help them to travel and study in other parts of France, and abroad. Young workers who leave school at the age of fourteen also need some training. The State spends 25 milliard francs on vocational training in industry, as against 1 milliard for agricultural training. So young people go off to the towns, where with some they can enter an apprenticeship organisations. Once again, Bernard's story ultimately leads us to the problem of organization, funds and government policy.

## THIRTEEN TELECAST

## "Summing Up"

Direct R. Louis — Summing up and conclusion. It is difficult, after a cursory a survey, to draw conclusions about so vast a field, where everything is interlinked, where we are always coming up against the same problems and the same needs.

The telecasts have prompted different reactions—some favourable, even to the point of enthusiasm, and others hostile, not to say furious. This was because they touched on vital points. One conclusion to be drawn is this : the peasant today must "change his skin", his outlook. There was a time when the farmer's life was one that people "put up with"; now it must become a trade to be learnt. Being born on a farm is not sufficient preparation for the art of farming; the lack of any serious vocational training is one of the chief obstacles to modernization. In this as in so many other fields, the authorities are clearly not doing enough.

Discussion — A discussion then ensues between the Director of the Federation Nationale des Centres d'Etudes Techniques Agricoles (National Federation of Agricultural Study Centres), the director of an agricultural college, and the assistant secretary-general of the Federation of Mayors of France. Their topic for discussion is agricultural training, its lack of rational organization, and its urgency.

Unfortunately, farmers themselves are not yet convinced that it is necessary. An information campaign should be conducted among heads of families, so as to induce them to demand the establishment of many more courses and schools. Another difficulty is the shortgage of funds. This is a general problem, and the second greatest obstacle to modernization. It is felt at the individual level by farmers themselves, and on a nation-wide scale by the State. But the funds available are not always put to the best use. The authorities should at long last define an agricultural policy : to strike a balance between the needs of town and country; based on genuine fellow-feelings; to make the commune the basis of all efforts towards modernization. Modernization does not "come of itself".

This is a sphere in which the ordinary citizen can do something. Within his own commune, each person can make some effort, launch ideas, try out experiments and demand the community's support for them. Without waiting for the answer to come (though knowing that a reform of the State's agricultural policy is essential), "you too can make your own individual contribution to bring about a change".

## References

1. The considerations which influenced the choice of hour for these telecasts are discussed in Appendix VI, p. 263.
2. Details of the budget allocated to this series are given in Appendix VI, p. 263.
3. The same difficulty arose in a slightly different connexion. On several occasions the tele-clubs complained that the programmes suggested no really practical solutions. This showed a misunderstanding as to the essential purpose of the series, which was: to

encourgae viewers to find their own solution, not to offer cut-and-dried proposals. This was due not only to educational considerations, but to the very nature of the televised programmes. These were intended for districts which varied considerably in character—those devoted only to wine-growing, and those with mixed crops—and for large farmers and small holders alike. No over-all solution was therefore possible. The programmes were also intended for town viewers, who would have been bored by a purely technical approach. Finally, television, as a public service, could not enter into questions of agricultural policy which were still highly controversial.

4. See footnote, p. 41.

5. These figures emerge from an investigation into the situation regarding individual and collective agricultural equipment and public or domestic facilities, which we conducted among the audiences of the 10 largest tele-clubs: initial referendum—method no. 2.

6. See Appendix VI for details of the team's equipment, p. 263.

7. See Appendix VI for the final production plan, p. 263.

8. See footnote on p. 41.

9. Arthaud, Le metier de l'agriculteur, Ed. Economie et humanisme.

# 6

# Results of the "Etat D'Urgence" Series

## The Problem

To find out the results of the "Etat d'urgence" series we adopted the same practice as for other programmes. But viewers' reactions to this series, and the educational value of the programmes, were analysed in greater detail. Once again, we both observed behaviour and sounded opinions without interfering with the regular work of the tele-clubs or their members' established habits in and outside the club. Our methods and techniques of psycho-sociological evaluation first had to be adapted to the particular outlook of club members. We had to be specially careful not to distort group or individual reactions to "Etat d'urgence" under the pretext of obtaining tidy but perhaps unreliable statistics. The "log-book" in which reactions during each programme were noted down was kept by the teacher-observer, with a few assistants who had been trained in the principles and methods of observation during the preparatory course at Marly. The initial and final surveys (Method No. 2) were conducted in the form of direct interviews by the leaders, who were already used to getting persons whom they knew well to fill up printed forms. Of course, with this method there is often a larger number of persons who fail to reply, and the answers are less detailed than with an ordinary opinion survey. But the main concern was not to force our countryfolk into giving replies that would have had no genuine value. It was even more important than with the general survey to telecasts to analyse only the absolutely genuine reacations.

If we were to assess opinions regarding the "Etat d'urgence" series and its effects on viewers, it was essential to have some standard of comparison. The attitudes of viewers to modernization were studied before the series, and were used as a yardstick in all subsequent evaluation.

We then considered the interest taken by viewers in the 13 telecasts. For this purpose our findings on attendance at programmes were supplemented by an analysis of the opinions voiced by viewers concerning the problems of producing the telecasts.

Lastly, we noted a few effects of the "Etat d'urgence" series on the ideas of viewers, the wishes they expressed and their behaviour both in and outside the club. During the programme we noted in the "log-book" any variations in members' participation in the discussion. We were also able to record the exact remarks made, and compare them with the contents of the telecasts and the ideas which the same people had expressed, before the series, to explain their attitudes. We tried to grasp the desires created by the telecast among viewers, by jotting down any wishes expressed during the discussion. Lastly, after the whole series of telecasts, attitudes towards modernization were assessed once again by asking the same persons the same questions in much the same way; and though the interval between the two checks was short we were able to record a few interesting changes which were borne out by new behaviour.

## Before "Etat d'urgence" : Attitude of Viewers towards Modernization

At the outset we had some inkling of the difficulties

facing the areas where our tele-clubs operate. The villages are poorly equipped and modernization is a vital necessity. To find out the attitude of the population towards this problem[1] we first wanted to know whether the existing equipment was considered adequate or not by the users themselves, and, where equipment was non-existent or inadequate, whether these people were anxious to purchase or improve it, as the case might be. The replies to these "closed" questions, covering a specific list of items used in individual and collective agricultural equipment, public equipment and household equipment, were cross-checked by the spontaneous wishes expressed in reply to the following "open-end" questions: "If, in 1954, you had an extra 20,000 francs (50,000, 500,000) income, what would you do with the money?" "If, in 1954, your mayor had sufficient extra funds in his budget to allow him to do something big for the commune, what would you advise him to do?"

First we put the questions about individual and group agricultural equipment just to the small farmers, whose produce forms the very basis of French agriculture and whose difficulties are accordingly in most urgent need of attention. Then we put the questions about public and household equipment to tele-club members of all occupations and ages, and of both sexes. This method gave us greater insight into the attitude of the small farmers, which could then be compared with the reactions of other groups, so as to isolate those groups most hostile to modernization.

### Attitude of Small Farmers Towards the Modernization of Farm Equipment on an Individual or Collective Basis

The attitudes adopted vary considerably. Each individual wishes to purchase—if he does not already possess—certain items of equipment which are now regarded as part of the bare minimum required for his work. Less than 10 per cent of small farmers without such equipment are against its purchase. It includes such widely varying items as a farm building in perefect repair, an all-metal wheel plough, a reaper and binder, artificial fertilizers, an electric motor or a diesel engine.

Then comes the equipment that froom 10 to 30 per cent of small farmers do not wish to purchase. Slightly over 10 per cent are not interested in selected seed and about the same number of farmers wish to buy it, whereas it is actually used by 70 per cent of farmers. The small farmer is contemptuous of artificial insemination; about one in three are against this scientific method of stock-improvement. The natural way is good enough for them: "I have a bull", "My neighbour has a bull", and so on. About as many small farmers see no need for new buildings. Barely 10 per cent wish to renovate dilapidated buildings. The others think it "useless", or "too expensive". About 85 per cent of the persons who replied to our questions have no modern machinery, such as milking and separating machines, and close on 30 per cent are definitely against them: "I sell the milk", "I buy the better" or "That is bad for the cows".

Equipment intended for the rationalization of work seems to meet with the greatest volume of opposition. It is true that about 80 per cent of small farmers have a bank account, as against barely 15 per cent who do not want one. But a progress table and an account book are considered utterly useless on a small farm; "pointless, useless", "I keep the accounts in my head", and so on.

Opinion is much the same on the subject of tractors; about 80 per cent have none, and barely 20 per cent would like to buy one. Over 30 per cent expressed very definite objections; they do not want a tractor and have no use for them. An even smaller percentage of small farmers (0.3 per cent) express the desire to buy a tractor when asked how they would like to spend an extra 500,000 francs. On the other hand, 16 per cent say they would like to spend the 500,000 francs on a car. The home also has priority over the tractor (6 per cent as against 0.3 per cent). Our small farmers seem to show an aversion for the best machine for raising agricultural output. "There's no money for it", "I get along all right with what I have". "The holdings are too small", or "They're bad for the land".

If they clubbed together, perhaps, the small farmers could buy and make good use of a tractor. What, actually, is their attitude to co-operation? Co-operative silos, cellars and wine-presses may be left out of consideration, as these items of equipment are not of equal interest to farmers and wine-growers alike. But close on 40 per cent of all categories do not belong to any buyers' co-operative, and less than 15 per cent would like to enter any such co-operative association. Eighty per cent of our small farmers have never heard of a users' co-operative which would perhaps give them the use of such large costly machines as tractors, and not even 20 per cent would like too set one up. Hostility towards co-operation is especially marked when it comes to a domestic aid such as a collective washing-machine: this is unknown or rejected by 90 per cent, and desired by less than 20 per cent. The reasons most often given against co-operation are: "There aren't enough of us", "It wouldn't pay", "I don't believe in it", "That wouldn't work with us", "It's better for each to have his own tools" and (in the particular case of the collective washing-machine) "It's unhygienic".

If rural workers are to be able to adjust themselves to the progress of techniques and ideas, they stand to increasing need of information and education. Nearly all of them have joined or wish to join school-extension associations. Tele-clubs come under this heading. On the other hand, roughly 85 per cent of viewers live in villages where there are no young farmer's groups, and only 40 per cent think that it would be useful to found one. About half of the localities still have no commission for the re-allocation of land, and only 18 per cent of the replies were in favour of the establishment of such an institution in the locality in question.

### *Attitude of the General Public Towards The Modernization of Public and Domestic Equipment*

Road and bridge building is the first favourite (22 per cent of replies) for large communal undertakings. But main water supply is a close runner-up. We know that only 65 per cent of viewers have water laid on, in addition to which 20 per cent consider their communal supply inadequate; whilst nearly 50 per cent of persons without running water want it laid on, or at least desire some badly needed improvements. An equally high percentage of persons are in favour of public sewerage, yet about one-quarter of the villagers do not want either main drainage of main water supply. The most refractory are the small farmers, of whom only 30 per cent want water, as against 65 per cent in the case of workers (highly significant difference). Yet more surprising is the fact that women, who are the first to suffer from this lack of comfort, are more hostile than men to such schemes. Running water is desired by 52 per cent of the men as against only 36 per cent of the women. The difference in attitude over public sewerage is even more marked—61 per cent of men in favour, as against only 36 per cent of women (highly significant difference). The arguments, whether well founded or not, are invariably the same: "The commune is too scattered", "The village is too small", "There's no money for it", "We get along all right as we are", and so on.

Everyone knows how unhygienic some villages are, though many villagers are hardly aware of the fact. Although 90 per cent of the inhabitants have a wash-house at their disposal, over 50 per cent consider it quite inadequate. Nearly 95 per cent have no bath or shower, or are dissatisfied with what they have. Yet barely 35 per cent want to improve the wash-house, while about 50 per cent are anxious to install a bath or shower. Here again, farmers express stronger opposition than workers, and women (37 per cent) show less enthusiasm than men (58 per cent) (highly significant differences).

What are the reasons for these objections? "The village is to scattered", "There isn't any water", or, more frequently, "That wouldn't work", "The brook isn't far off", "I've lived in dirt and I'm not going to change now", "Things are all right as they are" (49 times).

As everyone knows, it is often difficult to find entertainment in rural areas. Of the persons who replied to our questions, 70 to 75 per cent live in localities with no village hall or sports ground, or consider the existing facilities inadequate. About 40 per cent would like to "do something" about the village hall, and 25 per cent about the sports ground. Nearly 65 per cent of manual workers want to have a village hall built, as against 35 per cent is the case of non-manual workers and 30 per cent is that of the small farmers. The idea of constructing a sports ground met with equal support except from the small farmers, of whom only 10 per cent were in favour of the scheme. The women are of much the same opinion as the men as regards the sports ground, but the men are more staunch advocates of the village hall (45 per cent in favour, as against 30 per cent for the women) (highly significant difference). As was only to be expected, young people of under 25 years of age are the most enthusiastic supporters of the village hall and the sports ground—50 per cent in favour of the latter, as against about 15 per cent in the case of persons over 40 years of age !

With regard to work that would be carried out for the community as a whole, most viewers also advocated improvements to school, church and roads, in preference to the building of sports grounds and village halls.

We mentioned earlier, in connexion with our question

regarding the purchase of a television set of their own by members of tele-clubs, that requirements were given different levels of priority and urgency. The same applies to our enquiry into the attitude towards modernization of the home. Some expenses met with practically no opposition. We do not refer to the cooking-stove or to the radio set which practically all homes already possess (about 90 per cent), nor to the sewing-machine owned by approximately 70 per cent of viewers' families. But 55 per cent of those questioned have no water laid on in the sink, by means of a pump or a tap fed from a tank; this is demanded by nearly 50 per cent and particularly by the men.

About 40 per cent are without butane gas, and only 20 per cent of the persons who answered our questions would like to use it. Eighty per cent of our sample have no household sewerage, and less than 50 per cent want to install it. As for washing-machines of their own, 85 per cent of viewers have none, and only 45 per cent want one. Central heating is practically non-existent, and over half of our sample consider it an unattainable ideal.

These attitudes vary according to the occupation of the person concerned. Ninety per cent of non-manual workers have no washing-machine and 52 per cent want one, as against 80 per cent and 33 per cent in the case of the small farmers. Generally speaking, workers are far keener on purchasing and modernizing equipment than are the small farmers. In three cases (full repairs for the home, running water over the sink, and household sewerage), over half the workers were in favour of buying up-to-date household equipment—a percentage never reached in the case of the small farmers. Furthermore, only 36 per cent of workers have a rooted objection to central heating, as against 50 per cent in the case of small farmers (significant difference). The washing-machine met with 47 per cent of support among workers and 33 per cent among farmers. Sixty per cent of workers would like to improve their homes even though they are only tenants, as against 4.5 per cent in the case of the small farmers.

By and large, women's lukewarmness for the modernization of household equipment, though less marked and consistent than in the cse of public equipment, bears out the more conservative attitude of women as compared with men. A higher percentage of women than men are opposed to full repairs for the homestead, running water over the sink, and so on. The most striking instance of this difference is afforded by the fact that 53 per cent of the men want household sewerage, as against only 36 per cent of the women (significant difference).

Difference were also registered as between the various age groups. Only one instance will be quoted, so as not to labour the point. Close on 60 per cent of the young people want to buy a washing-machine, as against only 40 per cent in the case of men over 40 years of age.

The arguments most often put forward against up-to-date household equipment vary widely. "Butane gas? It might blow up." As for the electric cooker : "We have our wood for nothing" and "There are breakdowns". Sewerage: "What would I want that for?" or "I've got a cess-pit". Washing-machines: "They aren't perfect yet", "They're a luxury" or "They're hard on the linen". Central heating: "That's all right for the people in Paris", and so on.

This preliminary survey naturally prompts us to enquire into the reasons for this antagonism to progress, commoner among the small farmers than among other categories, among women than among men, and among men of over 40 than among the younger generation.

We made a comprehensive review of the reasons advanced in the replies to the initial referendum on the modernization of farm equipment. These reasons were then divided into two main categories: (1) genuine, material obstacles; economic, geographic obstacles; lack of resources, unsuitable land, etc.; (2) imaginary obstacles attributable to prejudice. This second category of reasons we then sub-divided into two sub-groups: on the one hand, attitudes due to in difference or conservatism with regard to technical progress ("We've been doing things like that for 20 years, so why should we change now?"); on the other asocial or anti-social attitudes ("I have my own wash-house; the others can look after themselves..."). This classificatioon, which we worked out most carefully and cross-checked by oral interviews, is, of course, based on a rough estimate. The result is therefore also bound to be approximate, and the figures will be rounded off to the nearest ten. As regards individual and collective agricultural equipment, of the total number of reasons put forward by small farmers against progress, 140 were based on economic and geographical obstacles and 250 were attributed to sheer prejudice, either against progress in general or against co-operation. It should further be added that with a considerable number of objections, "shortage of funds" were in fact a mere pretext (10 out of 20 per cent).

There are more genuine obstacles to modernization in the case of public and household equipment. But, especially with the latter, arguments based on lack of funds again seem to be a cloak for general unwillingness, to an extent that we cannot assess. Lastly, the number of objections dictated by indifference or hostility to progress or co-operation equals those which, according to the replies given, are due to economic or geographical obstacles (348 and 352 respectively).

These findings, which we suspected before the beginning of the survey, fully justify the choice of the subject-matter dealt with in the "Etat d'urgence" series. The question of modernization is a vital one for French agriculture and for the nation as a whole ; in every field—mechanization or credit, the re-allocation of land and the situation of women in rural areas, the community spirit, vocational training and the organization of recreational activities for young people—ignorance and prejudice and their weight to genuine obstacles, to put a break on the forces of progress. How far did the series succeed in uprooting prejudice and in creating a constructive approach? This remains to be considered.

## Variation of Interest in the 13 Telecasts

### *Variations in Attendance*

The chief aim of "Etat d'urgence" was to make an appeal to the small farmers. It was therefore specially interesting to find out whether this series attracted more small farmers than did other tele-club programmes; whether members of other agricultural and non-agricultural occupations purposely stayed away from this particular progrmme on the pretext that it was of less concern to them; whether women and young people were affected by its appeal; whether viewers of these different categories kept up their attendance at the "Etat d'urgence" series from early January to the end of March; whether attendance varied, and how its variation was to be interpreted. The assessment of results was to provide the first answers to these queries. Most of these replies are recorded in the log-book for each programme.[2]

The remarks which leaders noted down in the part of the log-book set aside for critical summing-up provide some preliminary information:

*Montfaucon:* Last programme before Christmas 1953: 2 persons present. First telecast of "Etat d'urgence": 24 persons, including 22 farm labourers.

*Viffort :* The day after the first telecast, two farmers who had never visited the tele-club said to a friend: "One must go and see that".

*Le Marais :* After the second telecast, "a small farmer's family who had only been two or three times to the tele-club came to buy a permanent card". Again after the second telecast, the leader noted: "A new audience" different from that attending the variety programmes, is being formed".

*Dammard* : "Two farmers with land bordering on Dammard came for the first time during the "Etat d'urgence" series."

*Nesles:* Three out of the six farmers in the locality came to the first telecast. When the second one was given, the agricultural officer brought along, in his own car, 8 farmers and members of their families living some considerable distance from the centre. "The Thursday programme" wrote the teacher "is the favourite with the small farmers, while the others attract a large number of farm labourers and factory workers, craftsmen and retired persons."

*Etampes:* "These telecasts brought me a new public."

Local notables who were not accustomed to frequenting the tele-club came to see the "Etat d'urgence" programme. In many localities, the mayor and municipal councillors joined the villagers in the discussions. The leader at Venteuil writes, on this subject: "I give; in this list, the names of the persons who were present at this viewing, as an indication of the interest shown in the programme: the mayor, the deputy mayor, the municipal councillors, the president of the trade union, and the heads of co-operatives and of the Agricultural Loan Bank". Thus the tele-club became for several evenings, a centre for discussions between municipal councillors and group of villagers. This survey is, however, only a starting-point; we now have to examine the precise variations in the detailed attendance figures for each of the 13 telecasts, according to profession, sex, and age group.

The attendance graphs for the various telecasts show, first of all, the wide variations in the figures. It is not easy to interpret these variations, since there are a large number of factors determining them, and these tend to overlap.

To begin with, "Etat d'urgence" is not the only item in the evening's programme, and we know that many viewers come for a whole programme rather than for one particular item. Another point is that attendance may be affected by weather conditions, local happenings and the requirements of everyday work, which have nothing to do with the telecast. People working in the field of popular education are familiar with the intricate effects of all these factors, which cannot be isolated with any degree of accuracy. In view of the time-limit set for completion of the survey, it was not even possible to make a systematic comparison between the figures for attendance at the tele-club before, during and after the telecasts in question, since we could not have allowed for seasonal variations and changing work conditions, although these affect the attendance figures. We were thus obliged to base our interpretation of the figures on the analysis of evidence and data collected.

One primary fact is revealed : "Etat d'urgence" certainly reached the public for whom it was intended. According to the evidence of the leaders, given above, many small farmers who had never been to a tele-club were attracted by and interested in "Etat d'urgence". They said so themselves, and proved it by their regular attendance. Did they remain after the 13 telecasts? Often, yes. But the end of these telecasts coincided with the peak period in agricultural work, during which the working section of the population in any case visit the tele-clubs less often than in winter.

Small farmers formed the bulk of the audience at the "Etat d'urgence" telecasts. They represent 70 per cent. In the following five graphs (1-5), the horizontally at the top represent the thirteen evenings covered by the investigation. The following list gives the title of the broadcasts in the series "Etat d'Urgence" corresponding to each of those evenings, together with an indication of other main features telecast:

1. 7 January : "What I saw among you"; "Pleasures of the Theatre"; "Animal Life".
2. 14 January : "Moucherelle farm"; "Pieces a conviction"; "Evening in Monte Carlo".
3. 21 January : "Credit"; "Pochades electroniques"; "Joyaux de Paris".
4. 28 January : "Partition and ownership"; "Eddie Warner"; Outside broadcast from the Saclay atomic research centre.
5. 4 February : "The Community Spirit"; Pleasures of the Theatre"; "Joyaux de Paris".
6. 11 February : "Co-operation no. I"; "Pieces a conviction"; "Lost in the Jungle".
7. 18 February : "Co-operation no. II"; "The Accident"; "Joyaux de Paris".
8. 24 February : "Co-operation Abroad"; Zorro; "Journey without a passport".
9. 3 March : "Over-production"; Zorro; "Journey without a passport"; Circus.
10. 10 March : "Women in the country"; "Animal Life"; Zorro; "Journey without a passport".
11. 17 March : "The Country Homestead" ; "Les Miserables"; "Chester Follies"; "Journey without a passport".

12. 24 March : "The Story of Bernard"; "Les Miserables"; Outside broadcast from the Orly airport.

13. 31 March : "Summing Up"; "Les Miserables"; Circus.

The agricultural audience as a whole; and indeed form the largest group—32 per cent—among the entire audience. This proportion is much higher than that of the small farmers who ordinarily frequent the tele-club, which in the past has been 25 per cent. These figures provide further evidence of the fact that "Etat d'urgence" has increased this category of the population's interest in tele-clubs.

As regards non-farming occupations there are more manual than non-manual workers (484 attendances as against 402); the next group, some considerable way behind, is that of the small clerks (115 attendances).

Taken together, agricultural and non-agricultural workers from a proletarian audience constituting 27 per cent of the general public. This is a higher percentage than that usually recorded in workers' educational establishments which do not cater exclusively for the proletarian element, even though they pride themselves on having a great success among the workers. This figure is particularly gratifying in view of the fact that the telecasts were designed fist and foremost for farmers.

Fifty-seven non-agricultural workers attended the last telecast, as against 37 for the first. They do not appear to have found the series dull. A curious point is that the attendance figure for this category was highest for the thirteenth telecast, which summed up the conclusions of the series as a whole; the attendance of the other three socio-professional categories, on the other hand, was roughly the same at the last telecast of the series as at the first.

Graph 1. VARIATIONS IN ATTENDANCE AT THE 13 TELECASTS OF THE 'ETAL D' URGENCE" SERIES

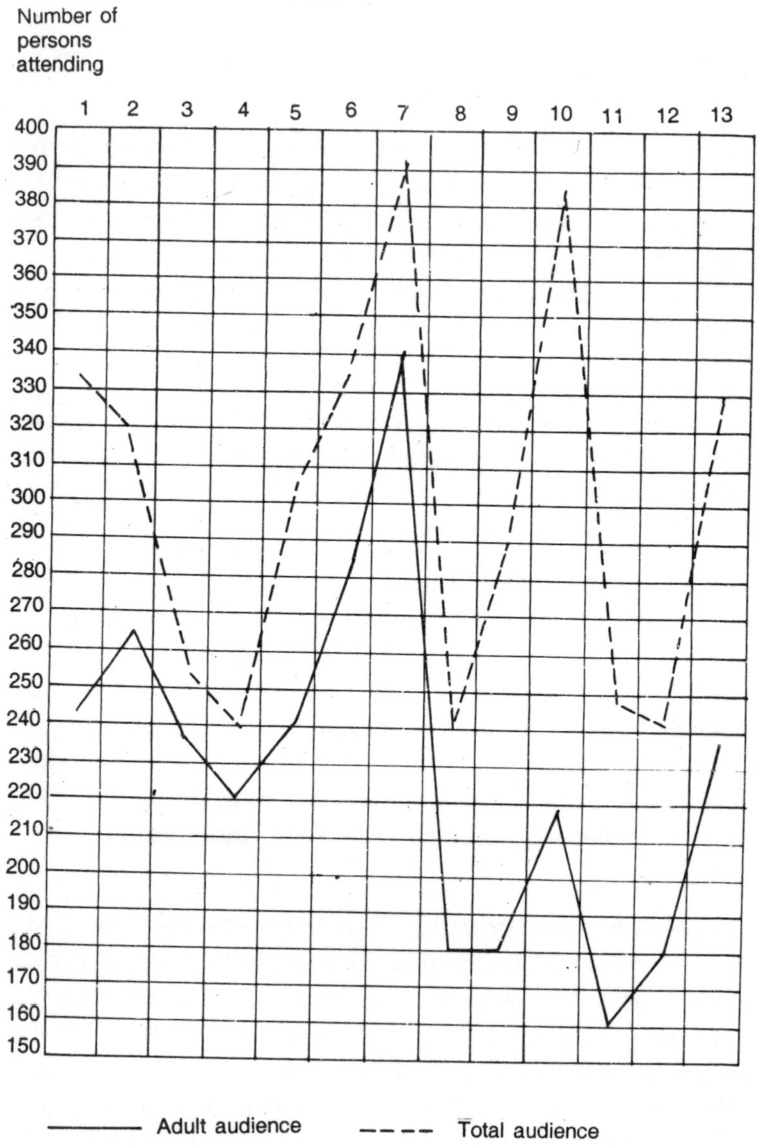

Graph 2 . VARIATIONS IN ATTENDANCE AT THE 13 TELECASTS OF THE "ETAT D' URGENENCE" SERIES, ACCORDING TO AGRICULTURAL OCCUPATION

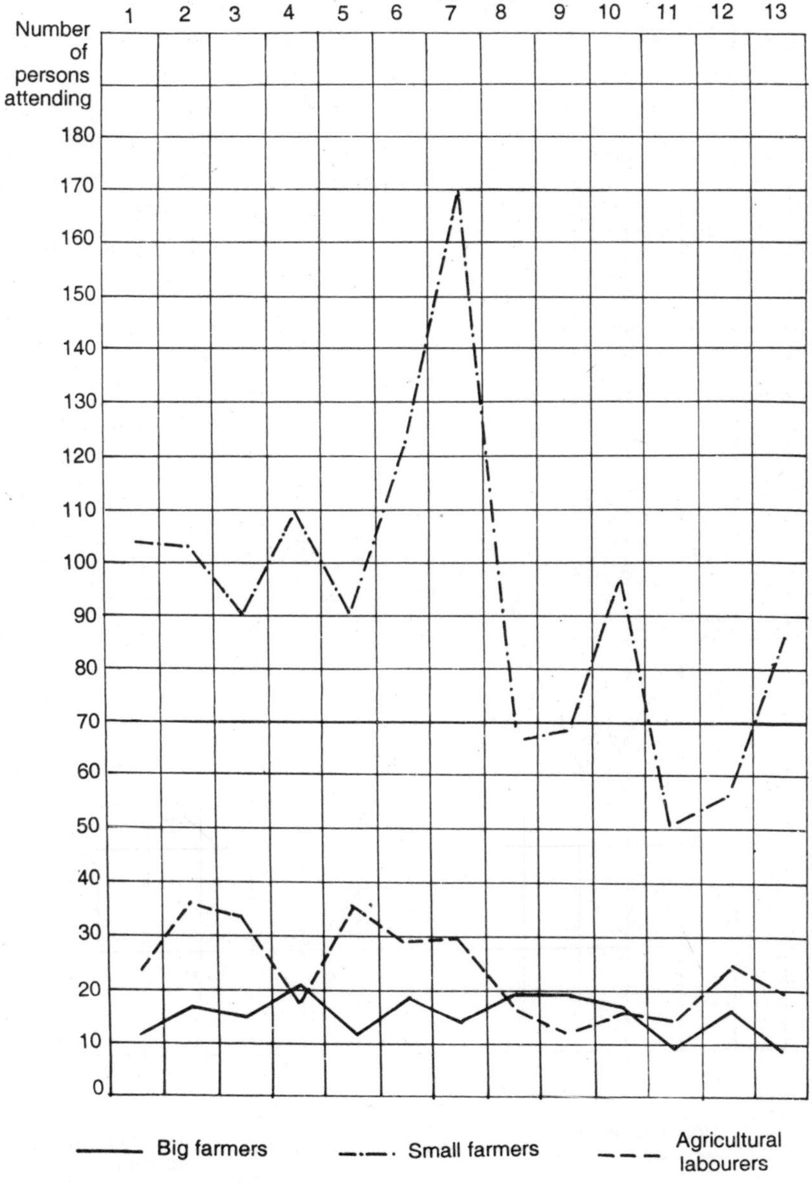

Graph 3. VARIATIONS IN ATTENDANCE AT THE 13 TELECASTS OF THE "ETAT D' URGENENCE" SERIES, ACCORDING TO NON-AGRICULTURAL OCCUPATION

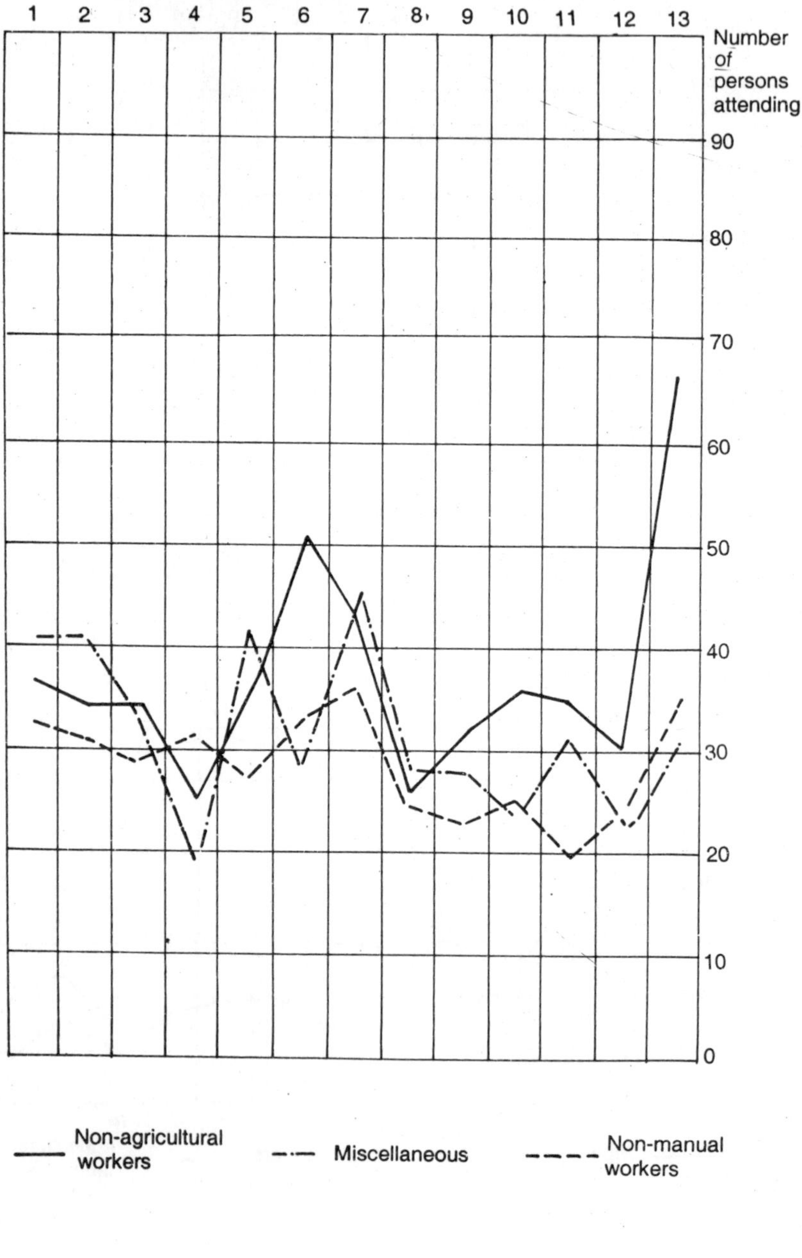

Graph 4 VARIATIONS IN ATTENDANCE AT THE 13 TELECASTS OF THE "ETAT D'URGENENCE" SERIES, ACCORDING TO SEX

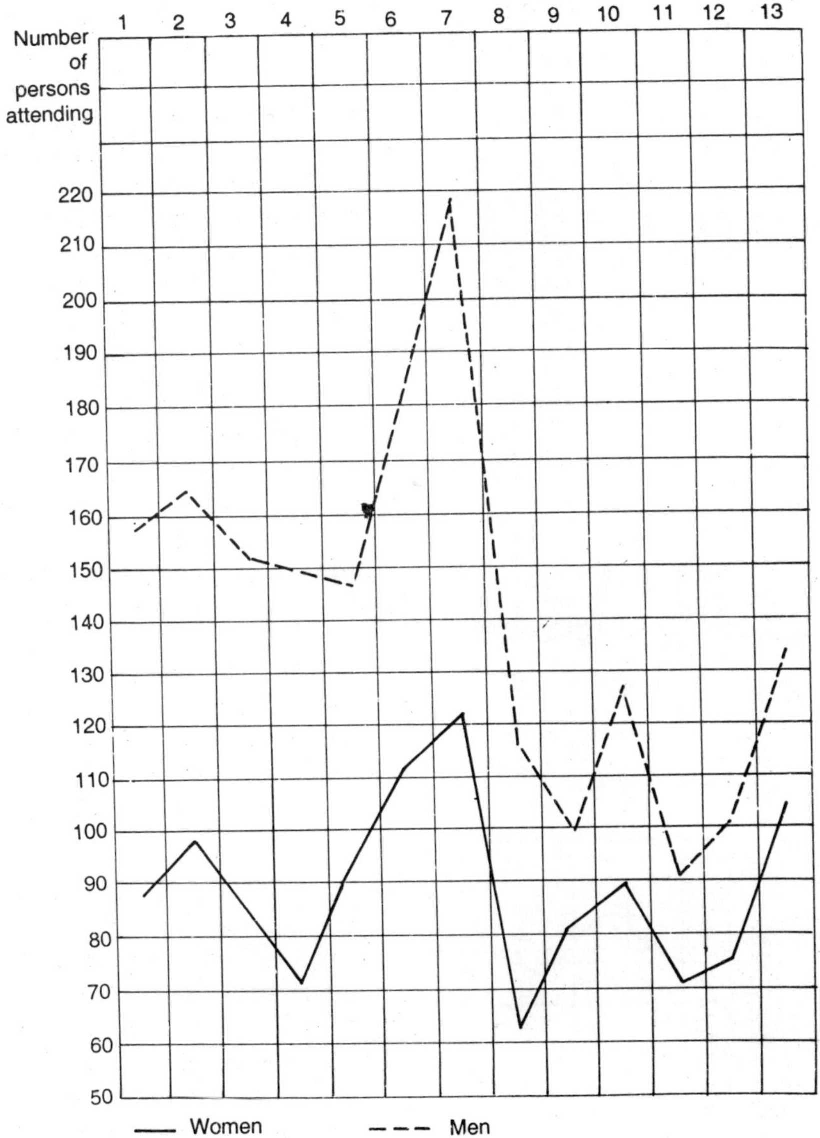

Graph 5. VARIATIONS. IN ATTENDANCE AT THE 13 TELECASTS OF THE "ETAT D' URGENENCE" SERIES, ACCORDING TO AGE-GROUP

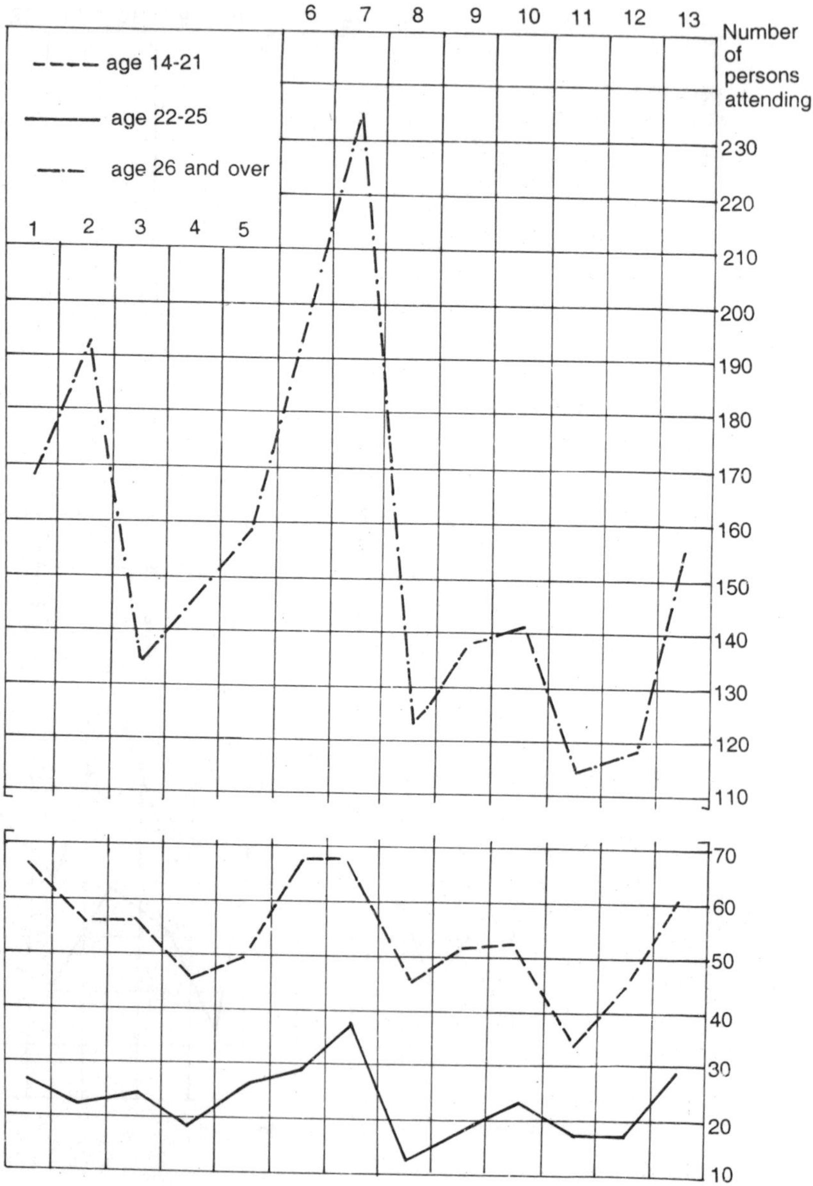

It will be noted that the attendance figure for non-manual workers remained almost the same throughout, in contrast to that of all the other agricultural and non-agricultural workers. However, this category was really too small, in our ten experimental tele-clubs, to be included in our analysis—which, we repeat, concentrated on the small-farmer category.

In any cae, it may be stated that "Etat d'urgence" did not cause a drop in the attendance of representatives of categories other than small farmers. Apart from agricultural workers and large farmers, members of non-agricultural professions, as well as urban workers and employees also showed an interest in agricultural topics and attended "Etat d'urgence" with remakable regularity. The women, although fewer than the men, also followed these programmes regularly, and finally young people were as regular in their attendance as men of over 40. On an average women viewers provided 39 per cent, as against the men's 61 per cent, of the audiences. These percentages are roughly the same as those for the usual attendance at tele-clubs.

The graph-curves for the first two age groups (11 to 21 and 22 to 25) are relatively stable. Does this indicate a steady interest in the programmes? No absolutely categorical answer can be given. There are the news and music-hall feataures, apart from "Etat d'urgence" . . . . But we might quote in this connexion one note made by the leader at Viffort: "I personally do not regret" said a small farmer "having seen these films; but I doubt whether the young people feel the same, they were often noisy". To which the schoolmaster, noticing that a fair number of young people had attended regularly, retorted: "All the same, some of the young people only came on account of that series".

Generally speaking, the attendance curves for the three age groups followed a similar course, and variations do not appear to have been due to age differences.

How are we to explain the differences in the attendance figures for the various telecasts of the series? The seventh, dealing with the foundation of a champagne-producers' co-operative, the Mailly-Champagne Co-operative was the best attended. After that, numbers fell sharply, and then rose again slightly for the telecast on women in the country (tenth) and for the final telecast (thirteenth). Does it follow that these three were more popular than the rest? It is possible, but the viewers do not know in advance how good each telecast is going to be. As we shall see, that which received the highest mark was the one on "credit" (third). But it was by no means the best attended. It cannot even be stated categorially that the success of one telecast invariably influenced that of the following one: for instance, the attendance at the fourth telecast was smaller than at the third, although the latter was so popular. On the contrary, the attendance figures appear to have been determined either by circumstances completely irrelevant to the telecasts (though decisive in the everyay life of the viewers), or by the interest of the subject of each particular telecast. We shall concentrate mainly on this second factor, bearing in mind the whole evening's programme in each case.

I. As between the first and the second telecasts, the number of children dropped sharply, whilst that of the adults rose.[3] This is attributable partly to certain parents' habit of taking their children with them to the tele-club—a habit discouraged, on this occasion, by the fact that the "Etat d'urgence" series was not "light" enough for children. The increase in the number of adult viewers appears to have been due to the favourable accounts of "Etat d'urgence" given by those who had attended the first evening's programme. These variations confirm the evidence of the educational experts, given above. The 14 January programme contained nothing else particularly calculated to attract an audience; moreover, people had not previously been in the habit of coming to the tele-club on Thursday evenings.

II. After the success of the second telecast, attendance figures were smaller at the third (credit) and the fourth (re-allocation of land). How is this to be explained? First of all, it is a matter of weather: this was the end of January and there was an exceptionally cold spell in the region during these two weeks, so that those afraid of the cold and unwilling to venture out on the frostbound roads refrained from visiting the tele-club. The composition of the programmes (report on the atomic laboratory at Saclay, and Eddie Warner's orchestra) failed to offset the effects of this weather factor, which tele-club leaders are unanimous in holding responsible for the drop in attendance.

III. The figures for the fifth telecast (the community spirit), the sixth (co-operation no. I) and the seventh (co-operation no. II) show a steady rise. The reason, this time, is to be sought in the interest in the films shown in these programmes, films which were shot in various parts of the region—at the Nogentel tele-club (fifth telecast), the Chateau-Thierry Co-operative (sixth) and the Mailly-Champagne Co-operative (seventh). At Nogentel, the fifth telecast was viewed by 114 people (as against an audience of 26 people at the fourth), who came to see the film on the foundation of their own tele-club; thanks to this stimulus, attendance thereafter continued to be much larger than in the preceding weeks.

The peak figures on our two curves (and on the adults' curve in particular) is reached at the seventh telecast, dealing with wine-producing co-operatives, which attracted a large number of wine-growers from Venteuil and Chatillon. (At Venteuil, 32 persons viewed the sixth telecast, 80 persons the seventh, and 19 persons the eighth). The same effects were observed at Chatillon and in other tele-clubs as well, owing to the fact that the particular co-operative in question is very well known for its championship of the small wine-producers against the large champagne-producing firms. With this telecast the curve, for male attendance, of the most dynamic and progressive age group (26 to 40 years) attained its peak.

These figures appear to confirm the fact that the most popular programmes are those most directly concerned with the everyday problems of a certain sector of the population, particularly when they touch on collective action by the "little men" against the threats of the "big men".

IV. After the eighth telecast, dealing with co-operatives (in India, Denmark and Canada). "Etat d'urgence" was transferred to Wednesday evenings—this led to an increase in the number of children in proportion to adults, an increase which continued up to the tenth telecast. But it is probable that this has nothing to do with "Etat d'urgence" itself. A glance at the programmes shows that, from the eighth to the tenth, they included "Zorro", an adventure film which children rave about. Note that there is no similar increase in the number of adult viewers at the eighth and ninth telecasts. On the other hand, the sharp rise in the number of children was doubtless partly accounted for by the latter spreading the news that "Zorro" was showing (several tele-clubs noticed how keen children were on the black-masked hero).

The fact that the number of adult viewers from the eighth telecast onwards fell below that at the fourth (at the time of the cold spell) probably indicates that some people are less interested in co-operatives abroad than in those at Chateau-Thierry or Mailly-Champagne. The opinions expressed by the televiewers confirmed this supposition. Moreover, spring work in the fields was beginning, owing to the early arrival of the fine weather. The small farmers were less regular in their attendance. Attendance figures are lowest for the eleventh telecast (the country homestead) on 17 March. It is obvious that the series "fell" badly in relation to the seasonal fluctuations of farm work. At the tenth telecast, on 10 March, Chatillon notes "now that the fine weather is here, work in the vineyards goes on fairly late in the evening, with the result that there are not many people at the telecasts. The wine-growers have resumed work on dressing the vines, and can no longer afford to stay up late at night, as in winter; we usually stop our programmes at Easter". At Montfaucon, the same thing was observed at the eleventh telecast (17 March): "we have noticed a sharp drop in the attendance at tele-clubs, coinciding with the beginning of ploughing and sowing. There are hardly any small farmers, though they constitute the bulk of our village's population".

Nevertheless, there was a marked increase in attendance at the tenth telecast, on women in the country. Why? The graph of variations in men's and women's attendances shows that the number of women viewing this programme was not much larger than the number of men but that, on the other hand, there was a sharp increase in the number of small farmers (97, as against 52 at the following telecast). It is clear that this increase was not due to the other items of the evening's programme, "Journey without a Passport" or "The Life of Animals", both of which were shown on other occasions without attracting correspondingly larger audiences. It seems to have been the subject which was responsible for the greater number of men viewers, a fact which indicates once again that men are more interested than women in modernizing women's work in the country.

Finally, the fact that the attendance rose again at the thirteenth telecast seems to have been due mainly to interest in the conclusions and practical advice—an interest, which incidentally, was even keener among the workers than among the small farmers: all the log-books are categorical on this point. A certain proportion of people who were discouraged by the length of the series returned for the final telecast. According to the leaders, the viewers, knowing that the series was coming to an end, were anxious to see "how Roger Louis finished up". In this connexion, there is one point which we consider important, namely that the large number of telecasts and the time they lasted represented a serious drawback. When asked: "Are there any items which you used to like but which you like less today?" 14 people replied "Etat d'urgence" (as reported earlier), after the sixth, seventh and tenth telecasts. Although "Etat d'urgence" continued to interest a large number of people, they were keener at the beginning than towards the end: in fact, a series of 13 telecasts at a stretch, on faily serious subjects, is too long. Tele-club audiences would certainly be very interested in shorter series, consisting of three or four telecasts on the same theme; after one series, a certain interval should elapse before embarking on another series of the same length on a kindred subject.

### *Difference of Viewers' Opinions on the 13 Telecasts*

Data on the interest aroused by the subject of the various programmes, and the conditions in which they were shown, need to be supplemented by the comments of spectators on each particular telecast. These comments may be useful to producers wishing to use this kind of cultural programme in dealing with important social problems.

In the best tele-clubs, as we already know, viewers assign "marks" to the items of the evening's programme, by raising their hands. This method of comparing opinions often leads to useful comments, based on sincere impressions. We adopted this normal tele-club practice in our survey, in order to avoid getting purely formal and meaningless answers. By this means, we were sure of obtaining data which reflected the real opinions of the club, despite the inevitable interaction of influences. A certain number of leading spirits influence the group as a whole; but since, in most cases, they are not alone, their effect is usually evened out. Moreover, in any group, imitation is at least as important as originality; this is a psycho-social fact which applies in tele-clubs as everywhere else.

The only instructions we gave the leaders, emphasizing

that they must be scrupulously observed, were the following: (a) after the "vote" has been taken, teachers are not to speak until last; (b) questions must be asked in the precise form laid down in the written instructions sent every week, before each meeting, to all leaders; they must be precise, and each one must be asked separately; (c) "free" questions (questions not given in our written instructions) should not be asked until all the questions set by us have been dealt with.

In order to obtain useful results, we decided to make this "referendum", held after every meeting, more precise by the introduction of a few standard questions designed to draw viewers' attention to problems of organization: "What parts of this programme did you like most? least?" "Classify the impressions made by the various sections of the evening's programme. What would you put first?" (take a vote on certain sections, or on some particular aspect of the picture and commentary).

This was of course a somewhat over-simplified way of stating subtle problems of aesthetics, but the purpose of these questions was merely to provoke comparisons and disagreement and so arouse a desire to seek the causes of similarity or differences between the various impressions received. The leader would then start a discussion on the problems of organization, but without influencing the course of the debate.

The questions contained in the log-books, it is true, often proved too complicated, but they did provide an opportunity for recording authentic individual opinions of members of all social categories, and of small farmers in particular, which would otherwise certainly have been expressed. The replies provided invaluable information on the reasons underlying the preference for individual subjects dealt with, and for individual production techniques employed.

What emerged from this survey?

It will be noted that generally speaking, although viewers warmly approved of the "Etat d'urgence" telecasts, most of them did not consider it necessary to award them the highest marks.[4] This confirms that the referendum was always carried out in a spirit of real sincerity.

As we noticed at the time of the general survey of the programmes of Radio diffusion-Television francaise, certain items were more popular than "Etat d'urgence": "series to be continued", reports the leader at Viffort, "provided it can be fitted into an amusing programme, such as the circus ..." A large number of people always prefer variety shows: "it would be more interesting to see a music-hall programme", exclaims a worker at Nogentel. At Chatillon, some people preferred "Chester-Follies" to "Etat d'urgence". At Montfaucon, the circus showing on the same evening as the thirteenth telecast of "Etat d'urgence" (5 marks) obtained 6 marks. The same preference was indicated at Saint-Aubin and Etampses. Only one tele-club (Chatillon) gave "Etat-d'urgence" and the circus programme the same marks; one club only prefer "Etat d'urgence" (Fossoy, 16 votes to 7).

On the other hand, when "Etat d'urgence" followed a moderately popular variety programme such as "Joyaux de Paris", there was a marked preference for the rural programme. Similarly, we found, that people preferred our series to travel films—"Journey without a Passport", for instance—whenever the two were shown in the same evening's programme.

The over-all marks awarded to the "Etat d'urgence" telecasts confirm these statements. Although no telecast received an average mark of 5 or more than 5, none was marked less than 4. They all, therefore, earned warm approval. The most popular were the first telecast, on motorization: the third, on agricultural credit; and the sixth and seventh, on co-operation. The least popular was the eleventh, on the country homestead. It is difficult however, to distinguish when examining their relative popularity, how

**Table 6.1**
**Collective Opinions of the Tele-Clubs on the 13 "Etat D'urgence" Telecasts**

| Telecast | Number of tele-clubs which organised a referendum | Maximum marks awarded | Minimum marks awarded | Average marks for each telecast |
|---|---|---|---|---|
| 1st | 5 | 6 | 4 | 4.8 |
| 2nd | 8 | 5 | 3 | 4.1 |
| 3rd | 12 | 6 | 4 | 4.9 |
| 4th | 9 | 6 | 3.5 | 4.2 |
| 5th | 7 | 5 | 3 | 4.2 |
| 6th | 10 | 6 | 4 | 4.8 |
| 7th | 6 | 5.5 | 4 | 4.8 |
| 8th | 7 | 5 | 3.5 | 4.6 |
| 9th | 8 | 5 | 3 | 4.4 |
| 10th | 9 | 5 | 4 | 4.7 |
| 11th | 5 | 4.5 | 4 | 4.1 |
| 12th | 4 | 5 | 5 | 4.4 |
| 13th | 5 | 5 | 4 | 4.7 |

*Note*: The significance of this method of marking is as follows: 6, exceptional approval; 5, warm approval; 4 approval; 3, uncertainty; 2, disapproval; 1, strong disapproval.

far the success of any particular telecast was due to the subject and how far to its treatment. The comments reported bear on a very small number of "subjects", most of which were considered to be well-chosen, except perhaps in the case of co-operation abroad (eighth) and over-production (ninth), both of which, as general" subjects, were rated less interesting than subjects taken from local life. On the other hand, there were many comments on "methods of treatment"; we propose to assemble these comments around a few main themes, in order to illustrate the reactions of viewers to the various telecasts of the series.

I. The main problem of treatment in television is obviously that of the relationship between pictures and "spoken" material—the emphasis placed, in a composite telecast, on film and "live material" respectively. In this connexion the first point to note is that the problem of the relationship between pictures and spoken material in television depends on a more general consideration—the importance of achieving a lifelike atmosphere. The agricultural workers at Dammard objected, in the second telecast, to the farmer's speech: "The farmer had been told what to say". The same criticism was reported in most of the other log-books; no one thought the farmer lifelike. On the other hand, the commentaries by both Mr. Demarck, with his plan, downright speaking in the first telecast (arrival of the tractor in the village), and the small farmer in the third (discussion on "credit" with an industrialist), were most popular. "We want something real and striking, that's what we want" said a skilled worker at Aux Marais; "We don't want any humbug" (a wine-grower at Venteuil). This seems to be the main reason why the most popular telecast was the first, followed closely by the third.

Anything smacking of propaganda and "effects produced to order" arouses the suspicions of the general public. By "propaganda" we mean, not sincere campaigning for an idea openly expressed, but a deliberate attempt, often disguised, too "put over" a distortion of the truth. After the telecast on the re-allocation of land (fourth), some of the viewers became suspicious. "Roger Louis had an axe to grind", "he protested too much", such was the comment at Aux Marais. "It was impossible to judge whether he was right or wrong" said someone at Venteuil, referring to a farmer whose objections were summed up too briefly by the commentator. "The 'live' discussion would have been much more animated if the pros and cons could have been put" (Viffort). All the tele-clubs were shocked because, in the telecast on over-production (ninth), a small farmer from Brittany who had said very little was refused permission to speak again by the organizer, who was pressed for time. At Venteuil, when this telecast was shown, there was an extraordinary incident : 23 people, all of them farmers, walked out of the hall as a sign of protest. A striking example, if ever there was one, of how people can be influenced by television.

II. In the case of eight telecasts out of thirteen, the comments reported show a preference for films, though this technique is welcomed only on condition that it conveys the impression of life and reality which viewers prize above all. On the subject of a film about co-operatives in India, a worker in Nogentel exclaimed, rather surprisingly: "It went too fast, you'd almost think it was the cinema", a comment which revealed a keener instinctive appreciation of the special style and rhythm of television than many professionals possess. Films on every-day local life, shot specially for "Etat d'urgence" at the Nogentel tele-club, the village of Chapelle-sur-Chezy and the Co-operative Cellars at Mailly-Champagne, met with universal approval—and the fact that the two latter films formed a large part of the sixth and seventh telecasts largely accounts for their receiving one of the highest marks (4.8). "That's right", "That's true to life", "So-and-so plays his part very well". Used in this way, the telefilm gives a new slant and a new interest to everyday life. Familiar though it is—and perhaps precisely because it is familiar—everyday life is an unknown quantity, which television sets out to portray.

Thus telefilms, when they succeed in conveying the impression of real life, are preferred to "live" transmissions. It is not the method as such which is popular: other subjects might be better treated "live". Aesthetic problems do not interest the general public except in connexion with the object of the telecast, and the impression of authenticity it conveys.

III. As regards the other five telecasts, the majority of

viewers preferred "live" discussions to films: this refers to no. 2 (the model farm), no. 3 ("credit"), and also no. 6 (co-operation no. I) despite the film on the dairy co-operative at Chateau-Thierry, which was very popular. The ninth and thirteenth telecasts constitute a special case, since they were composed almost entirely of "live" items.

It is true that a powerful minority protested from time to time that there were too many "spoken" sequences. Two tele-clubs in particular criticized the eleventh telecast (the country homestead) as being too dry; this item was in fact composed almost exclusively of discussions and technical plans: "It's boring, with discussions all the time" (Nogentel), and "Let's have fewer discussions please, a little more life and fewer plans which look so hard-and-fast" (Viffort). These comments coincide with the suggestions regarding the Television francaise programmes as a whole, which were analysed above.[5]

But when "live" programmes are clear and vivid, as in the discussion between the small farmer and the industrialist in the telecast on "credit" they meet with unanimous approval. We would emphasize this fact, which at first sight seems surprising. This telecast—the third—contained practically no film; it nevertheless received the highest average mark of the series (4.9 out of 6), and aroused comments such as the following: "Most discussions are boring, but this one was exceptionally gripping" (a farmer, Viffort). "It should be noted that this instalment was comparatively popular, although it consisted almost wholly of discussions, without much picturesque material" (Aux Marais). "Despite the dryness of the subject, Roger Louis succeeded in interesting the bulk of the viewers" (Nogentel). This seems to indicate that the spoken word can be just as interesting as film, on condition: (a) that the subject is a "red-hot" one (the subject in the present case was money); (b) that the other side of the argument is presented, or a variety of ideas put forward, by live people (a debate rather than a monologue); (c) that the telecast gives an impression of being authentic (first-hand accounts); (d) that it is clear (with an avoidance of over-general or over-specialized terminology—all tele-clubs criticized the use of words such as "criterion", "planning", etc.); (e) that warmth and passion in controversy, which liven up the discussions, are not deliberately eliminated (at the Fossoy tele-club the observer, whose comments were checked on the spot by our central team, wrote that telecast no. 3, on "credit", was followed as keenly as a boxing match). Ideas which appear to be stale suddenly take on a real meaning when "put across" by persons of striking personality. It is easy to express sentiments; but the difficulty which the producers of "Etat d'urgence" had to face and which, judging by the tele-clubs' reactions, they largely succeeded in overcoming, was how to express ideas through sentiments.

IV. The method of presentation is obviously a very important factor in composite telecasts such as "Etat d'urgence". The physical appearance of the commentator, who in this instance was also the leader of all the discussions, can from the outset establish a sympathetic atmosphere, or the reverse. In our case, Roger Louis, a teacher who had transferred to television, had already proved his worth in the "Life in the Country" series the year before. He made a good impression, and was known personally to many of the tele-clubs; in addition to which his experience of popular education enabled him, as a rule, to strike the right note. He generally addresses viewers as if he were passing an evening amongst them, and gives the impression that he knows how to put himself, "in their shoes". The shortcomings of his vocabulary, which tends to be rather too limited or else too general and abstract, are offset by his direct approach, which never verges on the vulgar. He has considerable "presence"; yet as the Etampes log-book comments, "he didn't put himself too much in the limelight". In this respect he was contrasted with a certain varieties producer, vey well-known but regarded as too "exhibitionist". The fact that he sometimes found difficulty in controlling stormy discussions did not shock the majority of viewers. Many of them tended to regard him as their champion: "he held his own very well", or again "he often got out of awkward situations". People like him very much. One evening, when he was bidding farewell to the viewers, a workman in the hall cried "Good-bye, old chap, see you again soon"; and at Nogentel, after the thirteenth telecast, the comment was heard: "He looked very tired, poor old chap, he can't have had a good sleep for quite some time". Incidents such as that which occurred at Venteuil, where the wine-growers walked out of the hall because he refused to allow the small farmer to speak, do not affect his general popularity.

Such are the main comments on the part played by films, discussions and methods of presentation in the "Etat d'urgence" series, as reported in the log-books. They show how important it is to adapt the tone and atmosphere of the telecast to the reactions of that section of the population for which it is particularly designed, and how useful the approach and direct methods of popular education can be in introducing the problems with which television deals.

We have noted that the series should have finished before the arrival of spring: that 13 telecasts at a stretch are too many; that some of the subjects were too "general", although interest as a whole was very keen, particularly among the small farmers and workers; and that serious subjects suitably treated by television can appeal to a "popular" public while "spoken" items can, in certain circumstances, be even more successful than films. But we have not yet examined what purpose the series served; what did it give the viewers, in what way did it change them—in brief, what was its educational effect?

## Effects of "Etat d'urgence"

### *Participation in Discussions*

The first sign of the effect of any educational activity is the verbal reaction it immediately calls forth. This reaction may take the form of participation in a discussion.[6] Such discussion is customary in popular education. Its educational effect may be considerable; it breaks the ice and serves as an introduction to social life. It may free the participants from inhibitions or feelings of inferiority, or encourage shy members to take on some responsibility from which they may hitherto have shrunk for lack of ability to express themselves. As we saw in our study of the operation of tele-clubs, it may train people to think. It is of particular importance to those whose schooling has been curtailed and who have been obliged to take up manual work as soon as they have left primary school. Did the "Etat d'urgence" programmes encourage the small farmers and workmen to take part in discussions?

At the beginning, many teachers thought it unlikely that our series would have this effect. "Countryfolk will never dare to say what they think in front of people from their own village... They are inarticulate ... " But in all the tele-clubs in our districts, even in those where it had hitherto been impossible to start any discussion whatever, the main themes of the 13 telecasts were debated. The animation was naturally not as great at Fossoy, for instance, as at Montfaucon or Nogentel. But in some clubs the discussions went on till two in the morning. At Venteuil, some wine-growers declared one evening: "We have arguments here such as we've never had in the cellars—we never talk seriously there". In many clubs, which had held no debates before "Etat d'urgence" came along, viewers found in them an opportunity of thinking out their daily problems together. At Coudray, a village in the Oise, the leader wrote: "No one is more surprised than I to

Graph 1. TOTAL NUMBER OF PERSONS VIEWING TELECASTS AND TAKING PART IN THE DISCUSSION : BY OCCUPATION

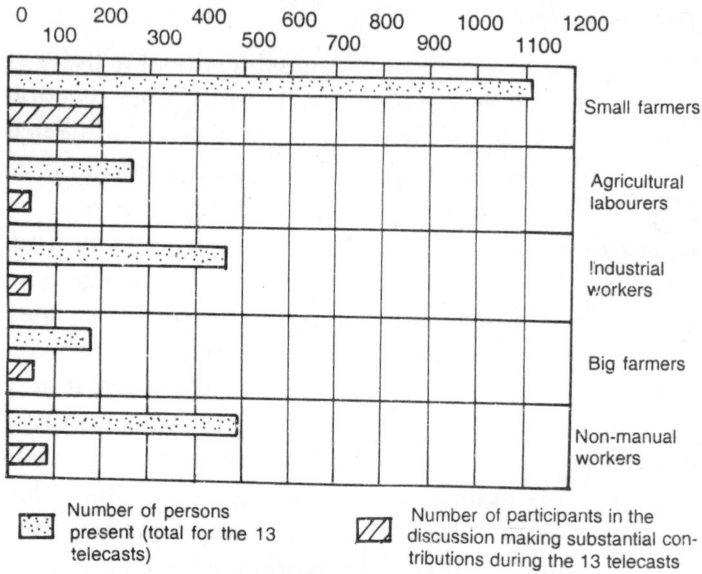


Graph 2. RATIO BETWEEN NUMBER OF PERSONS PRESENT AND NUMBER OF PARTICIPANTS IN THE DISCUSSION, ACCORDING TO OCCUPATION

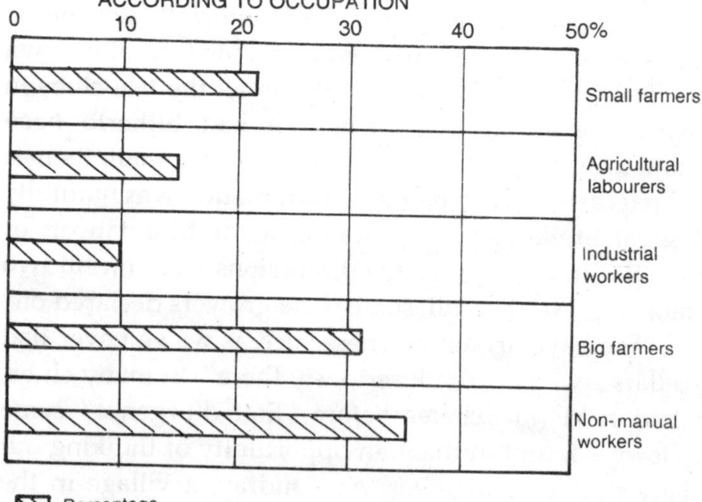

find that the viewers discuss with such energy". The leader at Nesles summed up the prevailing opinion when he wrote that television had introduced its audiences first to the cinema, then to the theatre, and finally, with "Etat d'urgence", to debating.

But who took part in the debates? Did differences of social status and education reduce them to mere monologues delivered by the village "notables" and educated persons—the big farmers, the teachers, the white-collar workers and local officials? It does seem that in certain tele-clubs the presence of big farmers embarrassed the small farmers. We find in the log-books. "The absence of the big farmers loosened the tongues of the small ones" or "It's better without people who are too influential—the mayor made great difficulties for me by repeatedly butting in to lead the discussion". In another tele-club, when the film on the Mailly-Champagne co-operative was shown (seventh telecast), a big farmer transformed the debate into a long monologue held before the farm labourers, who left one by one. At Dammard, on the contrary, the farm labourers stuck to the club and their "bosses" came less often. In these clubs, discussions of "Etat d'urgence" sometimes failed to establish any real exchange of ideas between groups with conflicting interests and habits.

It might, therefore, have been feared that even where men and women of different social standing continued to sit side by side in front of the screen, those with less authority or education would be too timid to open their mouths. Generally speaking, this was not the case. True, as many as 31 per cent of the large farmers spoke in the debates, they having the greatest command of words. But 15 per cent of the farm labourers who attended made some substantial contribution. This is an appreciable result, having regard to the social situation in some of the villages. As for the small farmers, who made up almost half the audience, they were responsible for the most numerous contributions, which came from 23 per cent of their representatives attending the 13 telecasts. Not only in actual number, but also in percentage, their speeches reached a much higher figure than those of the factory workers. So the first result of "Etat d'urgence" was to prove that, where certain problems of daily work and recreation are concerned, exchanges can be set up between different or hostile classes and social circles, enabling the manual workers to express themselves, despites the handicap of their position and lack of education. Let us now describe the views put forwards as a result of our programmes.

### *Themes of Discussion*

Words spoken or heard in a small group of people often carry more conviction than those spoken in a crowd or even between two people. This psycho-social fact may perhaps be explained by pressure of public opinion, the impulse to imitate, fear of making oneself conspicious, or an atmosphere which encourages the expression of wishes and decisions. Hence the importance of well-managed debates in a tele-club. What remarks were called forth by "Etat d'urgence"?

Before analysing what was said, we should discover whether these remarks resulted from what had been heard during the actual telecasts, or whether they were prompted by the questions put by the leader at the conclusion of each. In the latter case the discussions would have been in the nature of mechanical repetitions or docile recitals, of little use in estimating the effect produced on audiences by the "Etat d'urgence" series. It might also be wondered whether the discussions would not take up again what had been said before the transmission, to account for the indifference or hostility to modernization. Here again, what effect was to be anticipated from the showing of "Etat d'urgence"?

In order to answer these two questions, we made a complete list of the views expressed during debate, which were noted down direct in the log-books.

Since the present book is intended for an international public, we could not make an analysis of vocal comments and their meaning, so we confined ourselves to a study of the themes which we arranged roughly in two categories—approval and protest. It was not possible to make any serious study of frequency. We therefore restricted ourselves to a qualitative study of the general replies which seemed to typify the views of the club as a whole, or of individual replies which were characteristic of a particular social category. Original remarks are seldom heard at the tele-club; the members usually speak in order to express what their friends or "mates" are thinking in silence. In most cases we have avoided naming the village where the remarks were heard, in order to preserve the speakers' anonymity; but whenever possible we have mentioned a speaker's social position and occupation.

It will be seen that the subjects overlap from one meeting to another. Discussion usually dealt with what had been shown during the evening's telecast, but was not necessarily confined to it. We noticed that related subjects were often dealt with for about three meetings, and that the theme then changed. In our classification, however, we have taken the 13 telecasts in their correct order.

Here is the substance of the principal speeches, as gathered from the most characteristic phrases noted in the log-books.

### *Motorization*

The tractor is regarded with distrust: "Work in the vineyards is too delicate a job for it" objects a wine-grower. The whims of weather and soil make it inadvisable to buy one: "You can only use a tractor in certain years" (a farmer). At Montfaucon the farmers said the soil was too heavy and the ground too broken. The general opinion at Nesles-la-Montagne was that "the farms are too small". At another place a small farmer remarked sceptically: "We'd still need horses, to haul the tractor when it breaks down" or "One tractor isn't enough, there have to be at least two, one heavy and one light". And what will become of the farm labourers? "If tractors arebrought in there'll be the eight-hour day ... what will become of the farm labourers then?" asked several farm-hands.

Other farm labourers said, however: "We'd like our bosses to be well equipped, as long as it doesn't do us out of our work" or "It'll make the work less hard". And one big farmer declared: "If it weren't for the tractor we should all be selling our farms".

***Credit***

"Demarck has money" said the small farmers. "He's a multi-millionaire". "We can't afford to buy a tractor" was the general opinion at Nesles. "A horse lives off the farm, but petrol has to be bought" said Montreuil-aux-Lions. Besides, "If it takes five years to work off the cost of a tractor on a 230-hectare farm, how long would it take on a 30-hectare farm?" wondered one small farmer.

To go and ask for a loan is difficult. "My father told me that in his day people used to go to the bank after night-fall, because they werfe ashamed of it" said a big farmer. And there is no certainly that the loan will be granted. The young farmers in all the villages complained that "A young man who's just beginning finds difficulty in getting a loan". "There isn't enough credit for young men". This is perhaps because the agricultural credit system is short of funds, owing to the fact that it gets little help from the farmers themselves. "Farmers aren't lunatics—if they have any money they'll invest it at 8 per cent in industry rather than at 6 per cent in agriculture" admitted one small farmer.

On the question "Is it better to buy more land or improve

-RE-ALLOTCATION OF LAND AT BOULLAY-THIERRY
AND BOULLAY-MIVOYE

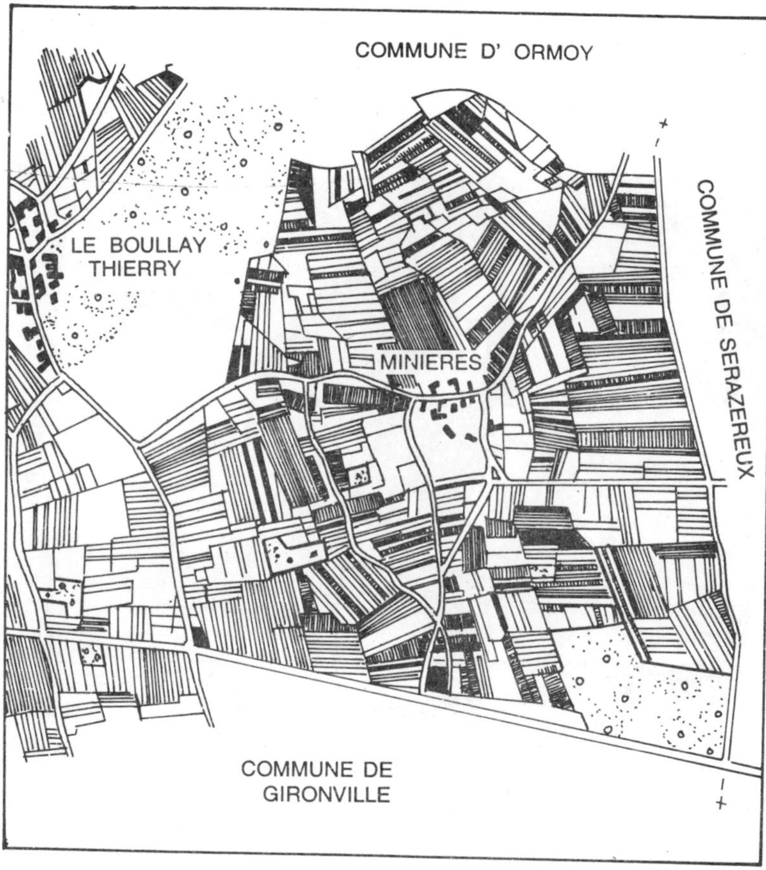


| | Total area | Reduction |
|---|---|---|
| (solid black) | 32 acres | 96% |
| (hatched) | 183 acres | 98% |

0 50 100 500 1000

scale (metre)

RE-ALLOTCATION OF LAND AT BOULLAY-THIERRY AND BOULLAY-MIVOYE

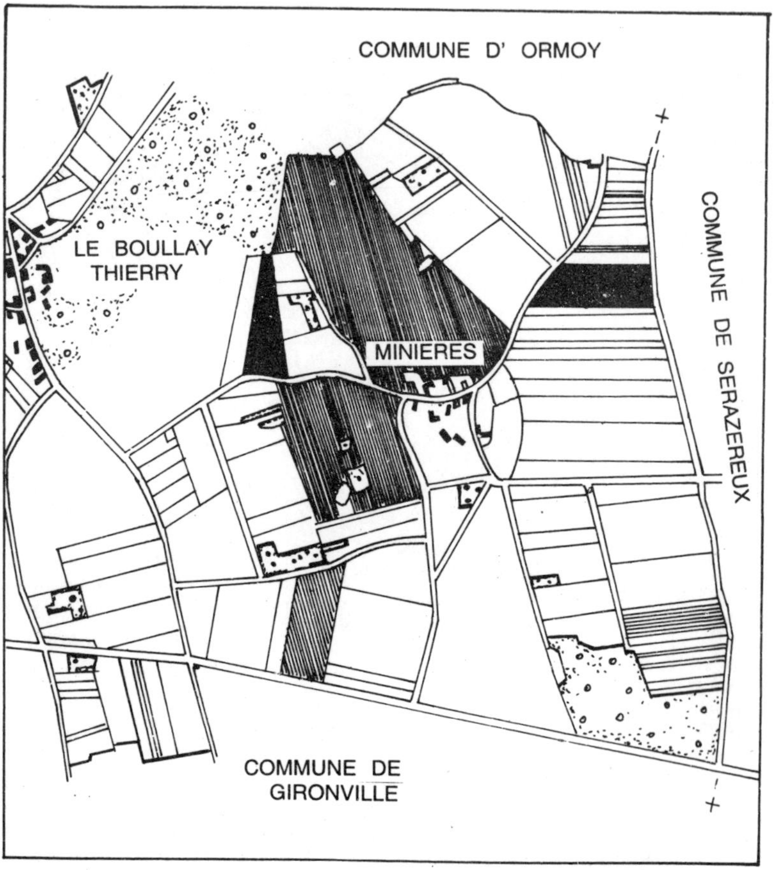


Results obtained :

Average size of a plot of land

Before: 1 acre

after: 7 acres

what one already has?" opinion was very much divided. "It's better to buy and increase one's holding"; "Land is an investment", was the general opinion at Aux Marais. On the other hand, "For young farmers" said one small farmer "it's better to improve the equipment".

Another question on which there was much disagreement was: "Is it better to use the old methods, or to ask for credit facilities?" A lot of people refrained from answering this. Nevertheless, there were seven speeches in favour of the old methods: but fourteen were definitely in favour of credit facilities.

One small farmer exclaimed indignantly "We'd be expected to give good land in exchange for rubbish". But a big farmer spoke on lines which may be summed up as follows: "It's the only possible solution". At Chatillon a vote was taken, and showed 60 per cent opposed to reallocation. At Venteuil, on the other hand, 60 per cent voted in favour of re-allocation. In the other tele-clubs, 16 lengthy speeches criticized this voluntary revision of ownership, against 14 which approved it. At Viffort, according to the club leader, "Everyone seems to angree that re-allocation is necessary, but they hesitate when they see the results in the neighbouring villages".

***Co-operatives***

This was the subject which produced the most sustained and heated argument. There were many negative replies to the question: "Do you think a co-operative could be set up in your village?" "People wouldn't like it" said a small farmer "Household co-operatives are impossible"; "We don't want any co-operative for agricultural machinery". At St. Aubin, for instance, five long speeches were made by farmers on this subject alone.

A small farmer expressed mistrust of his potential associates: "A co-operative? It might be all right for buying a tractor together, but some people always try to take the lion's share". Another said: "If one man handles it badly, everybody has to pay for the repairs"; and another: "They'd say, it wasn't me that broke it". A wine-grower thought a co-operative would never work: "Everybody would need the vine-sprayer on the same day". The apprehension expressed by one farmer sums up the general feeling: "There might be rows".

Others, however, energetically defended the co-operative: "We need to be less individualistic and have more confidence" was the theme of three important speeches by big or small farmers, in three tele-clubs. Six speeches of the same origin maintained that a co-operative was possible: "Yes, for buying fertilizers" or "Yes, for buying agricultural machinery".

Another question had been raised: "What criticisms do the members of co-operatives bring against them? Are they justified?" A big farmer proved that "It's more expensive than buying elsewhere". A small wine-grower complained that "Instead of paying out the dividends they put them into the purchasers' co-operative". Another protested that "They take no notice of our objections". "At the general meeting we feel awkward and daren't open our mouths" confessed one small farmer, while another pointed to a permanent unfairness: "The big fellows have time to think about it, we little chaps can never let up for a moment".

"The consumers' co-operative is hard on the small tradesman" said one baker "but generally speaking the co-operative system is needed"; "We have to remember that co-operation means not only organization, but a certain spirit as well" said a clerk. Several small wine-growers made declarations of faith: "We need to be less individualistic and have some confidence"; and at the end of one meeting, an agricultural officer said rather prompously that "the co-operative member is not working for himself but for his children, and for mankind in general".

The question "Is it desirable to expand the co-operative

system?" revealed widespread mistrust of the big co-operatives. "They're too centralized and impersonal" or "It's better to have small co-operatives, closely interconnected" (a small farmer at Montreuil-aux-Lions). At Nogentel, ballotting on the subject producd 4 votes in favour of large co-operatives and 26 in favour of small ones.

A final observation is that there were considerable differences in the general or majority opinion expressed in the tele-clubs on the occasion of the four telecasts dealing with co-operation. We tried to note the over-all conclusions reached in connexion with telecasts 5, 6, 7 and 8. We give these without comment (Table 6.2) as a sign of heated argument.

**Table 6.2**

| Club | 5th telecast | 6th telecast | 7th telecast | 8th telecast |
|---|---|---|---|---|
| Mon'taucon | against | ? | in favour | x |
| Viffort | x | in favour | in favour | x |
| Venteuil | in favour | against | in favour | x |
| Chatillon | x | in favour | x | x |
| Dammard | x | in favour | x | x |
| Saint-Aubin | x | x | x | x |
| Coudray | x | in favour | in favour | x |
| Aux Merais | against | x | x | x |
| Fossoy | against | against | against | against |
| Montreuil | x | x | x | in favour |
| Nesles | x | x | x | against |
| Nogentel | x | x | in favour | in favour |
| Etampes | x | x | x | in favour (with reservations) |

x: No definite reply

## *The Over-production of Farm Goods*

The questions we asked the leaders to put on this subject

were of a very general nature. Many of them had no replies at all. "Interesting discussions" took place in a few tele-clubs, at Etampes for instance; but there seem to have been no firm grounds for most of the conclusions reached, whether positive or negative. We give these replies, which were noted in most of the log-books by yes or no, without comment.

**Table 6.3**

| Question | Yes | No |
|---|---|---|
| "Do you think the domestic market in France can be expanded during the next few years?" | Dammard<br>Nogentel<br>Nesles (yes per-perhaps) | Aux Murais<br>Nesles |
| "Do you think that by improving the quality of certain goods and setting up an export organization, French agriculture could sell more to foreign countries?" | Dammard<br>Aux Marais<br>Nogentel | Nesles |
| "Are you in favour of a European market for agricultural produce?" | Saint-Aubin<br>Nogentel<br>Aux Marais<br>"Yes, but it's risky" (A small farmer) | Montfaucon<br>Nesles "Better keep inside our own frontiers" (A small farmer) |
| "Should the United Nations arrange to buy up excess agricultural goods and make them available to underfed peoples, in India for instance?" | Coudray<br>Etampes | Nogentel<br>Nesles "The French in Africa should be fed first" (a wine-grower) |
| "Do you think the French Government should assist such an undertaking with taxpayers' money?" | | Dammard "No tax payers' money for such as undertaking" general opinion). |

The first question—"Are you in favour of making things easier for country-women?" —raised objections of a financial nature on all sides, especially from the small farmers: "Modern machines are all very well, but they cost money";

"You have to be always paying out, there's no getting away from it". To the question: "Do you think outlay of that kind is as useful as buying an agricultural machine, for instance?" the president of the wine-growers' union at Chatillon replied that "Present conditions in the vineyards make it impossible to improve matters inside the home". "A machine gets on with the work, it helps us; there's not so much hurry about the inside of the house, we can carry on as we are" protested a small farmer at Nogentel. Besides, "women will have just as much work when the machines are there" (a small farmer at Viffort), or "before we have cooking apparatus we need to have water, electric light and power laid on all over the place".

"Do you think domestic science schools are useful?" "It seems likely" said a small farmer at Montfaucon "that girls who've learnt to make cakes in an electric over will have a hard time with our wood-burning stoves." "That's not a school, it's a chateau!" exclaimed a wine-grower when the domestic science school at Verdilly was shown on the screen. Finally, a very sceptical old agricultural labourer raised a peal of approving laughter by declaring: "When girls leave the school and come home they want to change everything; the old people throw them out, in less than no time!"

But "The schools are useful if they don't make the girls too ambitious" admits a small farmer. They are useful; "if attached to a farm and not to the sort of place that none of the pupils will find at home" (a teacher): "There's no doubt" said a farmer's wife "that the girls learn a lot of things I haven't time to teach my daughters". "There aren't five people who know how to give an injection, and the village stretches nearly two miles" explained a farmer at Montfaucon. "If classes were held here I should send my daughter" (a farmer at Coudray).

***Housing***

When the plans of a big farm rebuilt on modern

principles were shown on the screen, nearly all the viewers were dumpfounded..... To the question "What do you think of what you have just been shown?" there does not seem to have been a single favourable reply. Many speakers, on the other hand, expressed scepticism, often tinged with amusement: "Impossible here" said a small farmer at Viffort. "Let's begin by having water in our 17 hamlets, and that'll do" added another. Some workmen at Etampes found such unattainable luxury comic: "They must have been to the Ideal Home Exhibition before getting up this programme" they said; and a farm labourer exclaimed "Don't they ever put up curtains in the cowsheds?" "We should look fine with a grand farm and no modern equipment too work it with!" remarked one small farmer.

Others struck by the exceptional circumstances of the reconstruction, added: "Did well out of the war, didn't they!" "It's a pity" observed a factory worker ironically "that everything round here wasn't smashed up by the war, it would all be much finer!" And a farmer concluded "That's all very well, but we really can't order another war!"

"Would you like to build, or to do up the present buildings?" "Later on, when I'm sure of staying here" said one farm labourer—"but labour seems too be less in demand, and suppose we leave?" In conclusion, several small wine-growers and farmers declared "We've plenty of ideas, it's the cash we're shrot of"; "The most important thing is lacking"; "Where do we find the millions of francs?", etc.

***Drift of Young People to the Towns***

"Are many people leaving your village?" All the tele-clubs replied in the affirmative—except Etampes and Nogentel, the most highly urbanized.

The question "Is there enough work in the village?" called forth a majority of no's—Montfaucon, Viffort, Veneuil, St-Aubin, Nogentel.

"Why are the young people leaving?" A small farmer at Montfaucon replied "When they see the town folk, who can rest from Saturday to Sunday evening, it tempts them". But most speakers stressed the low wages—"Wages are too low"; "A farm labourer earns 77 francs an hour and a bricklayer 120 francs", etc.

"Do you think we should try to stop this drift, or does it signify adaptation to present-day life?" "When I was young" said an old farmer "it took four families to get in the harvest, now one lad can do it by himself." "Modernization means that some have to go" said a clerk at Nogentel. "The ground's too 'low' for them" grumbled a small farmer. "It's natural they should go"—such was the conclusion reached by the Viffort farmers in their discussion. "It won't go on for ever" declared a big farmer.

"How could the drift be stopped?" "Impossible"; "It can't", are the most frequent replies from the wine-growers and small or big farmers. Some fairly practical ideas were, however, put forward. "Revive the law of primogeniture" urged a small farmer. "Keep people on the spot by setting up factories for processing agricultural produce" suggested a country schoolmaster. "Organized recreation isn't enough: there ought to be vocational classes too" said a small farmer. "Why shouldn't people come to live in the country when they retire, to make room for young people in the towns?" asked someone at Nesles—a man with small private means.

***Summing-up***

Very straight questions had been suggested to the leaders at the end of the series: "Should countryfolk study?" "Would it be a good thing to start adult education classes?" "Will you send your sons to the school of agricultural?" etc.

The replies were everywhere favourable, but always a little stiff. One the whole, the questions were regarded as premature: "Give us time to think it over"; "We'll see next year"; "After the holidays"....

What conclusion is to be drawn from all these comments? They leave no doubt that sayings like "the countryfolk take no interest in anything"; "all they care about is making money", etc. are untrue. They are keenly interested in the basic problems of their daily life. Their ideas on the subject, though often limited, are clear and consistent, and are expressed in definite, albeit few words. Popular education, popular culture and popular art should start from this basis, in an effort to ensure a gradual improvement in the level and extent of knowledge and skills. Great cultural possibilities are neglected by most educators and producers, who ground their work on a "middle class", "aesthetic" culture, too often remote from the realities of village life.

It can also be said that "Etat d'urgence" succeeded in awakening an active response from the country audiences. The small farmers did not merely repeat, parrot-like, the arguments heard during the telecasts; they thought them over in relation to their own experience. Prejudices proved stubborn: but the people were brought up against real reasons for suspicion of or indifference to modernization. The views defended during the discussions were less blunt and better thought-out than the negative attitudes taken up, on the occasion of the initial investigation, against technical progress or social co-operation.[7] Insincerity? Perhaps. But the discussion initiated by "Etat d'urgence" provided a propitious atmosphere, a framework for the exchange of ideas which few of the participants would express so clearly if they were among themselves. An awareness of problems may be awakened, develop steadily or revive from time to time, and the education of the less advanced by the more advanced is facilitated. At Venteuil the wine-growers' representative was heard to make an open declaration of faith in the co-operative system. The discussion on "Etat d'urgence", which had no narrowly political bias, gave the opportunity for a public debate on social problems, which the majority of viewers do not discuss because they never attend party or trade union meetings, or the meetings of specialized groups. This discussion therefore constituted a lively social education circle.

Was it reasonable to hope that discussion on "Etat d'urgence" might produce not only ideas, but decisions? Our survey shows that the questions which best facilitated discussion were those which avoided two drawbacks. On the one hand they were not too specific—that makes the prudent countryfolk cautious and reduces them to silence. For instance: "Do you want to start a co-operative?" One leader mentions in this connexion that in his village the municipal council, when it has to take a decision, leaves an interval of three days between the meeting at which the decision is reached and that at which it is confirmed. "When the question is too precise, nobody answers" reported the Viffort leader. "I heard in one village that some of the farmers would like a co-operative threshing-machine; what do you think about it?" Silence, "Have you any scheme for reforming the local co-operative?" Silence.

But when the questions are too general they have an equally paralyzing effect on the discussion. The survey of the discussions which followed the ninth telecast (over-production) is very instructive in this connexion: many answers were confined to a yes or no, there were few original ideas expressed in direct terms, and many people remained silent. This shows that the discussion was not keen (except in a highly urbanized tele-club such as that at Etampes). Venteuil notes: "The questions were too general, they did not call forth replies". The yes and no answers recorded in the log-books that evening are of very doubtful value as indications.

The questions which obtained the most genuine and the most numerous replies were those which dealt with numbers and categories ("How many co-operatives are there in your village?" "How many young people go to work in the town?") and those which called for critical consideration of recognized problems (such as "Should a tractor be bought, or not?").

It can hardly be asserted that replies are valueless because, in many cases, they merely report facts. Attitudes take time to evolve, and it is very difficult to secure rapid results which are not illusory. Nevertheless, we noted the development, over a month, of the general opinion on the most controversial problem, that of co-operation. It is not surprising that this should have called forth far more numerous and more vigorous replies than did motorization or even re-allocation! One need only recall the vigour of certain anti-co-operative attitudes among the small farmers, as revealed by the initial investigation. Not until the four telecasts dealing with the community spirit and with co-operation do we find in the log-books remarks such as "We're waiting for the continuation"—as for a serial story. "The problem of co-operation interested everybody, all the social categaories in the tele-club—farmers, workmen and craftsmen" (Boullay-Mivoie).

It can be definitely stated that during the four telecasts on co-operation the atmosphere in the tele-clubs underwent a transformation, and that on the whole this was for the better. The leaders testify to this, and inspection of the log-books confirms it. It is true that at Fossoy the atmosphere remained hostile, and at Saint-Aubin uncertain; but at Montfaucon the predominantly negative atitude did not persist. Coudray, after undecided reactions, declared itself at the third telecast as "in favour". At Venteuil the atmosphere became such that, as we have already seen, the President of the Wine-growers' Syndicate declared himself openly in favour of the co-operative system. Nesles remained somewhat hostile. A favourable trend was observed at Montreuil and at Etampes.

These of course are only trifling indications of the effect of "Etat d'urgence". Can we discover some of a more decisive character?

### *Wishes Expressed by Viewers*

Television has been reproached for exerting only a superficial and temporary influence. "It may possibly suggest ideas, but it does no more. One programme is forgotten when the next comes along." We have already seen that, in the light of our investigation, this opinion seems exaggerated and prejudiced. Far from satisfying its public "Etat d'urgence" left it unsatisfied. Certain viewers wanted to see some of the telecasts again: the most in demand were the first, on motorization, and the third, on credit—a fact which confirms the statistical estimates. But above all it would seem that "Etat d'urgence" succeeded in awakening or re-awakening a desire to go thoroughly into the problems which the telecasts raised, touched upon or indicated. Wishes to this effect were expressed throughout the whole 13 of the series. Cross-checking them, on occasion, with those we had heard during the general investigation, we found that they often supplemented these and carried them further. It is a pity the tele-clubs did not then embark upon a systematic campaign to induce their members to take up suitable reading. There is here, we repeat, a considerable possibility, which has not as yet been adequately developed, of helping to inculcate a taste for reading, as the Seattle experiment showed could be done in the case of a juvenile public.

What exactly were these wishes, as revealed by a minute examination of the log-books? The relate first and foremost to vocational training. The countryfolk would like to know more about the plants they grow, the animals they breed and employ. They suggest, as subjects for telecasts. "Fruit-trees and the pruning of trees" (Montfaucon). "The life of insects and insecticides", "Lives of the animals on our farms". But they also use machines, which often take the place of animals for working purposes. So they must keep pace with progress: "Display of the latest agricultural machinery" suggests Saint-Aubin. "The upkeep of machines" is Venteuil's request. Farmers are not—as might be supposed from their relatively unfavourable response to the telecast on over-production (ninth)—averse from considering general problems. But they would like these general questions to be discussed in more concrete terms. They suggest, for instance, "The price of wheat" (Aux Marais)."Etat d'urgence" has engendered the wish for a comparative knowledge of different ways of living and working. Here are some of the suggestions: "How do farmers work in other parts of France?" (Nesles). "How does the farmer's life compare with that of the shopkeeper and industrialist?" (Viffort). "The hard life of the farm labourer" (Etampes, Boullay-Mivoie). The features on domestic and family life aroused the wish for the question of housing conditions in the country to be dealt with (Boullay-Movie)—and not merely the "model dwelling", as in the eleventh telecast. "Life in a farmer's home, summer and winter" (Montfaucon). "Leisure in the country, "The activity of the school co-operatives" (Saint-Aubin), "Fish and fishing", "Wild animals and shooting" (Venteuil). And the fact that the telecast on co-operation abroad was less liked than those dealing with co-operation in France, and attracted smaller audiences, does not necessarily mean that foreign questions are in general of smaller interest. This depends on the countries referred to and on the quality of the programme. For we find a great number of wishes expressed as a result of the feature on co-operatives in Canada and Denmark. "We ought to have more features on foreign countries"(Venteuil). "It would be a good thing to look into the problems of the agricultural proletariat, which are more numerous than those of the employers, and deal with the question of the drift from the countryside in comparison with foreign immigration" (Saint-Aubin). "Examples from abroad help one to make comparisons" (Nogentel). "Survey of the agricultural methods in foreign countries—especially those of Eastern Europe" (Nesles). "Let us be shown what happens in other countries, and especially in the U.S.S.R." (Fossoy). "More features on foreign countries" (Etampes).

This leaves no doubt that "Etat d'urgence" awoke or revived the wish for information and education on subjects connected with the work and spare-time occupations of countryfolk, not only in their own district, but also in the rest of France and abroad. As our series showed, introduction to local problems may lead to the gradual extension of general culture. But has it led to changes of attitude and behaviour?

### *After "Etat D'urgence": Change in Attitude Towards Modernization*

The results of any popular education undertaking can undoubtedly be measured by the change in attitudes and behaviour which it brings about in everyday life. It was unreasonable to suppose that century-old prejudices could be known down in four months; and even more unreasonable to hope, through education, to create a new type of mentality—which can only be achieved by raising the standard of living and effecting "structural" alterations. But what we could do was to seek a means establishing and, if possible, measuring the extent of the change in attitude as regards modernization, brought about as a result of our programme. After an interval of four months, therefore, we put the questions incorporated in the initial investigation[8] to the same people as before, and in exactly the same circumstances—without, of course, reminding them of their earlier replies which most of them had forgotten. We made our method of checking as sensitive and accurate as possible by allowing for the mentality of the population—drawing a distinction firstly between serious plans and a mere desire for acquisition, and secondly between vague plans, detailed plans and plans already being carried out.

The changes were not, of course, sufficiently numerous for statistical calculations to be made for each of the 46 articles of agricultural equipment—individual or collective, public or domestic—enumerated in Method No. 2. What we did, therefore, was to separate the replies into "positive" and "negative" changes—taking four categories only, for the main types of equipment.

Changes were considered to be positive when refusal to countenance modernization gave way to a desire for improvement or acquisition; when mere desire was replaced by a serious plan; or when a vague plan became a detailed plan or a plan in the course of implementation. Changes in the opposite direction were classed as negative.

In order to rule out, as far as possible, chance causes of change, cases in which replies were given to only one of the two sections of the questionnaire were not counted. These cases were too dubious, in either direction. They were treated according to the law of probabilities,[9] so as to calculate the exact significance of the change in question.

### *Change in Attitude of Small Farmers to the Modernization of Collective and Individual Agricultural Equipment, and of Public and Domestic Equipment*

The largest number of positive changes apply to the repair of buildings of the construction of new ones. Next in order come the changes as regards the use of artificial fertilizer and seed selection; and then far behind, changes as regards the use of tractors. So far as changes respecting individual agricultural equipment as a whole are concerned, 69 per cent are positive and 31 per cent negataive. This difference was checked by a test, and it is highly probable that it was widespread (highly significant difference).

The same is not true of collective agricultural equipment, which is not surprising when we remember how much anti-co-operative feeling was revealed by the answers to the initial investigation and in the discussions on "Etat d'urgence". In this case, the differences between positive and negative changes cannot be said to be significant. They may be due merely to chance. The former are, however, slightly more numerous than the latter (57 per cent as against 43 per cent).

As regards collective cultural equipment, on the other hand, the attitude of the small farmers has become much more positive, especially where influenced by considerations relating to the organization of after-school leisure activities. After "Etat d'urgence", the attitude to post-school agricultural courses also underwent a favourable change, but not that to the commission for land re-allocation. In regard to collective cultural equipment, the attitude of small farmers evolved in a positive direction: 68 per cent as against 36 per cent (significant difference).

Graph 20. VARIATIONS IN ATTITUDES OF SMALL FARMERS, ACCORDING TO CATEGORY OF EQUIPMENT

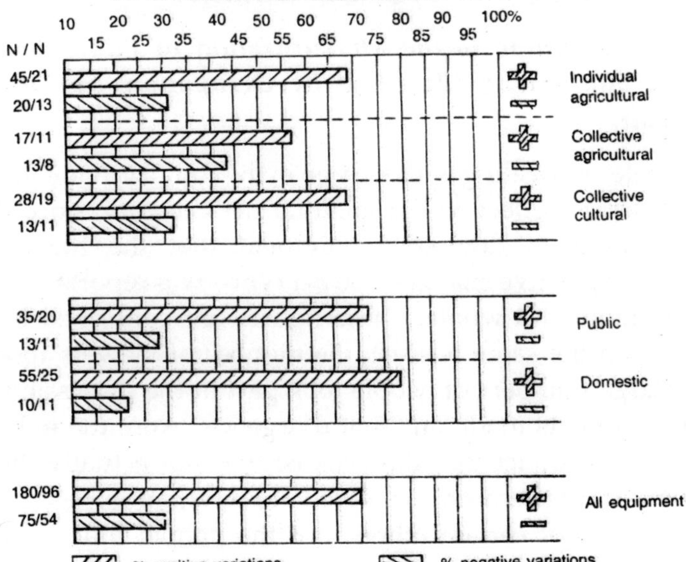


*Note* : N/N, = Number of variations / Number of individuals

Changes in attitudes to public installations were positive rather than negative, especially in the matter of shower-baths, provision of a village hall, and main water supply. But the most marked progress in the small-farmer category was in respect of domestic equipment, especially with regard to washing-machines, housing repairs and the installation of running water over the sink. For domestic equipment, there were 78 per cent positive changes to 22 per cent negative (highly significant difference). The person who stands the most chance of having conditions slightly improved as a result of the "Etat d'urgence" type of programme is thus the farmer's wife. When we recall the information yielded by our initial investigation on the condition of women in the coiuntry, and their attitude, we cannot but hope that there will be more programmes of this type.

In short, the changes noted in the attitude of the small-farmer category to the various aspects of modernization indicate a very significant positive tendency.

### *Changes in Attitude to the Modernization of Public and Domestic Equipment, Classified by Occupation, Sex and Age Group*

The telecast dealing with women in the country evidently had considerable effect on the small-farmer category, since it is with regard to domestic equipment that the highest percentage of positive changes—80 per cent—was reported for the population as a whole. These figures are confirmed by other data on the same telecast: the number of viewers rose sharply, large numbers of people took part in the discussion, and the comments made on "Etat d'urgence" were the most constructive. The fact that this telecast was not actually the most popular was because its method of presentation was less good than that of certain others; but the people found the subject stimulating, and the telecast was an undoubted success.

Graph 21. VARIATIONS IN ATTITUDES OF POPULATION AS A WHOLE TO MODERNIZATION OF PUBLIC INSTALLATIONS AND DOMESTIC EQUIPMENT

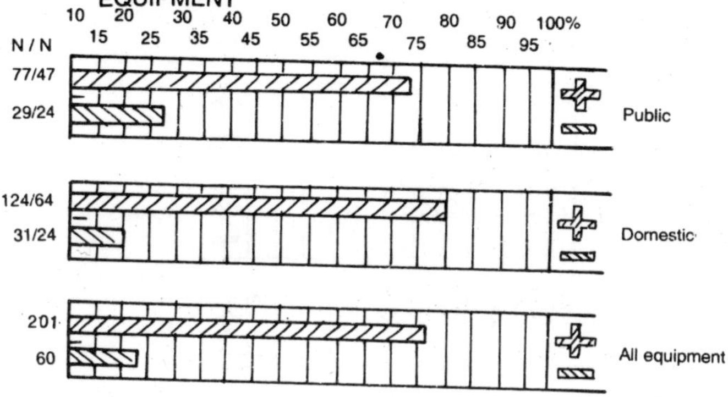


% positive variations — % negative variations

*Note* : N/N, = Number of variations / Number of individuals

Graph 22. VARIATIONS IN ATTITUDES TO MODERNIZATION OF THE PUBLIC INSTALLATIONS AND DOMESTIC EQUIPMENT, ACCORDING TO OCCUPATION

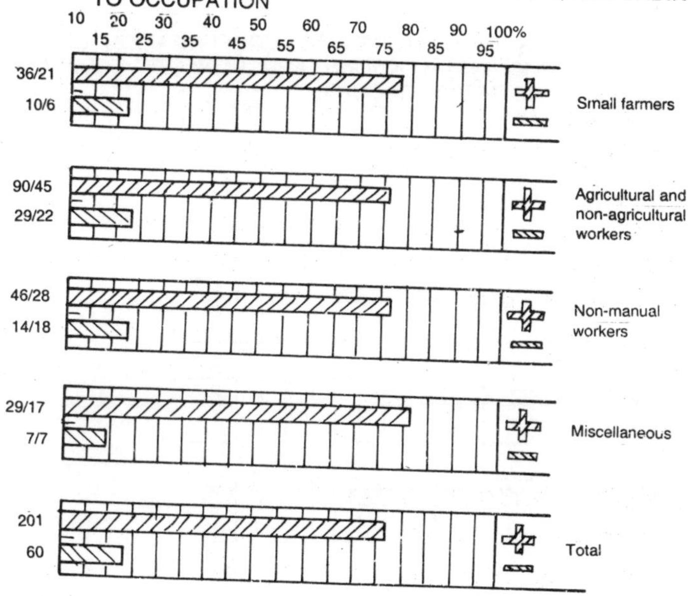


% positive variations — % negative variations

*Note* : N/N, = Number of variations / Number of individuals

Graph 23. VARIATIONS IN ATTITUDES TO MODERNIZATION OF THE PUBLIC INSTALLATIONS AND DOMESTIC EQUIPMENT, ACCORDING TO SEX

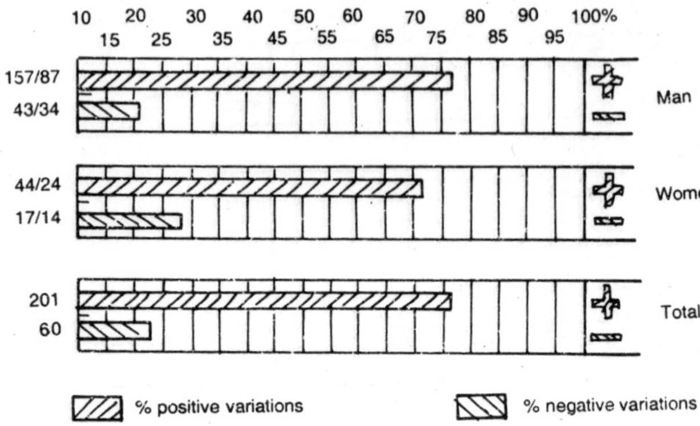


*Note* : N/N, = Number of variations / Number of individuals

Graph 24. VARIATIONS IN ATTITUDES TO MODERNIZATION OF THE PUBLIC INSTALLATIONS AND DOMESTIC EQUIPMENT, ACCORDING TO AGE GROUPS

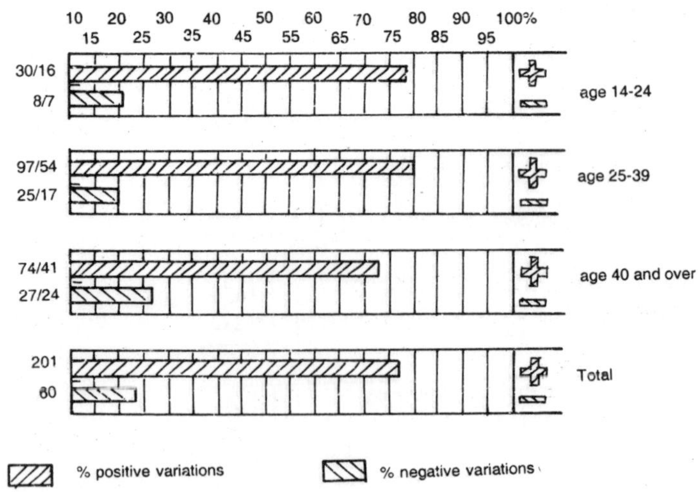


*Note* : N/N, = Number of variations / Number of individuals

In the case of both domestic and public equipment, the positive changes reported for the total population were similar to those occurring amongst the small-farmer category, which constitutes more than half of that population. The most positive changes refer, firstly, to the provision of shower-baths, village hall, water supply, wash-houses and sports ground; and secondly to washing-machines, repair of houses, installation of running water over the sink, and use of butane gas.

What is the perhaps even more important is that these positive changes occur, to some extent, in persons of all occupations and age groups, and of both sexes (highly significant difference). The main point to be stressed, however, is the change in the attitude of those persons who were shown by the initial investigation as being the most bitterly opposed to, or chary of, modernization. There are of course no grounds for claiming that they have been converted in bulk, overnight, to technical or social progress. But we are justified in stating that, as a group, they have changed more than the other categories. The evolution of the workers—who are less recalcitrant than the small farmers, and more open-minded about technical and social progress—does indeed take a different course, with 90 positive changes per 58 workers as against 36 such changes per 67 small farmers. On the other hand, 29 negative changes were reported among the workers, to 10 among the small farmers; with the net result that the proportion of positive and negative changes in the two categories was about the same: 78 per cent for the small farmers and 76 per cent for the workers, whereas the initial investigation showed that the latter category was much more favourable to modernization than was the former.

The same indications emerge, though not so clearly, from a comparison between the age group of over 40 and that of under 25. The final investigation showed that 6 per cent more of the younger age group took a positive attitude (79 per cent as against 73 per cent), whereas the difference in favour of the younger group, in the initial invstigation, was 21 per cent. The difference between the figures for the first investigation and those for the second is undoubtedly due to the effect of "Etat d'urgence", probably through changes brought about in the over-40 group—since almost all the young people showed a positive attitude from the outset, which could be little altered subsequently.

But have these new attitudes led to new ways of behaviour?

***New Behaviour Patterns***

Here again, the period of observation was to brief (April-June 1954) for a really exhaustive survey to be made, quite apart from the difficulty of carrying out investigations of this kind at the level of ordinary everyday life. We fell back once more on the invaluable evidence of teacher-observers living among the people of a village, where often they themselves were actually born and bred. We therefore give the comments entered in the log-books as they stand. The only criterion adopted was absolutely honesty; thus both the good and the bad effects of our programme are reported.

Some of the resulting attitudes and ways of behaviour are absolutely the opposite of what the authors of the programme were aiming at. Instead of feeling urged to combat the exodus from the country, a farm-girl of 20 drew the following conclusion from the series: "It's made me want to go and live in the town even more than I did before".

A 25-year-old office clerk, instead of showing more understanding of the farmer's difficulties, declared: "I used to think that the sacrifices (the word is not too strong) called for on behalf of the farmers in order to give a new impetus to agriculture (subsidies of various kinds, easy-payment schemes, tax exemptions) would be more appreciated by those concerned, that progress would be more marked, and that the community and country as a whole would stand to benefit therefrom. I am disillusioned".

Instead of feeling an urge to modernize his home after the telecast on "the fine models and achievements of rural housing", an agricultural worker commented, rather understandably: "It's all like a dream to us...."

Nevertheless, there are a greater number of cases in which the reactions correspond to the aims of the authors.

*Improvement of domestic equipment.* After the telecast on women in the country, a farmer criticized himself to the teacher for his indifferent attitude, concluding "More ought to be done to ease the women's position in the home; I'm going to do something about it".

*Improvement of farming equipment.* Some people who has vague ideas of modernizing their equipment took firm decisions. "As for me, I'm making an incubator—so is Lucien" (statement made by a farmer after the thirteenth telecast).

"Two farmers in the village have just bought themselves a washing-machine; the idea was certainly suggested or brought to a head by the telecast" (note by the schoolmaster at Saint-Aubin).

"Domestic science schools" remarked a farmer from the same village, after the tenth telecast "are often represented as a fancy scheme for big landowners". Now we see that an attempt is being made to provide them for everyone." Another farmer said: "It's given me the idea of sending my daughter to the school at Verdilly".

A farmer of 49, after the last telecast, said: "I'd never paid enough attention, before, to manure and the use of the tractor"; and another (aged 46) remarked: "I was using second-hand implements; I now think they cost just as much as new ones, and I can understand why the young people want to bring things up to date".

*Public amenities.* "The municipal council has just decided to lay on water, for which people have been asking for years" wrote, after the tenth telecast, the schoolmaster of a village whose mayor had attended the "Etat d'urgence" programmes regularly.

"The effect of the telecast on the community spirit (and what followed it) was certainly responsible for the decision of the trade union members to improve the tracks between the vineyards, with each man devoting one or more days to the work according to the size of his property" (report form the leader at Chatillon).

This brief summary of comments confirms earlier observations. The desires which found expression during the telecasts, the changes of atitude towards modernization, and the changes in actual behaviour noted in the village after the completion of the series, bear incontestable witness to the positive effects of "Etat d'urgence". The evidence of all reports, the observations of individual cases, and studies of statistics are all equally conclusive.

## References

1. Initial referendum on reactions to modernization (Method No. 2).
2. Log-books were kept by the tele-clubs in Montfaucon, Viffort, Fossoy, Venteuil, Chatillon, Dammard, Saint-Aubin, Nesles, Nogentel and Etampes. Comments are based on 230 log-books most of them (221) complete with extensive particulars regarding programmes. The nine remaining log-books had to be completed by means of extrapolated data based on the general trend of graphs and on comparisons with programmes preceding or following the programme not fully reported. The reasons for omissions were purely accidental (breakdown of current, illness of leade, loss of the log-book).
3. For the sake of simplicity, we shall speak of "adults". This in fact refers to persons not attending school, including young workers.

See Appendix II, p. 248; Categories of population used in the field survey.

4. If one is to judge by audience mail, "Etat d'urgence" was as popular with urban viewers as with rural ones. Of the 46 letters received in the three months during which the series lasted, 37 wre favourable, 4 voiced no opinion, and only 5 criticized the subject or its presentation. The large majority of these letters came from townspeople.

5. See Part II, p. 73.

6. It was difficult to keep records of participation in debates, and the quality of the records varies from one tele-club to another. Not all the log-books yielded suitable material for our analysis. Rather than make use of quantitative data of doubtful accuracy, we confined ourselves to the most complete records—those of Venteuil, Montfaucon, Dammard, Nesles and Nogentel.

7. See p. 266, Appendix VII, Tables recapitulating the reasons for indifference or opposition to modernization.

8. Method no. 2.

9. Cf. Methodological note: Application of Pearson's criterion, p. 232.

# Index

❑❑❑